MEN: From [illegible]
to Clone Age

BOB BEALE has been a writer for more than 20 years, much of it working as a journalist for the *Sydney Morning Herald* as Science and Environment Editor, Chief of Staff and European Correspondent. His work has won many awards and has appeared in many newspapers and magazines around the world. His previous book – co-written with Peter Fray – was *The Vanishing Continent* (Hodder & Stoughton, Sydney, 1990). He is now a freelance writer, living in Sydney. He writes regularly for *The Bulletin* magazine.

Bob Beale may be contacted at bob@beale.org

THIS BOOK IS

Inspired by the love of my life, Kathy;

Dedicated to our excellent daughters, Laura, Ellen and Jessie;

In memory of a fine and special man, Jack Weldon (1922–1999).

BOB BEALE

MEN

From STONE AGE to CLONE AGE

The science of being male

VIKING

Viking
Penguin Books Australia Ltd
487 Maroondah Highway, PO Box 257
Ringwood, Victoria 3134, Australia
Penguin Books Ltd
Harmondsworth, Middlesex, England
Penguin Putnam Inc.
375 Hudson Street, New York, New York 10014, USA
Penguin Books Canada Limited
10 Alcorn Avenue, Toronto, Ontario, Canada M4V 3B2
Penguin Books (NZ) Ltd
Cnr Rosedale and Airborne Roads, Albany, Auckland, New Zealand
Penguin Books (South Africa) (Pty) Ltd
5 Watkins Street, Denver Ext 4, 2094, South Africa
Penguin Books India (P) Ltd
11, Community Centre, Panchsheel Park, New Delhi 110 017, India

First published by Penguin Books Australia Ltd 2001

10 9 8 7 6 5 4 3 2 1

Designed by Susannah Low, Penguin Design Studio
Typeset in Minion 11.5/17 by Midland Typesetters, Maryborough
Printed and bound in Australia by Australian Print Group, Maryborough

National Library of Australia
Cataloguing-in-Publication data:

Beale, Bob.
Men: from stone age to clone age.

Bibliography.
Includes index.
ISBN 0 670 88810 9.

1. Men – Attitudes. 2. Masculinity. 3. Sex role.
I. Title

305.32

www.penguin.com.au

This project has been assisted by the Commonwealth Government through the Australia Council, its arts funding and advisory body.

CONTENTS

FOREWORD

Once there was a world with no sex, a planet of tiny Eves happily making more Eves just like them. There was no need for an Adam. That splendidly simple arrangement seems to have lasted for 1.5 billion years after life began on Earth. Then males were invented and all the trouble began. True, the multiplication game got much more interesting, but it got a whole lot messier and less sensible as well. Think about it: some bacteria can split in half to make two of themselves in as little as 20 minutes. Another 20 minutes later, there's four bacteria, then eight and so on. In less than two days, one bacterial cell could replicate enough to occupy the entire volume of the earth. I know, I know, there goes the neighbourhood. But the point is that all those little critters had it good, really good. Why risk everything on a crazy gamble with sex? To me it just doesn't seem, well, natural.

That puzzle – the man question – is what started bugging me one day and eventually led to this book. As a science writer, what started as a simple query in my mind led me into a fabulous smorgasbord of food for thought. Just take a random look at what's been happening lately in the world of science, technology and medicine to put the spotlight on men and maleness. Women are giving birth using sperm taken from dead men; the cloning of Dolly the sheep could, theoretically at least, mark the advent of a technology that makes men redundant; surgeons are planning testes transplants; molecular biologists are busy unravelling the very essence of every gene on the male sex-chromosome; a US$1 billion black market in testosterone has developed among body builders and confused teenage boys; the drug Viagra has revolutionised the treatment of impotence; alarming claims are being made that men's sperm counts are plummeting; the global incidence of cancers of the penis and testes is increasing, and more and more boys are being born with malformed genitals; the Internet has opened up whole new ways of accessing pornography; and cyber-scientists in Britain are working on implanted microchips that could for the first time enable men and women to directly experience their partner's sensations during sex.

As a man, however, it still pains me to say that males are largely useless. Oh sure, Mother Nature has cleverly arranged it so that we can be reinvented as the need arises. She's found all sorts of uses for us – things to keep us busy, helpful skills to employ, worthwhile roles to play and so on. We can thump our chests to scare off intruders, we can give piggy-back rides to the kids and we can bring home bacon. But we can't have babies and, when you get down to it, that's one heck of a drawback for a living thing. Yet we're still here 3 billion years later and, as you will see, we are still amazingly popular additions to the baby business. Males thrive and prosper everywhere in obvious, glorious and inglorious profusion. The one essential thing we do – whether we be guys, gorillas or ganders – is to fertilise females. The advantages of making offspring this way are apparently so great as to outweigh all the equally obvious downsides of having us exist at all. Makes you wonder.

Now, aside from the sex thing, men are plainly more useful than the males of many other species. By way of comparison, I invite you to consider angler fish. They have worked out a totally ruthless answer to the male question. These bizarre animals are noted for their canny hunting technique: they lie camouflaged on the ocean floor while dangling and wiggling a weird little fleshy protrusion from their heads, in imitation of a worm. Smaller fish coming too close for a peek at this lure are quickly devoured. Stranger still, though, is that for many years, no-one had ever seen a male angler fish. Then it was noticed that the females had other weird fleshy protrusions. Closer inquiry revealed that tiny young male angler fish drift around until they encounter a large female, then physically latch onto her body. In time, the two literally fuse together, becoming one individual – flesh and blood, Mr David and Mrs Goliath. Then his body shrivels away until only the genitals are left, totally dependent on her for life-support. Sometimes a mature female may sport as many as five or six sets of male genitals, from which she can fertilise herself. That makes human males an even greater puzzle.

As far back as we can tell, men have dominated human life to a degree that is vastly out of kilter with their essential reproductive role. They have often done so, of course, by dint of being larger and stronger than women, and more aggressive with it. Men are responsible for an overly large share of the world's violent injury and death. Plenty of women are willing and able to fight and kill, so it is far from being an exclusively male domain. Yet, as the prominent biologist Robert Sapolsky neatly puts it: 'Whether it is something as primal as having an axe fight in an Amazonian clearing or as detached as using computer-guided aircraft to strafe a village, something as condemned as assaulting a cripple or as glorified as killing someone wearing the wrong uniform, if it is violent, we males excel at it.' I'm not for a moment wanting to paint men as automatons unable to resist the age-old siren songs of sex and violence. They vary greatly in their conduct, as all people do. More to the point, human intellect, culture and civilisation are so remarkable and influential that we have long since broken free of many of the dictates of our genes and biology, at least where our behaviour is concerned. Yet there is a widespread perception – one I share – that the average man seems far more excitable about and interested in the sex thing than the average woman. No-one can say whether this is due to nature or nurture, biology or social double-standards. My belief is that on average there are real differences in male and female sexuality, but that the differences between individuals and at various stages of life are far greater. Some men seem to care little, if at all, about sex, while some women seem to pursue it with a sizzling passion. Indeed, a key theme of this book is that the middle ground between men and women is probably much broader than we all think.

Science is revealing that the supposed male–female divide is more of a large and subtle overlap. Perhaps that explains why one boy may grow up to be an aggressive thug or a rapacious tycoon, while another becomes a gentle guru or a tender healer. Did our ancestors simply bestow on us a culture that encourages aggression in men and suppresses it in women? Is male violence just the ugly unwanted side of an even more fundamental biological drive to compete and take risks for sex – a drive that might ultimately benefit the human race? Clearly, these are not dusty academic questions: we need to know and understand why these tendencies exist if we are to make the world a safer and more civil place.

Incidentally, I don't accept that men rape women because of some ancient Darwinian urge to spread their own genes, as some evolutionary biologists have recently suggested. Even if their hypothesis contains a grain of truth, it's just a hypothesis and there's a whole beachful of grains still to be sifted before any genuinely useful conclusions can be drawn on that score. But I do accept that good science is probably the most fruitful way to search for fresh answers and enlightenment about sex and men. Many wise and innovative people have turned their minds to these topics over the ages, with only limited success. More recently, feminism has added a welcome new momentum to the search.

There's no shortage of opinions out there about the differences and inequalities between the sexes but, as I see it, there's a crying need for more light and less heat. Facts, or at least more solid evidence, can help us make up our minds about which opinions should be given most credence. Facts don't just educate, they fuel constructive debate. Yet, despite our unusually avid interest in sex, we humans are strangely coy about discussing it publicly and about studying it. Pornography still sells in reams; self-righteous censors still hold sway over laws and individual liberties; homosexuals are still being bashed and denied legal rights; men still discriminate against women for the flimsiest reasons; gender politics is still a social minefield; too many boys and girls are still sexually abused; too many unwanted pregnancies still occur through ignorance and fear; and sex research still struggles for funds, respectability and influence. Being shy about all this isn't going to improve matters. Facts and understanding can help us overcome our shyness.

And while men are renowned for inventing and telling sex jokes, most are paradoxically loath to discuss and understand their own health, their bodies and their sexuality. One of my aims in writing this book, therefore, has been to help ease maleness, sex and gender out of the closet by pulling them into sharper focus.

Plainly, we still know far too little about men, and we need to know much more. Their reproductive health is under a cloud just about everywhere; their rising suicide rate in many societies reveals that all is not well with their mental health; their propensity for violence causes untold pain and suffering; and their tendency to take risks sends far too many to an early grave. We need to know why these things are happening, and a lot else besides.

This book will take you on a Cook's tour of maleness, from the Stone Age to the Clone Age. It begins, of course, by asking why males of any kind exist at all. Surprisingly, while the answer may at first seem obvious, science tells us that many species still get along fine with no sex at all. The book goes on to trace the impact of our long evolutionary history on the bodies and minds of today's men. Modern genetics and fossil studies are opening up whole new fields of research that help to explain, among other things, why men are larger than women and why men die younger. Next, we look at the animal world to find patterns of behaviour and biology that men have in common with males of other species, and how else maleness can be expressed. Then there's a whiz through some of what we know about men in prehistoric and historic times – why one was buried with his penis encased in gold, why another drew a picture on a cave wall of a man apparently attempting to have sex with an elk, and how the dawn of agriculture may have given men an early hold on social power that many still refuse to let go.

From there the focus switches to medical science. We discover how the sex of a human embryo is determined and how a recent but little-appreciated discovery has pinpointed a single gene as the source of a crucial difference between the sexes. Then we follow the tortuous travels of a single sperm from its formation to its successful docking with an egg, one of the most remarkable journeys known. Next, we look at why – despite our runaway population growth – men are duds in the fertility stakes, and why their prospects may be getting markedly worse. From there, we consider that ornery and undependable delivery vehicle for sperm, the penis. This much-abused and misunderstood organ has a colourful tale to tell about men – yielding some unexpected insights into men and women. And we learn how its failure to perform is being transformed by a new range of treatments.

Men and women alike will be intrigued by science's take on male sexual arousal, hormones and psychology: what turns a man on and what makes him tick is a rich field of study and speculation. You'll learn how some scientists argue that ancient evolutionary forces could explain why some women appeal to men much more than others, why men develop pot bellies and go bald as they age, why boys tend to ignore their mothers, and why many men retreat to their dens, stonewall their wives or even lash out with their fists during marital conflict. Also emerging from the research world are some intriguing, if controversial, clues as to why some men are aroused by other men.

Finally, we look to the future – and a strange, wondrous and sometimes daunting future it promises to be. I was astonished to learn, for example, that if I have a grandson it may be possible for him to give birth, and to breastfeed his baby.

I have three riders to add. First, I must freely confess here that I have many personal biases and that most or all of them are to be found in varying degrees in these pages. It's impossible to be objective. We are all products of our own genes, families, life experiences, times and cultures. For the record: I am male, pale-skinned, middle-aged, have three brothers and no sisters. My primary and tertiary educations took place in mixed-sex settings, my secondary schooling with boys only. I am heterosexual. I am married to a clever, beautiful and admirable woman whom I have loved deeply for 25 years. Our three inspiring daughters were all conceived naturally, effortlessly and with great joy. We have all enjoyed good health and have been spared much personal tragedy. We are, by historical and present global standards, among the most fortunate, secure and wealthy people ever to have lived. Inevitably, my privileged Western world view seeps into everything I think.

Second, I am not a scientist – I write about science. That gives me a lot of leeway to sacrifice precision for the sake of storytelling, whereas in science the story always comes second. So I apologise to any scientists who may feel that I have misrepresented, misunderstood, overlooked or trivialised their work in some way. Because of the vast scope of subjects covered here, I have had to read and consult hundreds of scientific papers and scores of books by other authors. I thank all of those researchers and authors: wherever possible, I have cited them as my sources. I am sorry if by oversight I have neglected some; the omission is not intentional.

Third, I confess that I think men have had an unfair rap in modern times. Their sexism and aggression have rightly been put under the microscope, but their many positive qualities have been undervalued; they have been harshly judged. Men are sons, brothers, uncles, lovers, husbands, fathers, and grandfathers. They are builders, doers, workers, protectors, providers, partners, creators, inventors and nurturers. They are straight, gay, bisexual, asexual, celibate, promiscuous, macho, effeminate and any other category or label you care to choose. They range from hulking great bundles of muscle to weedy little wimps. For every Adolf Hitler or Pol Pot, there is a Mahatma Gandhi or Nelson Mandela. For every bully, there's an empathic friend. For every absent father, there's a doting dad. Most men, it seems to me, settle happily into positive and mutually rewarding relationships. Most seem to cherish their lovers, families and friends. And, despite some inner-urgings from the evolutionary past, they're not 'natural-born' killers: in World War II, 80 to 85 per cent of the soldiers failed to fire their weapons in the heat of battle. Men may be born to compete, but it seems they have to learn how to fight and kill.

Knowledge is power. So, this is my modest contribution. It's not intended to be of biblical scope or authority; indeed it's very much an eclectic personal choice of facts and subjects to carry the story along. I hope it will introduce you to some facets of maleness you hadn't known or considered before, and will encourage you to make valuable connections with what you read here and your own life. Writing this book has been a rich and extraordinary experience for me, as fine a mental adventure as any writer could hope to have. It has changed for the better the way I think about myself and about all men. I hope that some of that sense of wonder and intrigue comes through, and that you will find this Cook's tour of maleness as fascinating and illuminating as I have.

1
ORIGINS: Why, oh Y?

WHY THE HECK were men invented? It defies logic. I mean, we humans like to think that when nature created us she came up with the smartest, most inventive and successful species ever to grace the planet. So why did she go and spoil it all by giving half of us the potential to be such a pesky, pushy, violent, sex-mad bunch of muscle-heads?

Let's face it, we men try to keep the top jobs for ourselves and take the lion's share of wealth and power, we exploit women, we can't take failure, we can't express our feelings, we're outrageously competitive show-offs, we have blatant double standards about fidelity, we form sexist cliques and we relish an elbows-and-all scramble up a pecking order. We take terrible risks, fight appalling wars, drink and smoke too much and have an endless thirst for watching mindless sports and playing with gadgets. We want affairs, not relationships. We seek allies, not friends. We want conquests, not consensus. We prefer to roam than be home. We live fast and die young.

But men are not alone in this. When it comes to expressing maleness, especially concerning sex, many other species don't do it by halves either. All those vain peacocks, kick-boxing kangaroos, head-butting mountain goats and spitting, wailing tomcats. They'll spurn friends and kin, forgo food and comfort, invade enemy territory and – if needs be – risk limb and life for sex. All that may often be true of some female animals too, but on balance males seem more prepared or more driven to take the mating game to greater extremes.

I have watched in wonder at the lengths to which some of my fellow men will go for sex. It's not long, for example, since 'the man with the most powerful job on Earth' – US President Bill Clinton – risked his alpha status, his job, his marriage, family, friends and reputation on a bizarre and foolish fling with a young woman.

It's obvious that life could be a lot simpler if there were no men. Women wouldn't have to bother with all that troublesome dating and mating. No beery breath, leering stares, groping hands, Friday-night football or fighting for a share of the bedclothes. If women could conceive children without men, no doubt they would get along just fine. Certainly, some lesbian couples manage well as parents. Let's be really generous and suggest that women might create a fabulous new feminine culture based on mutual care and co-operation, on empathy, equality, justice and harmony with the environment. Grannies, mothers, daughters and sisters only, and good riddance to guys.

As it happens, that idea meshes well with the real scientific puzzle about men – the great mystery is not so much why they behave as they do, but why they exist at all. In fact, plenty of other species have figured out how to survive and thrive without having males. Some of the most successful and numerous creatures on the planet do not bother with all that messy male–female business at all. When bacteria want to make more bacteria, for example, they simply split in half. They can still have sex: they simply hook up like refuelling aircraft, swap a few genes each way along a tube and off they go – gene pool mixed, dud genes repaired, no problem. Most plants avoid separate sexes, too: they either clone themselves (as any gardener can do by growing cuttings) or are hermaphrodites. Almost every dandelion seed is a clone of its parent plant. Some animal species can even perform the miraculous trick of virgin birth: female aphids can give birth to female aphids that are already pregnant with female aphids. And there's a species of lizard in Australia in which not a single male has ever been found: through a process known as parthenogenesis, females can activate their own eggs to start dividing and growing into female clones of themselves.

So why bother with males? After all, if the aim of the evolutionary game is to leave as many descendants as you can, it seems risky and costly to adopt a strategy in which half your children can't give birth and half your genes get dumped along the way. What if my mum, say, happened to be born with a perfect combination of genes for human success? If she cloned herself . . . a clutch of near-perfect daughters. But instead this superwoman goes and marries my less-than-perfect dad, has four less-than-perfect sons and undoes much of her genetic good luck.

And why opt for a reproductive system that causes all sorts of complications? Sex requires new kinds of behaviour, some of which may make life more risky for your offspring: many males, for example, perish in sexual contests with each other or get gobbled up by predators when they go searching for a bride. Therefore, to ask why males exist is to ask why sex exists. Despite many colourful scientific theories, the truth is that no one knows. It has been described as the biggest unsolved problem in evolutionary biology. There's no correct answer. Sorry if you were hoping for something more definitive.

So, in the beginning there was . . . what? Who knows? Scientists, like anyone who's ever wondered about it, would dearly love to be able to trace our ultimate origins. They are certainly on the case. But the trail is too cold, the tracks too faint, to make the search easy or success likely. It was so very long ago. All we can be sure of, because we are here, is that life began. We don't know much about where or when; we know even less about how. As for why it began, well, that's as much a matter of faith as science. But alive we are and, in the absence of some lost extra-terrestrial knocking on the front door and asking to use the intergalactic phone to call home, it seems to have been an event unique to Earth. But we can at least be content with the certainty that it happened. And as soon as it did, the struggle to prolong life emerged – and the need to reproduce was born. Eventually, out of that need came sex. But it sure was a long time coming.

Our beautiful planet is about 4.5 billion years old. But it wasn't such a gem at first: its atmosphere of poisonous ammonia clouds was further fouled by spewing volcanoes, raging electrical storms and a torrent of deadly radiation from the sun. So it took some hundreds of millions of years before the astonishing emergence of the first life – probably 'short stretches of nucleic acid floating in a chemical sea', as British biologist Steve Jones puts it. In time, more complex structures formed and eventually DNA – deoxyribonucleic acid – arrived on the scene. And here's where the trail warms up and tracks become clearer, because thanks to molecular biology we now know an awful lot about that amazing substance. What DNA provided in one neat little package was the master code for making amino acids, the building blocks of all proteins and enzymes, plus the ability for life to replicate itself pretty consistently.

If today's simplest bacteria and algae are any guide, those tiny pioneers of life used DNA to make accurate copies of themselves by dividing in half. In effect, they cloned themselves. This worked so well that they appear to have kept it up for another couple of billion years. We don't know how or why this process of replication changed. One theory is that a bit of 'selfish' DNA evolved and developed the neat trick of directing the individual that contained it to fuse with another one, then to divide, each new entity taking a copy of the DNA with it. It was so successful at this that it managed to spread itself far and wide and 'infect' whole populations.

Rick Michod, an American evolutionary biologist at the University of Arizona, has suggested another option – that sex could have emerged out of a bit of necrophilia.[1] In the 1980s he led a team that showed how some bacteria take into themselves bits of DNA from the corpses of their neighbours. The more damaged an individual's own DNA, the more it took in from corpses, suggesting to Michod that these microbes were actively repairing their own genes with the imported DNA.

Whatever form proto-sex took, sexual reproduction proper may have been 'invented' as a refinement of it, to create offspring that varied a little from their parents. That is a darned handy way for animals and plants to make themselves into harder-to-hit moving targets in their genetic equivalent of the arms race against parasites and viruses. This argument for sex is known as the 'Red Queen' theory (expounded in detail in Matt Ridley's fascinating book of that name), after the Lewis Carroll character who tells Alice that she must keep running simply to stay in the same place.[2]

As a way of staying one step ahead of your predators and parasites – which won't be able to prey efficiently on some of your more variable offspring – sex does seem worth all the trouble it puts you to. It also slams the foot down on the accelerator pedal of evolution, providing a steady flood of variety on which natural selection can act. This increases the chances of at least some of your offspring being better suited than others to the ever-changing world around them (the downside is that some of them won't be, but this is outweighed by the risk that all of them might not be). It also has the wonderful advantage, Michod believes, of enabling you to pair up your genes with another full set and use the extra set to repair any damaged ones on the original. It's like a vintage-car enthusiast having two vehicles of the same make and model and being able to cannibalise parts from one to keep the other going.

So, regardless of the original reason it came about, sex has likely served many different purposes since it first appeared. And sex itself probably evolved more than once in primitive species. What this means in the context of this book is that males have also been re-invented time and again. We should remember, too, that maleness is expressed in extraordinarily rich variety among the tens of millions of species on Earth. There are countless different kinds of males and countless different ways for them to fertilise females. They don't actually need to get together for fertilisation to take place. Take fish, for example: when it comes to their sex lives, well, you name it, they do it – everything from virgin birth to gender-bending, and from devoted lifelong partnerships to promiscuous mass orgies. For sheer inventiveness in the sex game, fish are probably without peer.

It's much more than simply unusual. It's also an object lesson in realising how maleness and femaleness, as humans know them, are relatively straight and narrow divisions. 'When you talk about sex and gender, fish are as fluid as they come,' says John Paxton, of the Australian Museum. Male fish still have to conform to some basic evolutionary rules – especially success in passing on their genes – but they give even the terms 'male' and 'father' a whole new meaning.

Let's sidetrack briefly here, to a coral reef, for an illustration of what I mean. Come snorkelling with me around the Low Isles, a couple of island specks of marine reserve in the Great Barrier Reef, off the far north-east coast of Australia. Beneath us, a flamboyant angelfish is weaving its way through the intricate maze of coral. It stops abruptly to hover beside a nondescript rock, then gapes its mouth and flares its gills, looking for all the world as if it is about to throw up. But no, it freezes in this odd position and glances sideways towards the rock. At this signal, a tiny torpedo-shaped figure with a fluoro-blue tail darts out from beneath a crevice and confidently approaches. Incredibly, the smaller fish gently swims head-first into the open gill covers of the angelfish and starts pecking away at the delicate blood-red fronds of its gills. We are witnessing one of the marvels of reef ecology. The little guy is a cleaner wrasse, who makes his living by setting up a drive-by cleaning station – in this case the rock – and waiting for trusting clients to cruise by to have their parasites picked off with surgical precision.

That's unusual enough, but his sex life is an even greater marvel. He is part of a social group of cleaner wrasse, usually about ten individuals, but he is the only male. The nine females in the harem follow a strict social pecking order, with the largest – the alpha female – dominating the next largest and so on. It's a finely tuned arrangement: experiments have shown that if the alpha female is removed from the group, the next largest one assumes her role and those below her all move up a step. But it's when the male is removed from the group that things get really weird in wrasse world. The alpha female immediately begins to change her behaviour. Within as little as an hour she begins to act like a male and starts courting the other females. Within a fortnight, her ovaries follow where her heart and mind have already gone – she develops male reproductive organs and her sex change is complete.

Sex reversal seems to have evolved independently in at least 23 families of fish, from moray eels to angelfish. They can either be born into one sex and later change into the other – some can do this within a matter of minutes – or they can be simultaneously male and female. Some humans change sex, of course, but as Paxton points out, 'the fish that change sex have no choice in the matter'.[3] They all have their reasons. Gobi fish, for example, are poor swimmers. Leaving their coral reef hideaways to search for a mate exposes them to a greater risk of being eaten. So when two females meet, they stop the search, form a pair and one of them changes into a male. That way, they can have all the advantages of sexual reproduction with fewer costs.

Sex is a spectacularly popular way of reproducing, even among simple life forms that are extremely unlikely ever to experience it as fun. The higher up the evolutionary tree you go, the more likely a species is to be a sexual reproducer. Indeed, 99.9 per cent of higher organisms do it. In short, sex works.

So even if we can't explain why, it seems we males are just too darned useful to dispense with. The flipside of that fact, however, is that men are plain useless without women. It is males who are the evolutionary afterthought, the add-on sex. Michod explains, 'As the biblical story of creation tells, the male came first and the female was created so that he would not be alone . . . What we know about asexual reproduction and virgin birth in other animals suggests the opposite: that females, or at least the female function, came first and can exist without the male function.'[4] It's quite possible, he says, that our distant ancestors did reproduce without sex and that humans have lost that capacity. But as we'll see in the final chapter, human technology has brought that wheel full circle. The birth of Dolly the sheep – a manufactured clone of her mother – seems to have put back into our hands the technical capacity for virgin birth. That raises some intriguing new questions about men, doesn't it?

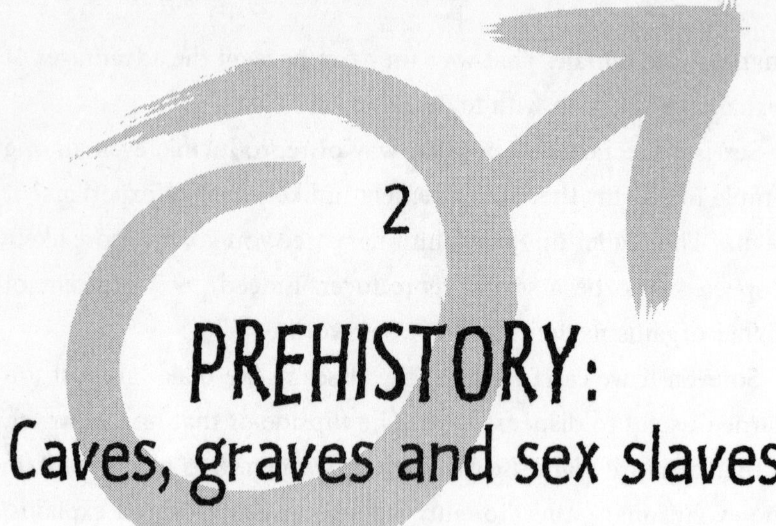

2

PREHISTORY: Caves, graves and sex slaves

'Why did people colonise the world? One answer is that it was the inevitable result of population growth within an intelligent, omnivorous, adaptable species. Humans are "super-tramps", ready to go anywhere and eat anything in order to survive and multiply.'

Peter White

IMAGINE YOU'RE LOOKING at a long, long queue of men stretching away over the horizon. Suppose that the familiar one heading the line is your father. Just behind him is your grandfather and behind him is your great-grandfather and so on, with each succeeding man being from the previous generation. Now imagine that a road travels beside the line and that you can drive down this memory lane to follow your evolutionary roots, back into the mists of time. Let's say the men are standing a metre apart and a generation ticks over every 25 years. So that robed fellow 80 metres back would be from the time of Christ, but dress him in Reeboks, blue jeans and a T-shirt and you wouldn't give him a second look if you passed him on the street today. The man 200 metres back (5000 years ago) has leather underwear and leggings held up by a suspender belt that also carries his portable tool-kit. He has a metal axe and is munching on some bread. The guy 800 metres back (20,000 years ago) is from the time before agriculture, wheels and cities – he is a pale, bearded and fur-clad hunter from the edges of the northern glaciers; next to him is a dark, loin-clothed gatherer of fruits from the tropical forests. One of them makes music, the other paints and they have tools and weapons made of stone, wood and bone.

After 6 kilometres (150,000 years) you see a lean, muscular African man. He is an early representative of *Homo sapiens*, although he probably does not use language as we know it. Even he would not look out of place, though, if you took him to a modern nudist beach.

Now pick up the pace and drive 160 kilometres (4 million years) down the line; by now you are struggling to see the family resemblance in the small, hairy-bodied males facing you there. Plainly not human, they stand maybe 1.6 metres tall and display diminutive penises: these guys would definitely cause a stir if they were to stroll the streets of New York or London today, although sadly no talk-show host would get much out of them. At 200 kilometres (5 million years) down the line, you meet the last blokes with faces that you might care to claim as far-distant kin, even if they do walk on their knuckles. At 240 kilometres (6 million years) you're unsettled to encounter a large, hairy and broad-shouldered ape: with his leathery skin, horny fingernails, flat nose, small sloping forehead and a jutting jaw featuring nasty-looking canine teeth, he is the last male ancestor you share with chimpanzees. Your sense of detachment increases as you continue down the line and pass the last relative you share with the gorillas, then with the orang-utans, then with the gibbons . . . by the time you pass the 800-kilometre mark (20 million years), the last nimble-fingered male ancestor of the apes has gone by.

You could keep driving down the line, of course: past monkeys, lemurs and so on, until at about 7000 kilometres (180 million years) you reach a nervous, furry little critter – one of the first mammals, which scuttled around at night while the dinosaurs snoozed. And you could carry on, right back to the first male, perhaps some tiny creature in the figurative primeval soup.

But by now you'll have got the idea: science tells us that we all carry a legacy of ancient genes and, as we now know in increasing detail, your father inherited some very important ones that your mother did not. One of these genes, in particular – or a linked group of them – was ultimately responsible for his beard, his muscles, his deeper voice and his genitals. Others were vital to his ability to make tiny packages of DNA that could fertilise one of your mother's eggs. But, like all humans, he carried many other genetic legacies as well. Gazing back down our evolutionary line of men, we see features we clearly still share with our male ancestors and many other species besides. The basic body plan that programmed his growth in his mother's womb, for example, is one your dad had in common with everything from the mouse skulking in the kitchen cupboard to the mighty blue whale. As a male, his penis and testes developed in ways that differ only marginally in design, construction and function from those of a rat or a stallion. But science also tells us that we are one of the apes which, in turn, are members of the larger group – mostly tree-dwellers – known as the primates, and of the larger-still group called mammals. To comprehend why men look and behave differently from women, then, we first need to see them in these wider contexts. I'm not going to re-tell the whole story of human evolution; a few examples will illustrate the point.

Breasts, nipples and wombs don't usually fossilise, but because all living female mammals – even the strangest of the lot, Australia's egg-laying echidnas and platypuses – produce milk, it's reasonable to assume that this fundamental trait goes back to the very roots of our mammalian ancestry, some 180 million years ago. And with one exception (a fruit bat), males in all 4300 or so known mammal species do not make milk, so it's also reasonable to assume that this fundamental sex difference goes back a very long way, men and women probably having been different in this respect ever since the first humans evolved. We can't be certain of this because men retain the equipment for milk-making, as do many other male mammals. Inject a male calf, guinea pig or goat with female hormones and he will lactate.[1] Men still have breasts, milk ducts and nipples and they can make milk – and do so in response to certain diseases or drug therapies. In the 1940s a 64-year-old man being treated for cancer was given estrogen and prolactin, the hormone that controls lactation in women, and he produced milk for the next seven years. Scores of malnourished prisoners of war held captive during World War II developed larger breasts and started producing milk once they were fed well again – at least until their livers recovered enough to bring their hormones back into balance. Some men who have persisted in putting their babies to their breasts have reportedly responded to the suckling reflex and produced normal nutritious milk.[2] Yet these eyebrow-raising rarities only serve to emphasise the overwhelming trend – male mammals don't make milk. It's no surprise, then, that mothers provide sole parental care in 90 per cent of mammal species. The fact that men share parenting duties puts them among a small minority of mammals.

But producing milk and caring for infants while they are still nursing makes special demands: women need reserves of fat to provide energy and healthy bones from which to extract calcium for the milk. So men have most likely always tended to be leaner and narrower-hipped than women. Humans are unusual among the mammals in having such abundant body fat, and women usually have proportionately more fat than men or children. Having extra fat leaves women less room for muscle, so a man's body weight averages 43 per cent muscle, whereas a woman's averages only 36 per cent. About a quarter of a woman's body mass is made up of fat, around twice as much as that of a man.

Female mammals typically store fat in the breasts, thighs and the base of the tail (or the buttocks in tail-less species), sites that place the extra weight near the body's centre of gravity to assist balance and locomotion, anthropologist Adrienne Zihlman realised – and thus men have been less affected than women by our ancestors' move to walking upright. That major change required our species to have an anatomical makeover, from one suiting a four-legged ape to one suiting a large-brained biped. Human bodies have become bottom-heavy, with massive lower limbs and light upper limbs (the reverse of our nearest relatives, the chimpanzees). Women's bodies have had to adapt in extra ways: their pelvis, for example, serves several functions – as an anchor for the legs, the opening for conception, the framework for the genitals and womb, the birth exit and even as a prop on which to carry a suckling infant.

It's obvious that men put on fat around the abdomen (which easily becomes hazardous waist!), while women tend to put on fat around the hips, bottom and thighs. If women were like men and did not have babies, they too would probably develop the male pot belly when they became overweight. Abdominal fat is laid down in men under the influence of genes and testosterone, the male sex hormone: the 'pot-belly' gene (if it can be called that) appears to be universal among men. The impact of testosterone can be seen in women with abnormally high levels of that hormone, who also develop abdominal fatness; depositing fat on the thighs seems to happen under the influence of estrogen.

Why do these sex differences occur? Clearly, the heavy demands of pregnancy and breast-feeding on women are the key. Humans, like other animals, lay down fat as a fuel reserve for lean times or periods of high energy demand (the camel's hump is the most famous animal fuel tank – it is made up of fat, which yields both energy and water when it is broken down). Women find it hard to lose their thigh fat in particular, because when fat is stored there it is less accessible for short-term energy demands. Men's abdominal fat is more metabolically active than women's and more easily broken down: that makes it much better suited to fuel the liver. In effect, a man's tubby tummy acts like a credit card for energy with a high daily cash limit that permits large withdrawals. A woman's rounded bottom and thighs, on the other hand, work like a credit card with a low daily withdrawal limit, to ensure her reserves can be eked out over a longer period. This system seems well-suited to the reproductive roles that typically face male and female mammals: males tend to need energy reserves they can call on quickly for the fight-or-flight responses required for male competition or defence of mate and offspring, while women need reserves that can sustain them more steadily through pregnancy and early motherhood.

Men also have a higher metabolic rate than women. Thus, because their body processes tick over a notch faster, they burn up relatively more energy. When women struggle to lose weight (and see men eating junk food and staying slim), they're fighting an uphill battle against biology.

It's a fair bet that since our species evolved, men have been taller and heavier than women on average as well. Most anthropologists believe this distinction goes way back, and that the size difference – known as sexual dimorphism – was even greater among our earlier ancestors. There's disagreement over which fossil species belong in our direct family line, but it's a trait we share with our closest relatives, chimpanzees, gorillas and orang-utans. 'We can't be certain, but I suspect that early hominids were sexually dimorphic since all three great apes are,' says anthropologist Dean Falk.

Chimpanzees and bonobos (also known as pygmy chimps) were the last apes to share a common ancestor with us, more than 6 million years ago – our genes and theirs differ by little more than 1 per cent. Among the earliest fossil evidence of human-like animals directly related to us is the group of species known as *Australopithecus*, which lived in Africa between 4 million and 2 million years ago. The famous fossilised partial skeleton of an individual nicknamed 'Lucy', who lived about 3.2 million years ago, was probably only 1.1 metres tall and weighed less than

30 kilograms. A similar fossil, thought to be that of a male, stood about 1.6 metres tall and weighed about 50 kilograms.

Different body sizes and functions, of course, suggest as well that men and women have always had different sets of sex-typical behaviour: it's not just our bodies that have been shaped by our sex, but our minds as well. We'll probably never know whether Lucy grumbled (or, more likely, grunted) about her mate hanging out having a good time with his friends every Friday night, or whether he thought she was moody and illogical. Jokes aside, we simply don't know whether *Australopithecus* society had clearly defined sex roles, or even whether the earliest humans did. Despite what you may have been told in the past about cave women sitting around the campfire tending the children while their big strong man went out hunting to bring home the bacon, it's all speculation. The oldest stone tools, from about 2.5 million years ago, reveal nothing in that respect.[3]

We certainly know that early humans had spiritual, or at least philosophical, beliefs. The oldest evidence for this comes from ancient human burial remains found in sand dunes at Lake Mungo, in south-eastern Australia. One grave there carries the remains of an adult man, known as 'Lake Mungo 3', who died between 50,000 and 70,000 years ago, according to the latest dating tests. His body had clearly undergone a mortuary ceremony, during which his bones had red ochre poured over them. Nearby are the more recent remains of a woman, revealing the world's earliest evidence of cremation. But, surprisingly, it has been virtually ignored that Lake Mungo 3 may also amount to the world's oldest evidence of human sexual self-awareness. Alan Thorne, a paleoanthropologist at the Australian National University, described the man as 'buried with his hands gripping, golfer-like, something between his upper thighs. Discussions with traditional Aboriginal people leave me in no doubt what the man was gripping when he was buried . . .' Penises, of course, don't fossilise. But some Aborigines today still bury a man with his hands cradling his penis, Thorne says. To them, it is a straightforward issue of 'a man protecting his most vital organ'. It is an action men reflexively perform when their genitals are threatened – witness the way soccer players stand when forming a defensive wall against a free kick.

Lake Mungo 3 is thus the first man we know of who seems to have belonged to a social group with this reverent attitude to sexuality and to the organ that is the vehicle of male reproductive power. As such, he surely deserves to be better known for this remarkable aspect of his life and death. Graves at the site also show an intriguing tendency for men to be buried and for women to be cremated. That trend may also reveal an ancient bias in the way men and women were regarded socially. If they were deemed to have a different status in death, it could well be that their social standing or roles – for some individuals at least – also varied in life. Sexism may thus have ancient roots. By the time Lake Mungo 3 was buried, he and other Australasian people were separated geographically from other races, yet there's ample evidence that similar spiritual and social beliefs have long been held by many of those other races. Colin Groves, also of the Australian National University, thinks this common global thread implies that these ideas had an early origin. Unless geographically distinct peoples each developed these ideas independently, they date well back into human history and were carried around the world as people colonised new lands.

The bracelets and ornaments found in human graves in Europe from 30,000 years ago were buried with both sexes, so they tell us nothing fresh about sex roles. It is only at later sites that more tangible expressions of cultural attitudes towards sex roles become apparent.[4] Cave art featuring Ice Age men hunting large game suggests that men were the painters – it doesn't tell us whether women hunted as well, or what else men did. The best-known Ice Age artworks are small sculpted images, rock carvings and cave paintings of women, mostly faceless and often with exaggerated breasts and buttocks. The most famous of them is the so-called 'Venus of Willendorf', a carved limestone figurine found in 1908 at an archeological site beside the Danube River in Lower Austria. The site had been occupied by Ice Age people in the Upper Paleolithic – between 40,000 and 12,000 years ago. Venus is a mere 13 centimetres tall: she is standing passively upright on chubby legs, has no facial features, is naked and displays plump, pendulous breasts and an apron of fat across her belly and hips; traces of red ochre have been found within the folds of her body.

Venus is one of about 200 such statuettes, carved over several centuries around 26,000 years ago and found widely dispersed, from the Pyrenees in the west to the southern Russian steppes in the east. Despite many colourful theories, no one knows who carved them or why.[5] They have been interpreted as images of a 'Great Goddess' from a time when women ruled Ice Age society, perhaps by dint of a spiritual belief in their creative power. However Timothy Taylor, a British archeologist, points out in his book *The Prehistory of Sex* that if this were true 'we should expect such a goddess to be doing something, as the vigorous goddesses of India do – slaying, giving birth, making love, and so on'. But none of them is shown doing anything much: even if they can be interpreted as depictions of pregnant women, not one is giving birth or nursing an infant. It has also been suggested that they may have been the Ice Age equivalent of male pornography, fertility symbols or grandmother symbols. Or perhaps they represented endurance and were images of women revered as great survivors – fat reserves successfully built up during good times making them better able to survive the cold and food deprivations of the northern winter. Taylor writes that the smooth figures seem to be well worn by handling. They certainly objectify women, leading to the untestable suggestion that women may even have been objects of exchange at the time. Perhaps marriage was practised by then, and the statues somehow represented a token of a bride. We will probably never know, but in contemporary hunter-gatherer societies, groups tend to be small and most people in them are related. Wives and husbands are usually acquired from outside the group, often through barter or warfare. Most human societies are patrilocal – that is, it is the woman who leaves her family group to marry into her husband's family group.

More recent Upper Paleolithic art features much more explicit sexual representation – engraved stones and paintings featuring male and female sexual organs, and a strange bone rod from the cave of La Madeleine, in France, depicting what seems to be a lioness licking the head of a huge penis hanging between the legs of a human figure. Other bones are carved and engraved into the unmistakable shapes of penises, including a double 'baton' somewhat suggestive of a modern double-dildo. Cave art from France and Spain often features male animals with obvious penises and, on occasion, male humans – perhaps shamans – appear with them, but their significance remains unknown. Even more recent paintings and engravings clearly depict sexual scenes: Taylor describes one from Adduara, Sicily, in which 'two young men are rolling over each other, their erections perhaps indicating some homosexual interest, while around them men and women dance'.[6]

Shamans, fertility cults and sexual symbolism are common in Paleolithic art. One famous image is of a 'sorcerer' from the Les Trois Frères site in southern France. Part-painted and part-carved, it combines human, deer, horse, bird and bear features; it is definitely male but its penis and testes are oddly positioned beneath a tail. The caves may also contain the first indirect evidence of male initiations. Well-preserved footprints have been found in some, and at least one set reveals a child's orderly dance pattern. At Niaux, in the Pyrenees, more than 500 footprints were discovered in a cave gallery more than a kilometre further into the mountain (and across three underground lakes) from the famous bison and horse drawings of the Galerie Noir. Many of the footprints are those of youngsters aged 13 to 15, intermingled with those of adults. 'Flutes and the remains of what may have been other musical instruments have been found in many caves, indicating that ceremonial dancing was accompanied by music,' reveals Swedish archeologist Goran Burenhult.[7] 'Within all traditional cultures, rites of passage are a crucial part of ritual and ceremonial life. They are related to birth, puberty, marriage and death. Male initiation rites – when young boys, under the direction of a master, are initiated into the mysteries of the adult world – are often associated with isolation, darkness and frightening experiences. Painful tests of manhood, such as tattooing and sometimes circumcision, are often an important element of these prolonged ceremonies.'

The evidence from Niaux conjures up vivid mental pictures of the scenes that may have taken place there. We can only imagine them now. But a revolution in human society was soon to follow, one that in Taylor's words 'was eventually to reforge women's economic inequality in bonds so durable that they persist into the present day'. It was the development of agriculture.

It's easy to forget today that for more than 90 per cent of their time on Earth, human beings sustained a plentiful and balanced diet with hunting and gathering, often requiring only a few hours' effort each day. The need for mobility keeps hunter-gatherer life materially simple, and such societies often limit their populations. But by making settled communities possible, agriculture sparked an economic, technological and cultural transformation. That revolution began in the Old World about 11,000 years ago, in the 'Fertile Crescent' of the Middle East, focused around the Tigris and Euphrates rivers, although there is increasing and often-overlooked evidence from the Australasian region that suggests agriculture may have developed independently several times, and much earlier. Strong hints can be found in the Solomon Islands, for example, that taro was deliberately planted and cultivated as early as 28,000 years ago.

There is no doubt, however, that what happened in the Fertile Crescent triggered a global human revolution. The region's archeological record shows the transition to farming villages took no more than a few centuries. Within two millennia, the food revolution had swept communities from Pakistan to the Balkans, with enormous environmental upheaval as forests were felled for crops and grazing. With surpluses, more individuals were freed from food production. The 'daily bread' is the reason craftspeople, artists, bureaucrats, social classes, crowded cities and epidemics could emerge. The first agriculturists could never have foreseen how their humble discovery would ultimately seed a population explosion.

The switch to farming required people to know about the reproduction of plants and animals – and to implement that knowledge. And, it seems, men seized this moment to exert control over human reproduction as well, and in doing so grabbed the lion's share of social power. 'The Old Testament, which was written by farmers, describes a world in which men are in control of society, where violence is commonplace, where God is male, and where the earth is female,' Taylor says. In that sense, the sexual symbolism of ploughing the earth seems obvious. Less obvious is that sex roles probably became far more clearly defined. At London's Natural History Museum, studies of Neolithic (11,500–7500 years ago) skeletons from what is now Syria suggest women got the lowly job of grinding grain – evidence for this is the peculiar wear and tear on their bodies, including bony growths on their kneecaps that would now be described as 'housemaid's knee'. Taylor points out, however, that when Caddoan mound builders in Texas switched from hunting and gathering to farming, women benefited more than men, because their skeletal remains show that the size disparity between them and men was markedly reduced by women growing larger – probably because of better nourishment. That implies, of course, that the men consumed either more food or more nutritious food before the switch.

A survey of 104 modern horticultural societies found that women were solely responsible for cultivation in half of them, while men were solely responsible in less than one-fifth. If that pattern of sex-based labour distribution reflects what happened in ancient times, the amount of time and energy women had available for nursing and rearing young children would certainly have suffered. Taylor wonders whether less frequent breast-feeding by women working in the fields reduced the contraceptive power of lactation – which depends mostly on hormones that are produced in quantities according to the frequency of feeds, not the volume of milk suckled – and so made them more fertile. The advent of communal longhouses and settled villages must have made the sexual activity of individuals much more public, so it seems at least likely that sex became more regulated during that time. It also seems likely that social violence increased. Farming communities stand to suffer gravely from encroachment of neighbours onto their lands or from the theft of their animals and crops, so conflict over resources may have brought men into battle with each other more often. One ancient gravesite in Germany contains 34 contorted skeletons in a single pit, the victims having been killed by stone axes, cudgels and arrows and stripped of their belongings.

By about 5500 years ago, European people were using animals to supply milk for human consumption, as attested to by a wide range of pottery vessels. When they first began using animal milk as a substitute for human breast milk for babies is unknown, but that move would have freed women to take on even more labour – perhaps they did so under pressure from men. At least one painting in northern Italy from the time shows what appears to be evidence of different sex roles in work, with men linked to heavy work with animals: men are shown ploughing with an oxen team while a woman uses a hoe and carries a baby on her back. Some bizarre sexual images from the same region depict a man with an erection apparently attempting intercourse with a long-eared animal that seems to be a donkey. Others from Siberia are stranger still: one shows a man on snow skis, standing directly behind an elk with an arm extended onto the animal's rump; the man has an obvious erection.

Whatever these images mean (whether merely symbolic or records of actual events), an association between men, sex and animals is plain. 'The fertilising power of the penis and the reproductive value of semen must have been well known to those who managed animals,' Taylor says. 'The control of animal sexuality by men may have had its analogue in control of the sexuality of human females. The rise of the idea of property, in land, in herds, and in women, would have placed new emphasis on exclusive rights of sexual access, as promised by certain forms of marriage. In an exploitative economy, virginity may have been valued in both land and women. Early farming societies were probably the first to formulate rape laws, not so much to protect women as to defend property and lines of inheritance.'

The male cultural role of husband probably dates from this time. The word 'husband' has old Scandinavian roots: the first syllable came from the word *hus*, meaning a house, the second from *bonda*, a dweller. So originally a husband was literally a house-dweller. The term has acquired other meanings, too: to husband your resources is to manage them well and economically (as in animal husbandry) and to be thrifty with them; another meaning, now obsolete, was to do with tilling the soil. Together, they suggest a positive picture of a married man, attached to his home, who manages his affairs well and labours to grow food, control animals and nourish his family. (This image of a cautious, nurturing, homebody is in stark contrast to the cliché of the roving, risk-taking exploiter of women. Yet early farmers are highly unlikely to have been peace-loving homebodies.)

Incidentally, we have recently gained an amazingly detailed insight into the life and times of one man from that era. Late in the northern summer of 1991, the deep-frozen body of 'Otzi', the Iceman, emerged from a melting glacier on the Austrian–Italian border. It was the earliest-known preserved human body – over 5000 years old – and a fabulous scientific find. The adventurous Otzi had the misfortune to be caught in a blizzard on a high mountain pass. But his bad luck proved a boon for science. Otzi's remains are currently being studied by 40 research teams. We know he was a mountain man from his rich tool-kit, adapted for alpine conditions in self-reliant ways any modern climber would recognise. His lightweight gear included a waterproof grass cloak, a backpack, a utility tool belt and plenty of sinew, leather straps and spare parts needed for running repairs. A leather case contained a firelighter, tinder, a dagger and repair tools.

Otzi may have walked to the pass from what is now Castle Juval, an ancient settlement about 8 kilometres away. He clearly had links with nearby agricultural communities and distant peoples. His last meal was of meat and milled corn, and the flint for his stone tools was almost certainly mined about 200 kilometres away at Monte Lessini. He carried 18 different kinds of wood, each chosen for specific tasks. His axe handle and 1.8-metre unfinished bow were of yew, his fur quiver was stitched with leather and stiffened with hazelwood and his 14 arrows were made of dogwood and guelder-rose. His soft axe blade had been rehammered for sharpening three times and his hair was heavily contaminated with copper and toxic levels of arsenic, suggesting exposure to copper smelting.

Otzi's mummified remains also offer insights into the illnesses and medicines of his time. Growth ridges on Otzi's chipped fingernails suggest at least three bouts of significant sickness in the four months before he died. Included in his kit were two tree fungi threaded on a leather thong. The fungi were apparently used as an antibiotic medicine. His 57 tattoos – groups of blue parallel lines and crosses – may have served to identify his tribe or personal status, or simply mark the sites of aches and pains that had been given ritualised treatment. He had badly worn teeth and stress fractures in his leg bones from much heavy load-bearing; osteoarthritis in his neck, lower back and hip; eight rib fractures; and signs of a very modern problem – high cholesterol and heart disease. A brain scan has hinted that he might have had a minor stroke, too. Cold feet apparently bothered him, because his roughly made fur shoes were packed tight with hay. Aged about 45, Otzi was probably a very senior man in his community.

Metals found in Otzi's axe may have come from the Bulgarian Black Sea coast, where one rich gravesite at Varna has attracted attention. It contains a man's skeleton and many well-made metal objects. He was buried holding a ceremonial copper axe and wearing golden arm rings, a gold medallion and clothing with gold buttons. But it is the gold-tipped object between his legs that is most unusual: it appears either to represent his penis or was designed to cover its end. Made of a single hammered sheet of gold, it is roughly the diameter of an erect penis but only about 6 centimetres long. The 'penis-piece', as Taylor calls it, has a hole in the tip, which could permit urination or ejaculation, and perforations on the rim suggesting that it may have been sewn to a garment. Taylor believes it was clearly an item made to be seen, either in life or after death, but otherwise the significance of the golden penis remains a mystery.

Early human writings make it clear that complex language skills had evolved by then, that people had discovered addictive drugs and that they routinely committed genocide. Sexual practices seem to have differed little from those of today: reference is made to homosexuality, transsexuals, transvestites and masturbation. Supernatural beings were accorded human-like sex roles and procreative powers. One ancient Egyptian myth told how Atum the sun god 'put his penis in his hand that he might obtain the pleasure of emission thereby and there were born brother and sister – that is Shu and Tefnut'.

The rise of megalithic culture in Europe, about 4500 years ago, led to a fantastic array of stone monuments – such as the famous Stonehenge – and burial mounds, many of which have been interpreted as having phallic overtones, although less blatantly so than the temples and phallic representations in later Asian culture. Priestly male cults arose and the symbolism of fertility rites is replete with evidence of men believing they held some sway over the reproductive power of nature. Burials differed for men and women; men were often buried with weapons at their side – readied for battle even after death. Ancient Greek texts record evidence of eunuchs, male homosexuality and cross-dressing shamans and priests. Taylor suggests that people born with ambiguous gender or sexual orientation may have been revered in some cultures, perhaps beginning a long tradition of priests wearing womanly clothing.

Attitudes to male homosexuality varied from culture to culture, with some embracing it and others reviling it. In 1904, two 'bog' bodies were found in the southern part of the Bourtanger Moor, in the Netherlands. They died between 160 BC and 220 AD: one was killed by a stab wound to the chest, from which some intestines spilled out, but the cause of death of the other is unknown. Both were naked and because one of them lay on the outstretched arm of the other, who is obviously male, it was at first though that the second body was that of a woman. They became known as the 'Weerdinge Couple', and much was made of their apparently romantic association in tragic circumstances. But in 1988 Wijnand van der Sanden, a former curator at Drents Museum in Assen and an expert in bog bodies, confirmed that the second body was also male. The discovery caused a stir, as he recalled in an e-mail message to me: 'The Dutch *Gay Krant* [gay newspaper] asked whether they were the first homosexuals in the Netherlands. I told them what I told you – there is absolutely no way we can find out if they were. I can think of many other, more likely explanations. Tacitus, in the first century AD, tells us that the Germanic tribes detested homosexuals (they drowned them in swamps!). However, the position of both men does not indicate that they were thrown in by people who detested them; the position they are in is one of caring.'[8] Van der Sanden believes most bog bodies are human sacrifices. The pair may have been father and son, brothers or best friends, but a romantic link between them remains a possibility. Other records suggest that women were killed and thrown into bogs as punishment for adultery, or because they had been sexually assaulted. Tacitus also asserted that the German tribes severely punished adultery: he describes how the husband of an adulterous wife would shave off her hair, strip her in the presence of kinsmen, expel her from their house and flog her 'through the whole village'.

The ancient Greeks had a more tolerant view, certainly in relation to homosexual behaviour: indeed, it was expected that even married men could have sex with youths 'without beards'. Some accounts suggest that certain boys were castrated as infants, or had their genitals manually crushed, to feminise them in preparation for later service as male prostitutes. Sex slavery and commercial sex – the 'oldest profession' – seem to have been well established by Roman times. Roman men could even acquire brothel tokens of differing values. A sexual act – such as fellatio or a particular position for intercourse – was pictured on one side of the token and a number on the reverse side set the price. 'Found all over Europe, wherever the Roman army went, they represented an institutionalised form of professional sex that crossed all language barriers,' Taylor explains. 'A mercenary from Libya or Dacia could decide what he wanted and obtain it from a Caledonian prostitute during his tour of duty on Hadrian's Wall. She, on the other hand, knew precisely what the man had paid for. The tokens imply an established sex industry that did everything from design and manufacture the tokens themselves to maintaining brothel premises.'[9]

Mystery surrounds the origins of a spectacular artistic expression of manhood, the Cerne Abbas giant in Britain. This huge chalk figure carved into a Dorset hillside has a body 55 metres long and carries a 40-metre club raised high over his head, as if poised to strike. His two nipples are depicted, as well as horizontal lines on his chest that seem to be ribs, and another line encircles his waist like a belt. But his most famous attributes are an enormous erect penis and scrotum. The giant's makers are unknown, as is the date when it was made (it may not be ancient at all). The site is recorded in historical texts as being used for maypole dancing, the maypole itself being a phallic focus for the fertility rites linked to celebrations of spring. Local legend suggests that women who wished to conceive should sleep on the giant. But it is the unusual combination of virility, aggression and technology in the figure that, for me at least, makes him a memorable symbol of ancient maleness. The rest, as they say, is history.

Although we know so little about how men got to be the way they are, we know a lot more about maleness from observing it at work in the much larger animal world. As you'll see in the next chapter, there are clues aplenty in that realm to help us learn more about why men are the way they are and what sets them apart – and links them to – other kinds of males.

3

ZOOLOGY:
All men are beasts

'In the spring a fuller crimson comes upon the robin's breast,
In the spring the wanton lapwing gets himself another crest,
In the spring a livelier iris changes on the burnish'd dove;
In the spring a young man's fancy lightly turns to thoughts of love.'

Alfred, Lord Tennyson

THE CAR HEADLIGHTS pick out our way along a thin black strip of road that winds between lush fields of tall sugar cane. Here in Australia's tropical far north the night air is balmy and still: conditions are perfect for our search for one of the strangest and toughest male animals on the planet. These guys are zoology's real-life equivalent of the cartoon character Yosemite Sam – ornery loners always spoiling for a fight. I am travelling with zoologist Graeme Newell to his field research site in a remnant patch of rainforest amid crop and dairy country on the lush Atherton

Tablelands of Queensland. Australia boasts many bizarre animals, but it's hard to believe that the one we seek here exists at all: it is the tree-kangaroo. Its famous ground-dwelling cousins are odd enough, but this is a 'roo with a view, one that spends most of its life in the treetops. It is a canny and intrepid climber that performs a hazardous high-wire act with no safety net, enjoys a steady diet of toxic fruit and has an occasional taste for meat. This is most definitely no cute and cuddly Skippy the bush kangaroo.

Unknown to the outside world until last century, tree-kangaroos are found only in dense rainforests in Australia and New Guinea, and precious little is known about them even today. And no wonder: they are secretive, mainly active at night and generally prefer the most rugged and remote terrain. The 10 known species range from about the size of a medium-sized dog to whoppers weighing almost 25 kilograms. That puts them among the world's largest tree-dwelling creatures. Some are also among the most spectacularly coloured animals of any kind, with lush fur in extravagant stripes and patterns. One has an almost human face and another leaves footprints like those of a child. Another stands erect, throws up its arms and whistles when startled. And the males are as macho and pugnacious as they come. Highlands hunters in New Guinea tell of a man who fired an arrow into one, only to have the animal rip out the offending projectile, throw it back and hit him. Careless hunting dogs can have their snouts crushed by a solid bite from the kangaroo's powerful jaws, or be disembowelled by its large and viciously hooked claws.

Newell soon pulls the car over on to the verge of a small side road serving several farms and we take in the sight of a calm, clear night blazing with stars and lit by a half-moon. The stillness of the air means that when we see leaves and branches shaking, we can be confident that animal movements, not the wind, will be responsible. Many crickets and grasshoppers are calling loudly (more males in competition) in a nearby sugar plantation and a few bats are winging their way overhead as we check our spotlights and heft heavy batteries into our backpacks. 'We can't predict where or whether we'll see any tonight, because they're so wary,' Newell warns. We head away from the road, skirting through long grass around the edge of the forest on foot. As our spotlights pierce the darkness, we are looking for the telltale 'eyeshine' of animals hiding in the treetops. The species that lives here is Lumholtz's tree-kangaroo, a medium-sized animal that is less bothered by living near people than other tree-kangaroo species.

Even so, this is not easy going. Our feet and legs are soon soaked by dew and itching from the scrub mites and small grass ticks that latch on to us for blood. The ground is rough as well and we must watch our step to avoid twisting an ankle – seeking tree-kangaroos at night is not for the faint-hearted. Likewise life up there in the canopy, as I soon realise when our thoughts are shattered by a sudden uproar from high in the tall trees almost directly above us. Two tree 'roos are crashing about up there, sending down a rain of torn leaves and snapped branches; they are almost certainly males intent on a riotous mutual assault. Then we hear with dismay an almighty crack as a branch breaks, a brief silence, then a heavy thump on the ground just metres to our right. A big 'roo has just hit the deck with an unforgettable and sickening thud. Yet moments later we hear him hopping rapidly away through the undergrowth, apparently unscathed by the drop of some 15 metres. We shake our heads in wonder at such resilience.

'They've been known to fall from 20 metres or more, then carry on as if nothing had happened,' Newell says. 'They must be extraordinarily tough.'

They are also highly aggressive and frequently fight each other, especially around breeding time. Their bloody battles and strong territorial urges can take a heavy toll. As with orang-utans, mature males of this species are largely solitary, patrolling a territory whose size depends on the individual's strength and fitness but which overlaps with the territory of several females and their young. Only during the brief mating season do the males seem to have anything much to do with their mates and offspring. When males first mature, they are driven out by their fathers to claim and fight for a territory of their own. Many are killed in the process. Radio-tracking collars placed on males by Newell frequently had to be replaced because they were torn off in violent conflicts. Older males often carry an array of battle scars, are missing patches of fur, have gouged eyes or one or both ears chewed.

Roger Martin, of Monash University, spent years trekking through rugged forests further north of here to compile extensive studies of another species, Bennett's tree-kangaroo. Martin found that males of this species can weigh up to 14 kilograms. They are much larger than the females and extremely intolerant of each other. Fights are common and all adult males carry many scars; some lose their lives in these altercations. The male combat points to a complex social order among the tree 'roos, but very little is known about this aspect of their lives. Newell tells me that the males boldly advertise their presence to each other with smells. They mark trees with a distinctive and foul-smelling yellow secretion from special large scent glands. 'The males can smell disgusting up close,' he says. 'I used to keep road-kills for study in the deep-freeze at work and my colleagues complained that you could still smell them even then.'

In and along the creeks and rivers that flow through the tree 'roo forests lives another extraordinary and surprising male, the platypus. This amphibious oddity is found in waterways right down Australia's east coast. The first specimen sent to England by early colonists was denounced as a sewn-together fraud, so incredulous were the scientists at the sight of this bizarre animal, with its webbed feet and bill like a duck, yet also warm-blooded, fur-covered and with females that lay eggs like a reptile and nurse their young with milk.

Among the many intriguing discoveries in recent times about these unique animals is that adult females greatly outnumber males. Field studies led by scientists from the Taronga Zoo Conservation Research Centre, in Sydney, have shown that the ratio of females to males surges from roughly equal at birth to about 6:1 after five years. It turns out that this is another case of an outwardly endearing animal having a mean streak; the young males probably disappear because older males systematically kill them. Although direct evidence is lacking, researchers at the centre believe mature males use the potent venom in the sharp spur they carry on the inner side of each hind leg to kill younger males in territorial fights. The females do not have such spurs, and in males they do not emerge from protective sheaths until about two years old, when they begin to pose a potential threat to older males. 'It seems pretty logical that this is the means by which dominant males assert their position,' says researcher Cliff Gallagher.

Australia's extremely variable climate, which can swing suddenly and unpredictably from extended drought to heavy flood, may account for such a deadly strategy. It has the effect of keeping overall platypus numbers low – thus easing the pressure on resources for females and young – but still leaves them able to recover their numbers quickly after droughts. If older males die in extreme climatic conditions, many young males are soon available to replace them. It is likely that an older male effects his kill by manoeuvring on top of a younger one, then grasping it in a bear hug and stabbing with his spurs. Venom is a serious weapon in the platypus male's offensive and defensive arsenal. It contains a potent nerve irritant, as one zoo worker discovered to her cost. Karen Firestone was hospitalised for days after she was accidentally spurred in the hand: the site of the wound quickly became heavily swollen and discoloured, and she excreted urine the colour of dark tea as the venom ruptured her red blood cells and muscle membranes, causing her agonising pain that not even morphine could relieve. Studies of her blood showed that the platypus venom contained an enzyme found only in some snakes, including the feared tiger snake. For male platypuses, sexual competition is a take-no-prisoners affair.

The pursuit of sexual success is no easier in elephant seal colonies. These remarkable animals perform amazing physical feats. They can dive down to 1.5 kilometres beneath the surface and stay submerged continuously for more than an hour when they do so – the deepest and longest dives recorded for any mammal. They can also store up enough energy and water in their body fat to allow them to fast for weeks or months during the breeding season. They need such rich reserves because breeding and parenting takes a heavy toll on them. Elephant seals are among the most polygynous mammalian species known and the most sexually dimorphic – in other words, adult breeding males mate with as many females as possible and are much, much bigger than the females. The males can weigh over 2.5 tonnes, which is up to seven times heavier than a typical female (picture a woman paired up with a man weighing 450 kilograms and you'll get the idea). But very few males ever get to be that big. Joanne Reiter of the University of California and her associates have studied northern elephant seals for many years and their research has revealed depressing statistics for the males.[1] Only 1 in 5 ever reaches breeding age and, of them, fewer than half actually get to have sex – but the lucky ones may get to have hundreds of 'wives'. In one group of seals followed over their lifetimes, 75 per cent of the females were inseminated by less than 5 per cent of the males. So the odds of becoming a parent are 1 in 10 for males, as opposed to 1 in 4 for females. But few females produce more than 10 pups in a lifetime, whereas the most successful males can father thousands.

The breeding season for elephant seals typically starts with males arriving from the Pacific Ocean at established rookery sites on islands and beaches in late November and early December each year. Males must survive for four years to become sexually mature, but they must survive another four to become fully equipped to win the reproductive prize. At that stage the males have become extraordinary individuals. Not only do they boast great size and weight, but their chests have developed a large layer of corrugated, calloused tissue – like a medieval knight's shield – and their noses have become bloated and pendulous. For the next 90 days they do little else but fight, clash chests, roar and bellow and have sex. Young males don't get a look in and are quickly driven off by the larger ones, who then turn their attention on each other to establish a 'dominance hierarchy', or pecking order. Their battles can be torrid and bloody, with injury, death or banishment to some vulnerable corner of the rookery for the losers. The victors lay claim to a prime piece of waterfront real estate that can attract thousands of females, when they arrive later. But the more females in each harem, the more energy these top-ranking males must expend on guarding them. It is a severe test of their fitness, and one that requires powerful motivation. Their enormous sex drive is one such force: 'Males do not discriminate among the females with which they mate; they will attempt to mate with any female, and some will attempt to mate with newly weaned pups, yearlings, dead seals and even fibreglass models of elephant seal females,' Reiter explains. 'Females do not appear to "choose" individual males but behave in such a way that only the highest-ranking males will have an opportunity to mate with them.' Before or just after she goes into estrus, a female will pull out all the stops to reject would-be suitors (sometimes these clashes are so violent that she is badly injured or even killed). Her protests advertise her readiness to mate, which attracts many other males: in the ensuing melée, the highest-ranking male in the vicinity gets to inseminate her. And that, in effect, is his parental duty done.

Male and female pups differ in size and behaviour almost from birth. Male pups are born slightly heavier than females and suckle their mothers' rich milk a little longer than their sisters before weaning about four weeks after birth. But newly weaned male pups are cunning: they risk hostility, even serious bites, to sneak back into the harem and steal milk from still-nursing females. Reiter's team found that male pups are six times more likely than female pups to do this and are far more persistent in their efforts. They succeed in part because their teeth erupt two weeks later than those of the females, so the mothers they rob often don't notice that the interlopers are weaners. Getting a head start on growth over his competitors must boost a male's chances of success later in life, since size differences between young individuals are usually maintained into adulthood. Once weaned, male and female behaviour diverges even more. Males playfight much as adults do for real, rearing up at each other, biting and slamming necks. By the time they are ready to go to sea, the strongest young males already seem primed for eventual success.

Male animals can be sneaky in their pursuit of reproductive success. Where I live in Sydney, for example, you can still be lucky enough to see an attractive bird known as the superb fairy wren. These busy little birds with their perky tails and sweet trilling call are much loved by people. But science has shown that they're loved even more by each other. Indeed, the crown of the world's most promiscuous bird now rests on its tiny head. Despite the fact that male and female pair for life in their own territories, genetic fingerprinting tests have shown that 75 per cent of these birds are fathered by males other than the one that devotedly raises them. This is the highest rate of 'extra-pair' fertilisation known among birds. Unless a male superb fairy wren zealously guards his partner during their spring breeding season she will happily receive a new suitor as often as every three minutes.[2] It stands to reason that she can do so because her own mate is so often away from home in search of hanky-panky with neighbouring females. This practice is known as 'kleptogamy' – literally 'marriage theft'. But a boffin with a sense of humour invented the more memorable term 'furgling', combining a well-known vulgarity with 'burgling'.

Patient research has revealed that male wrens spend much time and energy slipping into nearby territories to show off their wares to the resident females. Raoul Mulder, one of a team of evolutionary ecologists at the Australian National University who have been studying superb fairy wrens for years, has recorded hundreds of these displays. Males fluff their cheek feathers, lower their tails and twist from side to side to show off their striking blue breeding plumage. They often carry a yellow flower petal in their beaks as well, a flag of romantic convenience that contrasts nicely with the colour of their feathers. Strangely, though, resident males almost never bother to strut such stuff for their own partners, and are hardly ever seen to copulate with them either. But Mulder has found that the dandy intruders seem to have no better luck; their displays are virtually never rewarded with mating at the time. It seems that the deed is done quite secretively, when a female later slips away from her partner and actively solicits her chosen mates. Mulder suspects that the displays actually serve to advertise each male's finest features, and that the female eventually furgles with the flashiest fellow. The males that father the most offspring are those that moult earliest each year, ready to grow their breeding plumage – so the length of the display period seems to be the key to being chosen by females to copulate. The fittest males best survive early moulting.[3] Exposure to cold in late winter and the extra risks of predation by being so visible in their bright blue breeding plumage mean that many males die in their quest for sex.

Life is not all bread and circuses in a duckpond, either. Female choosiness can make life extremely difficult for the Pacific black ducks that frequent ponds in many Australian cities and towns. The females of the species, it seems, are social climbers whose tastes include not only choice real estate but a preference for the most successful and aggressive males, even when they are from another species. In fact, wherever mallard ducks are found in Australia, female black ducks are tempted to pair with them instead of males of their own kind. Mallard drakes are renowned aggressors: they compete vigorously to reach the top of their pecking order and are known to commit a kind of pack rape on unguarded females (including other waterfowl and even, in one reported case, a sleeping owl). But mallards are not native to Australia, having been introduced into the country in 1871. So why would an Aussie black duck be so strongly tempted to cross the species barrier and pair with an exotic, randy, violent mallard drake? Well, it seems that such a female doesn't just choose any old mallard. If she picks a dominant drake, one that has pecked and hustled its way to the top of the mallard social ladder, she reaps several benefits. In particular, she suffers less harassment from other males and gains access to the best feeding sites for herself and her hybrid offspring. Those offspring are fertile, but if the species-crossing process was common and prolonged, black ducks would be in danger of being genetically swamped.

The problem is confined to urban areas, because mallards have stayed in or near human settlements since their introduction, according to Walter Boles, an ornithologist with the Australian Museum. Pacific black ducks are numerous, and their much wider dispersal enables large breeding populations to remain unsullied. However, in New Zealand the same species (where it is called the grey duck) is faring much worse, having virtually disappeared around the main cities. In the US a related species that is prized by hunters, the American black duck, may be heading the same way. American black duck males are passive and subordinate in the company of male mallards, and readily acquiesce in competition over females, one study has found. Hybridisation between the species is extensive and, coupled with destruction of habitats, the trend poses a real threat to black ducks in the US. It may well be that other closely related species have already gone into genetic oblivion in such a way and that we are watching evolution at work in our duckponds.

By now you will have seen themes emerging in all these animal stories. Males and females can differ markedly in size and behaviour. Their reproductive strategies can be at odds with each other. Their degree of commitment as partners and parents can vary enormously, from lifelong devotion to wham-bam, thank-you ma'am. Sex may only take place at strictly defined times and in pre-programmed ways, or it may be possible for much improvisation to take place. For males, competition and a lusty sex drive are integral to their reproductive success as individuals, with some passing on their genes far more successfully than others. The behaviour of males towards each other and towards females can also vary greatly from time to time, depending on the context of their meetings. And there are different strokes for different folks: each species has its own variations on the sex theme that most suit its biology and way of life.

Humans are truly remarkable in this scheme of things. Our incomparable ability to acquire, store, reassemble and pass on information from one generation to the next makes us unique among animals. It has enabled us to effectively sidestep genetics to some extent and 'evolve' much more rapidly through our culture. We don't have to wait for large numbers of people to die out or thrive to be able to adapt to changing environmental circumstances – we can invent technology and develop ideas, acquire new knowledge and skills and share them rapidly with each other. But we are still very much influenced by our animal biology, which is firmly under genetic control. Our capacity to have children, for example, is governed by obvious biological constraints. We experience puberty, and until that landmark has been passed boys do not produce sperm and girls do not ovulate: we can't breed sooner than that, even if we want to. And, of course, our biology dictates that it is females who have babies and males who inseminate females.

Our anatomies and life cycles clearly point to our roots being among the mammals. There's no scientific doubt, either, that we belong among the primates, the mammal group that includes lemurs, monkeys and apes. So, to better understand men, we first need to rattle the skeletons in the family closet and look at the sex-related legacies we have inherited from such ancestors. As Mary McDonald Pavelka, an anthropologist at the University of Calgary, puts it: '. . . our precultural evolutionary history is not so remote as to render us unique in all respects and isolated in the world of living things. Human sexuality is primate sexuality, and an understanding of human sexuality requires that we know something about our basic primate sexuality.'[4]

Primates as a group – and there are hundreds of species – follow familiar patterns when they reproduce. They have small litters of well-developed babies, for example. Most have only one baby at a time, although the occasional twin can be accommodated since most female primates are equipped with two breasts. Primate offspring go through some well-defined phases as they grow: they spend a relatively long time being nursed by their mothers, they are slow to mature sexually, they have long pregnancies and they live relatively long lives. In short, primates have opted for quality over quantity, and parents must invest a lot of time and effort in their kids. Other mammals have taken the same tack – including whales and elephants – but the primates are exceptional in allowing their offspring so much time and resources to develop their brains. Correcting for relative body size, the brain of a primate fetus is about twice as big as that of a non-primate fetus. Humans have specialised even further: our babies are born utterly dependent on their parents and their central nervous systems keep developing for another year after birth. This seems to be largely because humans have evolved such large brains that they cannot develop further in the womb; any bigger and the head simply would be too large to fit through a woman's birth canal. If that mechanical hurdle did not exist, human babies would probably be born at about 21 months – the sum of the nine months they spend in the womb and the extra year they spend being nursed closely by their mothers.

These inescapable facets of our biology have major consequences for men and women, just as they do for the sexes in all other mammals. Patricia Draper, an anthropologist at Pennsylvania State University, points out that among species living in multi-male or mixed-sex groups, males typically take a dominant role in the social hierarchy as a result of their competition for access to females. But for mammal species in which the young's survival is critically dependent on both parents being involved in looking out for their welfare, male and female interests more closely coincide. Mate-guarding is practised by both sexes, since either can be disadvantaged by the desertion of their partner for another mate. Jealousy displays by males are typically more intense, though, because they are far more vulnerable to being cuckolded. A 'sneaky' male – such as a furgling fairy wren – may impregnate a female and so trick her more faithful partner into raising offspring that are not his own. It's much harder for a female to be duped into raising offspring that are not her own.

Humans carry the primate specialisation trick of dependent offspring to an extreme, and the consequences of this are more significant for women than men, especially when it comes to parenting. 'Women are committed to a disproportionate amount of this parental work since, unlike males, they cannot recoup one or a few infant deaths by finding another mate,' Draper says. 'A woman who loses a child has not lost only that individual with whom she has personal ties, but she has lost irreplaceable reproductive time. A man who loses even all his children may experience an acute sense of personal loss, but he can replace them by establishing one or more additional mating relationships with other women.' The all-time paternity record is held by Morocco's Emperor Ismail the Bloodthirsty (1672–1727), who had 700 sons and probably as many daughters.

And it's this reproductive inequality between the sexes – with parent potential skewed so much in favour of men – that fosters many of the physical and behavioural differences between them. 'Following this line of reasoning, one sees the human female is encumbered to an extent not seen in other species. Because of the extremely dependent state in which young are born and because of their slow development, any roles that conflict with a woman's reproductive roles are generally avoided by her as an individual or denied her by other interested parties, especially her kin and her mates. The human mother must continue to invest high levels of parental care in several young simultaneously. Unlike other primate females who greatly reduce care of the next oldest offspring (by no longer nursing or carrying the sub-adult juvenile) when a new infant is born, a woman maintains not one but several dependent offspring, albeit at different stages of dependence. With each new child, she adds further to her encumberment and goes farther and farther into "debt" in the sense that her dependents multiply, but her physical reservoir of energies remains the same. In order to rear offspring, a woman must have help. Some aid comes from her kin, but nearly all human groups attempt to regulate access to the reproductive capabilities of women by designating a mate (husband) and making him and his kin share in the work of rearing and defending the children.'[5]

So, just as women are pressured by biology into devoting so much time and effort into raising their children, men are likewise pressured by culture into behaving in ways that may at times run counter to their biological tendencies but that promote the survival of their offspring. If men had free rein, for example, to be like elephant seals – compete violently with other men, mate with large numbers of women and provide very little parental care – it's obvious that human society would be very different (and, I'd guess, far less pleasant or successful). If we look at how other mammal species manage this reproductive dilemma, we can see a wide range of responses: 'It is important to note how much variability there is, among species and subspecies, in the amount of parenting investment made by males. It would seem that biology has left males flexible in this regard, permitting them to adapt to the variable social conditions that determine whether or not male investment is needed to permit offspring to grow safely to maturity,' says veteran American developmental psychologist Eleanor Maccoby.

A key feature of sexual maturation that humans unquestionably share with their close animal relatives is that they go through a social adolescence, and this imposes special restraints on young males. We know from experience, for example, that an adolescent boy's first ejaculation does not clearly define the end of his childhood in the way that a girl's first period seems to do. Alice Schlegel, an anthropologist at the University of Arizona, points out that in some cultures the criterion for the start of transition into manhood is the first successful demonstration of a skill: killing a large animal, memorising a set of laws or simply getting a driver's licence. Doing so in some societies means that the youth can then take a wife: Hopi Indian boys, for example, become men by being initiated into a man's fraternity, then marry soon afterwards.[6]

♂ Chan's story

Chan is 18 and 'very much heterosexual'. He lives at home and has recently finished high school. He is working part-time and enjoying a busy social life, but his main focus is skateboarding with male friends. Here he reflects on his awakening to being male and to sex.

'I've always known I'm male but I never really thought much about it as such before I had sexual feelings. Even though boys and girls were often separated – for toilets and sports and things like that – I didn't think of myself as being different to them. I guess it's when you start seeing girls as romantic figures that it starts to hit home.

'I remember in early primary school my first crush was on the girl character named Penny in the TV cartoon series *Inspector Gadget*, which seems pretty strange now. She was the brains of the operation and she had a dog and carried a computer book. That's one of my first memories of respecting a girl.

'My first kiss happened when I was about 12. I was scared shitless, but it was done on a dare at a party with everyone else watching. She had to start it and it was like pure adrenalin for 14 seconds. I was really quite afraid of girls back then and I didn't want to overstep any boundaries.

'It was a very insecure time when we all started to get sexual feelings. You become aware of your penis in a new way once you start to realise that you don't just pee out of the thing. Your voice is cracking, which is embarrassing, and everyone draws attention to it. Slowly adults start realising you're not a little kid anymore and they start treating you more like a friend than a guardian. You don't need their compliments and approval so much.

'I clearly remember my first wet dream. I woke up and was shocked at what had happened. I felt really guilty and embarrassed about it and I was anxious to get rid of the evidence.

'I'm not exactly sure how I found out about masturbation and how to do it. I think your erection feels quite good, so I guess you just go on from there. Everyone seemed to be doing it or talking about it.

'Later on in high school it became the done thing to go to

parties and try to get girlfriends. You'd just try your luck, but I was very cautious and I'd never make a move unless I knew I'd get a favourable response.

'Sexual encounters with girls just went in small steps and built up. I remember touching my first breast. It was this girl in Year 8 who had really large breasts for her age. We were kissing and hugging and I had the old sly feel on the outside and then put my hand inside her T-shirt. I liked it.

'The next landmark, I guess, was mutual masturbation with a girl. It was at a party and she took the initiative. She said: "Would you mind if I put my hand down there?" It wasn't the most romantic thing and it was not like a sexual thing either, more like experimenting.

'After that it was having sex. I was 16 and I was at a friend's party and I was drunk. It wasn't exactly the most intelligent thing to do but it just happened. I didn't really enjoy it much or see it as anything great at the time, more like something that just had to be done eventually. Take some teenage hormones, add some alcohol and an empty bed – it's not the perfect equation but it's a popular one.

'I don't really know why I decided to go ahead with it. The courting thing is pretty equal these days. Both guys and girls can take the initiative – but I think the final decision really is up to the girl. She gave me oral sex first. I was really scared about going further and I had to borrow a condom from a friend. She was much more experienced than me sexually and it wasn't a problem for her. That was just a one-off for us. We're not really the best of friends now. I think I took it all a little too flippantly, really. I won't forget her, of course, but more because of the incident than the person.

'I'd much rather have a relationship. I think you enjoy sex more if you have love and respect for the person – it adds a lot more to it.

'As for the lifestyle I'm living now – which is mainly skateboarding – I think I'd only be doing this if I was male, so I'm very happy that I am. Still, if I was female I might be twice as happy . . . who knows?'

Adolescence in human males is generally longer than it is for females and many teenage boys find it a frustrating experience. Their sexual impulses are strong, as they are for teenage girls, but adults in most societies try to limit the opportunities for youths to give vent to these lusty urges. If everyone married when they reached puberty, teenage sexuality wouldn't present so much of a problem, Schlegel suggests. But premarital sex has a potentially serious negative outcome – of producing a baby to parents who are neither ready nor committed to fully care for it – meaning that relatives must step in.

'Marriage is widely seen as a licence to reproduce, and in fact most human reproduction occurs within marriage. If young people are biologically capable of reproducing, why are they not given social licence to do so?' Schlegel asks. It's been suggested that one good reason young primate males are restricted in their sexual access to females is that they are most likely to die – especially from risk-taking behaviour – during this period of their lives. One study of a species of macaque monkey, for example, found that more than 72 per cent of males die during adolescence. Although young men are most at risk of death and serious injury during this period, they don't die at such a high rate as to explain why most societies contrive to make them wait longer than girls to marry and reproduce. Older men, in particular, seem to feature strongly in this process of control by flexing their social and physical muscles. But they do not succeed completely. Teenagers still manage plenty of sexual activity with very little commitment. Even after marriage, older couples do their fair share of furgling as well. Various medical surveys have shown that 5–10 per cent of British and American children are adulterously conceived. A well-publicised report that the rate was as high as 30 per cent in one Liverpool housing estate seems strikingly unrepresentative, if indeed it is correct. After all, men do pay close attention to their likenesses – or lack of them – in their children.

Yet the sexual contract adopted by most societies – marriage – is essentially based on women providing certainty of paternity for men in exchange for economic resources and protection. In technologically simple societies at least, children are for some years left wholly dependent on a mother's nurturing if she enters a dud contract – that is, marries a man who cannot or does not keep up his end of the marriage bargain – so she must judge carefully indeed. Her children's survival depends on it. In terms of our evolutionary past, then, these realities meant that women enjoyed less freedom of choice than men. 'I do not suggest that women are without choices or strategies, nor that they have been selected for passivity,' Draper says. 'I do argue that women relative to men must be extremely cautious in their economic and reproductive careers because, unlike men, they have only limited ability to recoup their losses.'

This caution in mate choice among women is thought to have been a powerful force in the way men have evolved. When females are choosy, males must compete to get their attention. Those who are chosen – or who survive to get chosen – get to pass on their genes; those who don't face genetic oblivion, as we saw with the elephant seal and the platypus. This process of sexual selection is what shaped the peacock's tail, the lion's mane and the tree-kangaroo's surly disposition. In humans it is thought to explain why men are larger than women. In ancestral times, the theory goes, women must have selected men to be that way. And, as many scientists have pointed out, the differences in body size between the sexes in animal species is usually a good indicator of their sex lives. Where males and females are a similar size, they are more likely to be monogamous. When males are larger than females, the males tend to have multiple mates – to be polygynous. The bigger the male, the more polygynous he is (witness elephant seals). That trend suggests that our early human ancestors were at one time mildly polygynous.

Roger Short, a reproductive biologist at the University of Melbourne, found more convincing evidence for this by comparing the testes of the various male apes. He found that body size and testes size don't necessarily tally. The best predictor of mating systems is the size of the testes in relation to body size. Male gorillas, for example, weighing around 250 kilograms (twice as big as females), nevertheless have minute 18-gram testes, whereas 50-kilogram male chimpanzees that are only slightly larger than females nevertheless have enormous 60-gram testes. Despite having a harem of three or four wives, the polygynous gorilla may only get to copulate once a year. In multi-male mating systems, competition for access to females can result in males being larger than females, but if all males have unrestricted access to the estrus female, the size difference between the sexes may be slight.

Evolution has also produced some powerful tools in mammals to help the male engine of desire fire smoothly into action and to keep running as long as it is needed. Helen Fisher, an anthropologist, has suggested that mammals exhibit three main mating emotions. Stimulation from testosterone, for example, provides the initial push: the sex drive that sparks a male's generalised craving for sexual gratification. His emotions kick in next, with a sense of 'preferential attraction', as Fisher puts it – he may experience an energy burst and focus on one or more specific potential mates, accompanied (in humans, at least) by feelings of exhilaration, as well as 'intrusive thinking' and an emotional dependency on a certain female or females. A successful courtship leads to sexual activity and the pleasure men experience from ejaculation and orgasm provides a memorable reward for persistence. (Of course, other mammal species can't tell us whether they enjoy sexual climax as we do, but we may assume that they do. Chimpanzees and bonobos, for example, make faces and noises that to human eyes and ears come across as pleasure, and the enthusiasm with which they and many other mammal species pursue sex suggests strongly that the rewards for such behaviour go beyond mere reproduction.) Then a sense of attachment develops to maintain close contact between mates, accompanied (in humans again) by feelings of calm, comfort and emotional union. All of that sound familiar? Our capacity to experience each of these emotional states evolved to direct a specific aspect of reproduction, Fisher argues, yet although they are inter-related they are distinct from each other, so it is possible to feel attached to your wife or husband yet at the same time attracted to another person and even to direct sexual energy towards a third – as has become plain in modern times with the relaxation of divorce laws in many Western societies.

We can imagine how our social organisation and sex lives would be very different today if our ancestors had never left the protection of the lush African forests and taken to a predatory, male-dominated and often unpredictable life on the open savanna. What if women had come to rule the social roost, for example, or if we had remained peaceful, largely vegetarian and adopted the hippies' catch-cry of 'Make love, not war'? The bonobo seems to have done just that.

Bonobos were discovered in 1929 and serious studies of them did not begin until the mid-1970s. They number only in the thousands in their shrinking wild-forest habitat in Zaire. Recent studies of captive and wild bonobos have delighted feminists, intrigued evolutionary biologists and revealed some steamy surprises. When chimps face social conflicts, they often resort quickly to aggressive threats and violence – especially the males, but females can be fierce, too – then use sex and mutual grooming later for reconciliation. But bonobos defuse conflicts by having sex first. Indeed, they do it in virtually every partner combination – with the possible exception of some close family members – and more often than any other primate. Frans de Waal first witnessed this sexual bent at feeding time – normally a tense and argumentative period among common chimps – among 10 bonobos at San Diego Zoo: 'As the caretaker approached the enclosure with food, the males would develop erections. Even before the food was thrown into the area, the bonobos would be inviting each other for sex: males would invite females, and females would invite males and other females.' Male and female bonobos often copulate in the so-called missionary position (once thought to be uniquely human), and engage in sporadic oral sex, massaging of each other's genitals and intense tongue-kissing. 'Practice' sex between young bonobos and between young and adult bonobos is common, as are homosexual encounters. Adult female bonobos have devised a unique form of mutual genital-to-genital rubbing in the missionary position. Males also engage in sexual contact with each other: they sometimes practise 'penis fencing', in which two will hang face-to-face from a branch while rubbing their erect penises together.

If humans suddenly started doing such things there'd be a massive upheaval in society. Homosexuality (a behaviour now recognised in more than 200 animal species), pedophilia, marriage, adultery and many other social concepts would have to be radically redefined. So why do bonobos practise all this hanky-panky? De Waal believes that sex is the glue that holds bonobo society together. 'The species is best characterised as female-centred and egalitarian and as one that substitutes sex for aggression,' he says. If a male discovers food first, females often have sex with him before sharing the meal. If a female discovers food first, the males often have to wait for an offer to share it. Indeed, male bonobos are wimps by human and chimp standards, real 'mother's boys'.

Bonobo and chimp society seem to have elements in common with dolphins when it comes to sex. These boisterous marine mammals practise masturbation, promiscuity and homosexuality. Studies at Shark Bay, in Western Australia, have revealed a surprising range of sexual behaviour among the wild dolphins that regularly come inshore at Monkey Mia. A team of American scientists reported in the late 1980s that they witnessed 'constant sexual interaction, both heterosexual and homosexual' among the animals. The dolphins were promiscuous, although much of their sexual interaction appeared to be purely social, said a member of the team, Richard Connor. 'The males are constantly mounting each other and mounting females not in estrus,' Connor told me. 'There'll be a group of four or five males and it seems like one of them goes, "Let's get Pointer!" And the other males start mounting him with erections.' Two-day-old dolphins have exhibited erections – and dolphins, both in captivity and the wild, apparently masturbate. Male dolphins have been reported to mount small boats, and in the US two heavily scarred male dolphins were seen to keep each other constant company for many years. Pairing in male dolphins may promote co-operation in hunting and protection from attack, but teams of males can also work together to isolate a female and keep her with them. Dolphin researchers have found that male bottle-nosed dolphins have unusually large testes and almost certainly feature sperm competition (a sort of 'survival of the fittest' for sperm) as part of their mating system.

Among primate species, humans and chimps seem to be exceptional in having males that form close bonds with each other. In the wild, male chimps stay in the troop of their birth and team up with their male kin to drive off other males. Within each troop, males do form friendships with females, but they are far more likely to form coalitions with other males to help them climb the social ladder. These male alliances are not stable, though, and males may unexpectedly abandon each other if other, more promising allies emerge – their political expedience contrasts sharply with the more enduring and consistent friendships between female chimps. Barbara Smuts, of the Center for Human Growth and

Development at the University of Michigan, comments: 'Male primates also form bonds with other males, but I am not sure that it is appropriate to label these relationships "intimate". For example, in my baboon troop over a six-year period, only one pair of adult males, Alex and Bz, formed a stable, long-term coalition. They used their alliance to protect one another from other males and to acquire sexually receptive females from younger and stronger rivals. Yet despite the importance of their partnership, I never saw them touch one another except during highly ritualised greeting ceremonies. These greetings, during which both males typically remain very tense, are as close as male baboons ever come to "intimacy" with one another.'[7]

Field studies of wild chimpanzees show that they can be almost as promiscuous as bonobos, yet male chimps dominate their social groups and can be particularly violent, committing gang rape and infanticide, kidnapping females and murdering rivals. Richard Wrangham, a prominent British anthropologist at Harvard University who has conducted field studies of chimps for many years in Africa, reports that humans and chimps also practise violence on each other. People kill chimps for 'bush meat', for example while one male chimp that Wrangham's group tracked for four years in western Uganda made eight known attacks on human children, killing three of them before local villagers eventually killed him. Wrangham's team also saw the gut-wrenching results of a murder by some of the group of chimps they had under study. The victim was a male chimp from a neighbouring community. His trachea had been ripped out and his limbs had been pulled as though he had been spreadeagled by his attackers; they had then broken open his scrotum and removed his testes. Investigators of human war crimes and homicide police could no doubt relate details of many human murders that were equally gruesome, if not worse.

Recent research findings into the genetic links between the various subspecies and communities of chimps in Africa raise some mind-bending questions about all this. A German team led by Svante Pääbo of the Max-Planck-Institute for Evolutionary Anthropology studied some key genetic markers for clues about the diversity of these subgroups. They carefully analysed DNA from blood taken from eastern, central, and western African subspecies of chimpanzees and the bonobo. They found that all the common chimps were quite genetically diverse, although those from the central group were the most varied and appeared to have the oldest lineage: 'The central chimps are the most genetically diverse and other groups seem to be derived from them. Thus, if you like, the chimp "Eve" of this sequence lived in central Africa,' Pääbo says. The study also reached the surprising conclusion that some common chimps are more genetically distant from each other than they are from bonobos, a startling outcome considering that the two are separated at species level. That suggests they had a very recent common ancestor. The researchers believe as well that the high degree of genetic intermixing between the chimpanzees and bonobos makes it unlikely that genes are responsible for any cultural differences between these populations. 'Rather, these differences are probably truly the result of cultural evolution, the transmission of learned behaviours from generation to generation,' says Pääbo.

These findings suggest that a peaceful or violent society of animals can emerge from virtually the same gene pool, so long as they are intelligent enough to have developed a flexible culture. It seems to me that Pääbo's conclusions are crying out for further scientific and public debate. Is the well-known human male tendency for violence largely learned behaviour that is much more amenable to change than we have previously thought?

As the saying goes, biology is not destiny. Just because a behaviour is rooted in ancient biology does not mean it is permanently fixed that way, or that we do not have the potential to behave in other ways. The fact that women, for example, tend to dress more flamboyantly than men in Western societies would suggest to an evolutionary zoologist that men are the choosy ones and women are competing for their attention. And a man would be unlikely to succeed in trying to justify cheating on his wife by laying claim to some polygynous ancestry. Yet some human societies are, or were, polygynous or polyandrous (one woman taking several male mates), just as some are promiscuous and others puritanical, some egalitarian and others extremely male-dominated. Biology is important, but modern people are now far more creatures of their own cultural making.

Strangely, though, we cling to some fairly rigid ideas when it comes to the influence of biology on our minds and bodies. Next, we look at science's take on how genes influence sex – and find that when you put them under the microscope, many surprises are emerging in the intriguing story of how boys are made.

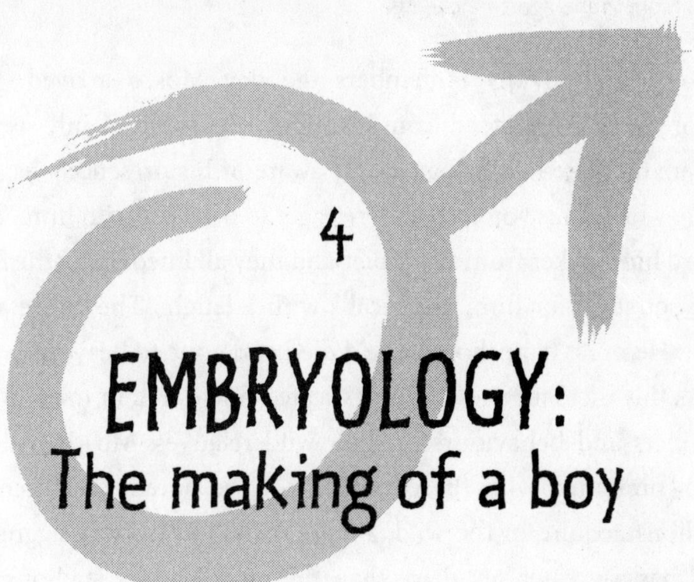

4

EMBRYOLOGY: The making of a boy

'What are little boys made of?
What are little boys made of?
Frogs and snails and puppy-dogs' tails;
That's what little boys are made of'

Anon – nursery rhyme

ON A PLEASANT green hobby farm near Madison, Wisconsin, Marijo Kent-First has assembled a small band of very special Arab horses. Her exceptional herd includes a dozen highly unusual mares and a very confused stallion named Mosco. In his youth Mosco was a pampered star of the Texas show-ring scene, famed for his masculine physique and prized for his success in competition. Ever since his move to the farm, though, he's had trouble working out whether he's Arthur or Martha. But it's not his fault. It's the mixed-up mares in the adjoining fields who have given poor Mosco an identity crisis.

Kent-First vividly remembers the day Mosco arrived. Even before he was unloaded from his trailer, she could plainly see that the mares were more than simply aware of his presence – as soon as they heard his voice, they were eager to have sex with him. 'They heard him nicker from the trailer and they all lined up by the fence and squatted for him,' she recalls with a laugh. 'They were all in heat. He must have thought he'd died and gone to heaven.'

As this incident shows, domesticated horses retain many of the instincts and behaviours of their wild relatives. Mosco had just been presented with the equivalent of the harem that breeding stallions acquire in the wild. A harem stallion is more aggressive and has a greater sex drive than the more passive stallions that form non-breeding bachelor groups. Within a few months of taking his multiple wives, his testes will grow, his sex glands will swell and he will produce much more sperm (the reverse happens when he leaves a harem and rejoins the bachelor group). Clearly, spending time around normal breeding mares affects a stallion's body chemistry and his behaviour, and those changes occur courtesy of the male hormones produced by his testes.

While a harem stallion is fully primed for sex, he must be patient. He is usually forced to be celibate most of the year as he waits for the mares to reach their annual spring breeding season – of only a few weeks. He is not idle while the time ticks by. He spends much time in the mares' company: he will quietly stand with or near them, pay them special attention and frequently sniff their urine and faeces, presumably to keep track of their estrus cycle and health. As he receives cues from them that breeding time is near, he may go through a more active 'teasing' sequence of behaviour that usually precedes copulation. After his long wait, he is clearly eager and excited when the time for sex at last arrives.

I once lived in a farmhouse at a horse stud and it truly was a wonder to see the change in the behaviour of the resident stallion at 'service' time – all rippling muscle, snorting machismo and rampant randiness. Nor is a mare in estrus a model of passive decorum in signalling her readiness to mate. She seems to flirt, calling out to the stallion, approaching him head on, sniffing and nuzzling and perhaps even nipping and pretending to physically challenge him to get his interest. It's not long before he's moving around behind her, getting an erection and trying to mount her. When they are both ready, they mate vigorously.

So, presented with 12 eager mares in heat, it wasn't long before Mosco's sexual instincts were being put to the test. He was already a successful father, but all his progeny so far had been the result of artificial insemination – his only sexual experience had been mounting a dummy and ejaculating into an artificial vagina. His first effort at the real thing was worse than clumsy: he mounted the head of the first mare to reach him, and unceremoniously ejaculated into her ear. With a little tuition he soon found the right way for a stallion to do such things. But if he had any thoughts of being in horse heaven, he must have changed his mind pretty soon. Like Mosco, the mares didn't know the 'right' way to behave. Unlike him, however, no amount of teaching would or could make a scrap of difference. They pestered him constantly for sex, never seemed to be satisfied and simply would not take no for an answer. Matters reached their lowest ebb one day when the biggest mare – over 17 hands tall and solidly built – leapt the dividing fence and aggressively chased Mosco down until he yielded in tired defeat. Then she promptly mounted him.

Mosco may have been shocked by this indignity, but Kent-First was hardly surprised. As an expert in genetics, she knew the mares' hidden secret. Like Mosco, all of them were in fact genetic males. They may have looked like normal females outwardly, but their genes and reproductive organs suggested otherwise. They were also quite aggressive and muscular and were so keen on sex that they made normal mares seem like total prudes. They were almost always in season and some carried their ongoing courtship of the resident stallion to extraordinary lengths, says Kent-First.

These remarkable horses highlight some key insights into how our sex, gender, biology and behaviour are ultimately orchestrated or influenced by genes. Without the right genes, you simply can't make a boy. And unless those genes are fully functional, you still don't get a 'complete' boy – you get something much more like a girl.

All the Madison mares were descended from a sire named Hal Gazal, a stallion noteworthy not just because of his success on the racetrack but because as a father he had a very strong tendency to produce daughters. Of his 500 or so documented offspring about 70 per cent were female. His daughters were sought after because they included a high proportion of successful racing and show horses, noted for their strength and aggression. The best of these fetched US$1 million or more and among the buyers were some of America's blue-chip breeders. But trouble ensued when their owners tried to breed from these mares: good racers they may have been, but many had low fertility or could not conceive at all.

Through scientific detective work, Kent-First figured out why. She initially found tell-tale physical signs that the mares were of an ambiguous sex. Many had a greatly enlarged clitoris, for example, one of which even featured the beginnings of a urethra, much like a part-formed penis. Others had testes within their abdomens – and it is these which were producing the male hormones thought to have made them more aggressive and muscular and so constantly interested in sex. Her laboratory studies revealed that instead of having the usual XX female sex chromosomes, they had the XY pattern of males. Kent-First led a research group which discovered, in the mid-1980s, that males or females could carry a gene or factor causing sex-reversal, a condition in which an individual's genes suggest that it should be one sex but its body appears to be of the opposite sex. Hal Gazal was a particularly rare and special case, also having an abnormality known as a 'germ-line mosaic'. The sex chromosomes in his sperm were highly variable, so his offspring were ticket-holders in a sex lottery: he was capable of fathering normal fertile sons and daughters, infertile daughters and genetically male 'mares' with varying degrees of maleness expressed in their bodies.

When she first revealed her findings as a young graduate researcher, Kent-First realised to her cost that her discovery was no mere scientific curiosity but was in fact painful news to all those owners and would-be breeders of the affected mares. The market value of Hal Gazal's male offspring was affected as well, since it was found that they could be carriers of the genetic glitch and pass it on to their offspring in turn. Big investments hinged on this crucial question of sexuality, and the owners of Hal Gazal were quick to respond with lawsuits against Kent-First and her university, seeking hefty damages over her revelations. After a protracted legal battle, the case was eventually settled out of court in her favour. As part of the settlement, Kent-First sagely decided not to seek recompense for financial costs on her part, but won a most unusual concession from the sire's owners – a lifetime supply of sperm, blood and tissue samples from Hal Gazal. The stallion has since died, but the deal enabled the Wisconsin herd to be bred, and they continue to yield fascinating scientific insights.

Sex is said to be biological, the combination of the sex chromosomes and sexual anatomy with which you are born. But gender is acquired – the sexual role or identity you adopt socially. Science has been able to cast plenty of light on the former but much less on the latter. What it has shown most clearly, though, is that the whole concept of differences between the sexes – a rich and long-running source of social and academic debate – rests on shaky biological foundations. The mares' rare condition is just one of a surprising range of variants in what we generally think of as male and female. Indeed, it shows that however much we may think that sex comes in just two distinct packages, in reality it doesn't quite work like that. Modern molecular studies have shown that sex occurs within a spectrum of states: sure, most individuals are clustered towards male at one end and female at the other, but there's a whole swag of in-between cases where the differences between the sexes don't or can't fully apply.

How and why these variations occur has become much clearer in recent times. In turn, this has led to new insights into the remarkable sequence of events within the womb that lead to the making of a boy. These insights really are exceptional when you consider how long – and creatively – people have wondered about how maleness and femaleness occurs, especially in themselves. To explain the division between the sexes, a marvellous range of ideas has been invoked over the ages: divine intervention, supernatural spirits, special foods, social practices, phases of the moon and so on. It was even supposed at one stage that each of a man's two testes produced differently sexed 'seed' – left for girls, right for boys. Thanks to recent genetic discoveries, however, we can now pinpoint with great precision exactly what first instils sex into a human embryo. While scientists working in this field may know the story, most of us haven't yet grasped it – nor have its implications fully sunk in. So I hope you'll excuse some of the jargon and technical details needed to tell the fascinating story of this important discovery. Let's begin at the beginning, with what we know about those sex chromosomes and the role they play in the recipe.

Myriad genes that shape us as people – about 30,000 of them – are arranged in tightly packed groups on chromosomes, the little sausage-shaped structures found in the nucleus of our cells. They contain a vast amount of information – the entire recipe for a human being. There are normally 23 different kinds of chromosomes in each cell, with two copies of each kind lying side by side in matched pairs. We inherit one copy from our father, via his sperm, and the other from our mother, via her egg. They first meet during conception, each chromosome pairing up with its counterpart.

Human chromosomes are identified by number, in descending size order. Imagine them all as ballroom dancers with numbers on their backs, lining up for the crowd before a competition. Couple number 1 is the tallest pair, and so on down the line. Couple number 23 stand out – not just for being the smallest, but also for being a hopeless mismatch. Indeed, they are so unalike that they hardly merit being called a pair at all. They are the sex chromosomes, X and Y. One is large and the other is small: the runt is Y, the one linked to maleness.

In the late nineteenth century a German biologist, Walther

Flemming, first used synthetic dyes that could stain a cell nucleus well enough to make visible its tiny inner details under a microscope. Flemming's work soon allowed other researchers working on insect cells to notice that one of the newly recognised chromosomes had no apparent partner, and it was dubbed with an anonymous 'X' to signify its shape and its unknown role. A decade or so later its involvement in influencing sex was realised, and soon after that its missing partner was found, again in insect cells. It turned out to be a dwarfish chromosome only a third the size of the X, and it came to be known as the Y. Side by side, they were like Laurel and Hardy.

The Y's role in the male story soon became apparent when two American researchers, Nettie Maria Stevens and Edmond Beecher Wilson, independently found that unfertilised beetle eggs always contained an X chromosome, while the chromosomes in beetle sperm were variable – they could contain either an X or a Y. When an X-bearing sperm fertilised an egg (making an XX pair of chromosomes), the baby beetle turned out female. But when a Y-bearing sperm was involved (making an XY pair), the baby was male.

In the 1940s, biologist Alfred Jost took the story a step further when he demonstrated that events in the womb play a vital role as well, and that maleness doesn't develop without male hormones. Jost surgically castrated male rabbits in the womb, while they were still embryos and before their other reproductive organs had developed. The embryos were then allowed to carry on developing as normal in their mother's womb. When they were born, these rabbits had female bodies. Jost had shown that testes were necessary for a genetic male to develop a male body. He also concluded that a foetus is programmed to develop into a female unless otherwise instructed, famously remarking: 'Becoming a male is a prolonged, uneasy and risky venture; it is a kind of struggle against inherent trends toward femaleness.'

It wasn't until after World War II, though, that it became clear that the Y chromosome was also the source of maleness in humans. But how exactly does the Y perform this amazing feat? In the 1980s researchers were able to peel back another layer of the mystery of sex and start to study the chromosomes in extraordinary detail – at the level of the tiny genetic building blocks of which they are made. Insights gained from studies of people with unusual sex chromosomes paved the way for the next big breakthrough in understanding.

As with horses, there can be sex-reversed XY women and XX men. In probing this puzzle more deeply, two high-profile teams of scientists led the field in homing in on the gene or genes on the Y chromosome that control the development of testes in an embryo. One team was in Britain, led by Peter Goodfellow of the Imperial Cancer Research Fund, and the other was in the US, led by David Page of the Whitehead Institute for Biomedical Research. They found that bits of the sex chromosomes can sometimes be deleted or swapped over onto each other, or even shifted across to other chromosomes altogether. Thus, someone who was a genetic male could actually be missing a tiny but crucial piece of the Y and so become female. Or a genetic female could have that same small fragment of the Y tacked onto one of the X chromosomes and develop as a male. It became clear that the entire Y chromosome wasn't needed to induce maleness – indeed, it was probably just one key gene. That gene would control the development of testes, and the testes would provide the hormones that steered the growth of a male body.

Finding just one gene within the whole human genome would be a bit like trying to pinpoint the location of just one house in a city. The entire genome contains billions of chemical bases strung out along 1.6 metres of DNA, with the tens of thousands of genes interspersed among vast stretches of 'junk' DNA sequences. But now the quest for the real kernel of maleness had been narrowed down dramatically: the scientists at least knew what suburb of the city to search, and roughly in which neighbourhood to concentrate their inquiries. It had to be somewhere in the missing piece of the Y in sex-reversed men, or in the bit added onto the X in sex-reversed women.

Page thought his group was the first to find the gene. They were studying a man and a woman with very unusual sex chromosomes. The man had a Y chromosome, but it was so incomplete that only a tiny piece of it could be found – yet that fragment was enough to make him male. The woman also had a Y chromosome, but it was missing an even tinier segment – yet that absence was enough for her to have developed a female body. The man's tiny Y chromosome was likely to have only a few genes on it, one of which had to be the target of the search. By cross-checking the relevant DNA from these two individuals, Page's group soon found the sequence of a gene. They called it the 'zinc-finger' gene, or ZFY, because of the way it acted on other genes. They found this same gene on the Y chromosome of all the other mammals they checked and promptly published their exciting discovery. On the other side of the planet, though, a young Australian scientist soon had bad news for Page. Andrew Sinclair, at LaTrobe University, was researching his doctoral thesis in molecular genetics. Working with his supervisor, Jennifer Graves, Sinclair was using the latest techniques to map the genes of marsupials – the bizarre animal group that includes kangaroos and koalas – and comparing them with human genes. If Page was right that ZFY controlled testes development in all mammals, Sinclair reasoned, marsupials would also have it on their Y chromosomes. Page's group had not checked the marsupials, so Sinclair did. 'It wasn't there,' Sinclair recalls. 'It wasn't on the Y chromosome at all.' Marsupials had no ZFY, but they did have testes. The wrong gene had been fingered.

So the hunt was back on, and Sinclair happily accepted an invitation to join the search as part of Goodfellow's team in Britain. Just before Christmas in 1989, the team received a telephone call from some collaborators at the Pasteur Institute in Paris. They had identified four unusual sex-reversed people. All four had men's bodies, including testes, but they were infertile and were genetic females. Further studies showed that they had an extremely small fragment of Y chromosome tacked onto one of their two X chromosomes. What's more, it was in an entirely different region from that where ZFY was found (it later emerged that the sex-reversed XY female studied by Page's group had this second region deleted as well, but no-one had noticed). Now the race was on to isolate the genes in this new region. Sinclair's marsupial gene maps helped him to narrow the search even more – to just 35,000 DNA bases. By cross-checking against other mammals (including London Zoo's tigers and chimps), he identified an even smaller region – a mere 2,000 DNA bases – that was present in all of them. 'Basically, that covered the entire gene,' says Sinclair. All the males had this gene on the Y; the XY females also had the gene, but it was malfunctioning. Eureka!

On a wet Sunday afternoon in London in June 1990,

Goodfellow's elated team decided to call this gene SRY – for the sex-determining region on the Y chromosome. A mere month later, the team made the front cover of one of the world's most prestigious science journals and Goodfellow's team basked in a wave of international publicity.[1] It certainly was a landmark discovery, the significance of which is still emerging. The SRY gene is the daddy of them all, the ultimate origin of maleness in mammals, the key difference between the sexes. 'It's the kingpin,' Sinclair says. 'It's the only one that really needs to be different. It's what makes males different from females.' Take SRY alone – ignoring all of the rest of the Y chromosome – and inject it into a fertilised mouse egg and even if that egg is genetically female the mouse will be born male, as researchers at Britain's National Institute for Medical Research subsequently demonstrated. The animal in question was nicknamed Randy, and he was the first sex-reversed mouse ever to be produced in this way. His testes were small but he was otherwise male in every discernible way. Just to make sure, Randy was placed in a cage with some females, with whom he behaved in a typically male-mouse way and mated up to six times a night. 'He thought he was male, they thought he was male and we thought that was pretty good evidence,' Sinclair says. 'It tells us that SRY is the only gene you need on the Y chromosome to develop testes and become male.' How SRY does this remains unclear, but it's worth noting here that SRY is not the only gene on the Y chromosome. Because it carries so much junk DNA that has no apparent function, many scientists suspected it might be a wasteland containing little else but SRY. After all, the X chromosome is a powerhouse by comparison, carrying about 5,000 genes. But over the past decade detailed studies have revealed that the Y does in fact carry a few dozen genes, at least 12 of which are active only in adult testes. These probably help to make sperm (men with fertility problems often have deletions in some of those 12 genes), so we now know that other genes on the Y, apart from SRY, are clearly vital to the development of a man who can reproduce.

And SRY is not the only gene involved in sex reversal. Only about 1 in 10 XY women, for example, has a detectable mutation of that gene: the other 90 per cent have it intact. As for sex-reversed men, 10 per cent of them don't even have an SRY gene. It's not at all clear what's going on in such cases. It may be that in some circumstances another gene can block SRY or, conversely, take on the role of SRY. It's now known that some sex-reversed women, for example, have a deletion on the tip of chromosome 9 that involves an ancient gene linked to the embryonic development of maleness in mammals, birds and reptiles. A mutation in the ATRX gene on the human X chromosome can cause sex reversal in genetic males, along with mental retardation and the blood disorder thalassemia. (Incidentally, ATRX doesn't have a matching gene on the human Y chromosome, but a counterpart – ATRY – has been found recently on the Y of at least one marsupial, a tamar wallaby. It seems to be involved in testes development in marsupials, and may be the gene that determined maleness in mammals before SRY evolved.) In fact, several sex-reversing genes have been identified on the X and other chromosomes. Perhaps SRY's role is simply as a master-switch for maleness, or it may stop other sex-determining genes from being expressed or repressed. Femaleness may not be a default state for humans after all.

The rest of the known genes on the Y chromosome seem to be mainly involved in basic housekeeping functions. Their presence there and their similarity to genes found on the X chromosome 'reinforces the theory that the X and Y chromosomes evolved from a common X-like ancestor before the Y acquired its male-specific genes and adopted its role in sex determination', according to Bruce T. Lahn and Karin Jegalian.[2] So it seems that the Y chromosome's role in determining maleness in mammals is a relatively new thing – at least on an evolutionary timescale. 'Birds, reptiles, amphibians and fish show a great variety of chromosomal sex-determining mechanisms, and many species have no differentiated sex chromosomes at all, preferring to leave the matter to environmental forces,' notes Jennifer Graves.[3] Variations abound. In laboratory strains of the common housefly, females and males have the usual sex-chromosome pattern. But in some wild fly populations, the male and female sex chromosomes are indistinguishable from each other and the masculinising gene is carried on another chromosome altogether. In Eurasian wood lemmings – small rodents that live in mossy forests – some females have male sex chromosomes, plus an additional gene on the X chromosome that overcomes the male influence of the Y: they give birth only to daughters, so females in this species outnumber males by three to one. Several other rodent species have multiple sex-chromosome systems, in which genes from elsewhere have jumped onto their X or Y chromosomes. The fact that closely related species of the fly and the wood lemming don't boast these innovations suggests that the way sex is determined can evolve rapidly. No SRY gene has yet been found in the monotremes (comprising the oddball platypus and echidnas); and in some other mammal species, the Y chromosome contains different active genes. Meanwhile, the sex chromosomes of birds and many reptiles have entirely different gene contents, which must have evolved quite independently from those of mammals.

Inevitably, some parasites have learned to hijack the entire process. Bizarre bacteria known as wolbachia, for example, parasitise many insects, which then pass on the infection to their offspring. Wolbachia are sexually selective, often killing off most of the males in a host population or forcing males to change gender. In one species of woodlouse, it is the presence or absence of wolbachia that determines whether an egg develops into a male or a female.

The fact that some kinds of animals rely on environmental forces to determine sex shows that specific sex genes are not even necessary. In many reptile species, for example, the incubation temperature of their eggs dictates whether their offspring will be male or female. Temperature changes appear to trigger the release of hormones that sway the developing embryo's sex one way or another. A good example of this phenomenon occurred in 1999. About a quarter of a million endangered olive ridley sea turtles showed up at the world's largest known nesting site, the Bhitarkanika sanctuary on the east coast of India. The turtles usually arrive in January, but they held off until April, possibly because the females had been deterred by fishing trawlers. The delay, along with unseasonably warm spring temperatures, meant that they laid their eggs in beach sands about 12°C warmer than normal. The effect was that the hatchlings were almost all female. Climatic variability over the years helps to balance the sex ratio in the populations of such long-lived species.

Environmental effects such as temperature may yet be shown to have some influence on human sex determination, although the evidence put forward so far seems a little contradictory. Exposure to floods, earthquakes and even smog has been associated with a reduced proportion of boys among babies conceived at the time. There's also evidence that sex ratios swing in favour of boys after wars. More recently, German biologist Alexander Lerchl matched five decades of birth and weather records in Germany and found a correlation between unusually long, hot summers and higher numbers of boys being born in the following year. Lerchl suggests that excessive heat may be less damaging to the development of Y-bearing sperm than X-bearing sperm in the testes, resulting in a sex ratio more in favour of boys 10 months later.[4] Another recent study found a significant correlation between 'severe life events', such as the death or hospitalisation of a woman's partner or child, around the time she conceives and a lower proportion of boys among the subsequent births.[5] It's not known what mechanism might lie behind this observation. Perhaps such events somehow affect the way sex is determined: severe stress might cause some decline in semen quality or result in a higher rate of miscarriage of male embryos, or some other factor entirely may be at work. The jury is still out.

Graves says there is now clear evidence, however, that the heritage of human sex chromosomes goes back at least 200 million years. That was when the platypus and echidnas branched off and decided to go it alone. The mammal family suffered another split sometime between 130–170 million years ago, when the pouched marsupials – the kangaroos, possums and so on – branched off from the placental mammals, including our own ancestors.

It is thought that from an original matched pair of X chromosomes in mammals, one later began to evolve into the Y as a result of a mutation or rearrangement of at least one gene. It is still unclear how and why the X and Y came to differ from each other so much. Recent research by Page and Lahn suggests that the 20 or so genes still shared by X and Y are essentially living fossils: 'Sex chromosomes are the only chromosomes with a long intellectual history, but those . . . genes can tell us a great deal about their evolutionary history as well,' says Page. The shared genes are clustered into four groups, physically arranged as four consecutive blocks – 'essentially like the layers of rock are arranged in geological strata,' Page says. Those groups seem to be scrambled on the Y chromosome. Most probably, the X and Y diverged from each other one group at a time, with their order gradually becoming more and more scrambled on the Y as their ability to pair up became more compromised. Today, X and Y have become so different that they can only pair up along very tiny regions of their tips, whereas the other 22 chromosomes pair up along their entire length. That change has serious implications, because it means that X and Y can normally swap very few little genetic information. Such exchanges are vital pieces of housekeeping. It's a bit like checking a file on your computer against a back-up copy. If the original file becomes corrupted or a piece of information is deleted, its integrity can be restored by salvaging the relevant bits from the back-up. So as the two sex chromosomes diverged, the Y lost the opportunity to restore corrupted files because it had no way to compare itself with a back-up copy. That hasn't happened to the X because whenever a female is conceived, a damaged X inherited from one parent can still team up with a healthy X from the other parent and be repaired. But if there is anything awry on the single copy of the X when a male is conceived – well, tough. That's why a number of inherited diseases show up only in men. Hemophilia, the potentially fatal condition in which the blood does not clot properly and which has blighted some royal families in Europe, is a classic example. The mutant gene that causes hemophilia is on the X chromosome (as are the genes for gout and colour blindness) so women are 'carriers' but don't get sick from it.

As for the Y, it is passed on – warts and all – from father to son virtually unchanged, accumulating damage and suffering copying errors down through the generations. Much of the 'human recipe' it carries has now become corrupted or lost and it is doomed to forever haunt the singles bar of the gene pool, an aging figure becoming more and more degenerate. So the Y chromosome is a much-diminished player, although nonetheless still with remarkable influence when it comes to sex. Yet it may have acquired some new genes – perhaps within the past 50 million years – that do not have counterparts on the X chromosome. These genes must have come from one of the other chromosomes and, considering what a risky place the Y chromosome is for a gene to reside, there must have been a good reason for them to move house. Sherman Silber, of the Infertility Center of St Louis, notes that the 'degeneration of the Y chromosome is well documented in fruit flies and is clearly an ongoing process in all animals'. It is not thought to be mere chance, however, that the few genes that remain on the Y in humans are either common-as-muck relics of the X or are male specific, as Silber points out. In theory at least, genes that primarily benefit one sex or the other are more likely to accumulate on the relevant sex-specific chromosomes – almost like an act of self-defence in the war of the sexes. Bit by bit, genes that determine some key aspect of human maleness, such as those controlling sperm formation, seem to have made their way to the Y, huddled together near the SRY gene for mutual support, like the remnant core of a once-mighty force. Clearly, the Y chromosome is 'in the long run a very dangerous place for any genes because of the lack of recombination', Silber says. The Y chromosome thus has a salutary tale to tell, one which suggests that the very essence of human maleness is suffering an inexorable decline. That doesn't mean that men are doomed – it's always possible for them to evolve or be re-invented. What it does mean, though, is that genetic sex as we know it is not some immutable rock on which our biology is forever founded.

Meanwhile, let's get back to what that vulnerable Y chromosome and its genes still manage to do in the here and now. Later in the book you'll find the amazing tale of how a sperm actually reaches and combines with an egg, but let's jump ahead a little here and look at what happens after that in the making of a boy.

Whether a child is genetically male or female is a matter of chance. But we should highlight here that women play no part in the toss of the coin. Whether it falls heads or tails is entirely up to men, because only they can influence a baby's sex. If that statement surprises you, remember that sperm and eggs are made differently from all the other cells: they each have only one copy of the 23 chromosomes. In human eggs, the 23rd chromosome is always an X, but in human sperm it can be an X or a Y. If we backtrack, we'll see why only one kind of egg is made but two kinds of sperm. When sperm are made from 'germ' cells by division, or meiosis, they split their chromosome pairs in half to make two sperm. A man's germ cells contain the XY combination, so when that pair unzips, one sperm gets the X and the other gets the Y. When a woman's germ cells divide, every egg gets an X. So when a Y-bearing sperm fertilises an egg, the embryo's genetic maleness is effectively preordained – the outcome of the sex game is decided before a ball is kicked, so to speak. That being so, you'd think an XY embryo would go straight down the path to developing as a male, but this doesn't happen. Instead it grows in a neutral way at first, neither male nor female. That's because genetic sex is all about potential, about creating the capacity to veer one way or the other. It is primarily the SRY gene which controls that potential: as we've seen, without it being present and fully functional only one sex can develop – female. But more important in influencing how sex is expressed – the catalyst that actually shapes a baby into male or female form – are the hormones made by the testes or the ovaries.

Early on, the embryo develops a pair of gonads that are neither testes nor ovaries, but more like little neutral sex buds that could bloom either way. Each gonad has two parts that can grow, an inner core known as the medulla, and an outer covering known as the cortex. It is only at about the seventh week of gestation – when the fetus is already thumbnail size – the SRY gene starts to work its magic. It switches on and directs the buds to start flowering into testes. The cells in the medulla multiply and form into a testis, while the cells in the cortex regress and virtually disappear.

It's hard to overstate the significance of this step in understanding what it is to be male: here is where it all begins, and everything we associate with maleness – biologically, at least – depends on and flows from this event. As Graves puts it: 'Of all the differences between male and female mammals, the primary one seems to be the development of the testis in males. Early in development the mammalian embryo is ready for anything. Male and female embryos are morphologically indistinguishable . . . and the embryo is equipped with both male and female internal ducting. The development of the testis triggers a cascade of hormone-controlled changes, so once this decision – testis or no testis – has been taken, the sex of the embryo is determined.' All of this happens, of course, long before the mother starts to feel her belly swell and often before she even realises she is pregnant.

In the absence of the SRY gene's vital influence, the embryonic gonads will keep hedging their bets until about the thirteenth week of gestation, when the basic architecture of the embryo is in place and it becomes a fetus. Only then do the gonads commit to femaleness: the medulla shrinks away and the cortex develops into an ovary. It is often argued that being female is the default state for mammals, that an embryo will develop in a female way unless the SRY gene imposes itself on the process. Some embryologists argue, however, that the default state is really just a sexless one, a case of dual potential. Just as the Y chromosome is needed to trigger male traits, they say, the X chromosome, or two of them, may be needed to set the embryo on the path to femaleness. There's no definitive answer on this issue yet, but the reasoning certainly is appealing in the context of modern gender politics. It gives no support to either of the two more extreme views expressed on this issue – that men are some kind of aberration from a 'natural' feminine human state, or that men are more 'advanced' than women in an evolutionary sense. If anything, science highlights the fundamental similarities of the sexes rather than their differences.

In any case, within a week of a gonad starting to transform into a testis, it begins to make testosterone. At first it does so without any apparent control, but a restraining system of some kind develops so that by about four to six months after a boy is born, testosterone production is limited and kept low until puberty, when the restraints are lifted again. The embryo's new testes also emit another hormone, known as Mullerian inhibiting substance (MIS). This is the next vital step towards maleness. These potent chemical compounds, testosterone and MIS, circulate in the embryo's bloodstream and are carried to its developing tissues and organs. When they make contact with the tiny ducts of the reproductive tract, they each perform special roles in sorting out the embryo's ultimate somatic sex – that is, whether it is born with a body that is male or female. The outer genitals, for example, grow from another AC/DC bud of tissues. Without testosterone, the bud develops into the clitoris and the inner and outer 'lips' of the vagina (the labia minora and labia majora). Under the influence of testosterone, however, those same tissues develop into the head and shaft of the penis and the scrotum.

As for the internal plumbing, the embryo has two sets of ducts ready to go, the Wolffian ducts and Mullerian ducts. A shot of testosterone sparks the development of the Wolffian ducts into the vital organs needed for storing and transporting sperm – the seminal vesicles, the vas deferens and the epididymis – and that process is completed by about 12–13 weeks. The MIS stops the Mullerian ducts from developing; otherwise they would develop into a womb, fallopian tubes and the internal part of the vagina.

That canny piece of chemistry is the third and final key stage in the making of a boy, but we're still discovering how these remarkable processes are then refined as the fetus grows to maturity. There is, for example, a special enzyme devoted to fine-tuning the construction of the penis and scrotum. This enzyme, called

5-alpha-reductase, is found in the genital skin and when it comes in contact with testosterone it has the power to give the hormone a little turbo-charge, converting it into another form – dihydro-testosterone – that focuses more precisely the building of the penis, scrotum and prostate gland. Hormones also circulate through the growing brain, and undoubtedly have sex-related effects there as well, but we know far less about those – and about whether they also cause us to think and behave in male or female ways – than we do about the way they make our bodies look. Even so, we've still only scratched the surface of how a boy or girl is made. 'The pathways for the determination of a male or female body type involve many steps, and each step is controlled by an enzyme or other protein made by a gene,' says Graves. 'In this sense, then, there are probably hundreds, or thousands, of sex-determining genes in the pathway that determines maleness or femaleness.'

About the twenty-sixth week of gestation, testosterone also prompts another sex-specific change in the growing boy. It triggers the growth of the bulbo-cavernosus muscles and the nerves in the spinal cord that control them. Both men and women have these muscles: they circle either the base of the penis or the opening to the vagina and they play an important part in sexual intercourse. In men, however, both their nerve control centre in the spine and the muscles themselves are much larger, possibly because they have a vital role in spasmodically contracting to expel semen during ejaculation. Testosterone gives the developing muscle a boost to ensure that it will be able to do so successfully, even though it may not be needed until many years later.

Surprisingly, the germ cells – which are destined to be either sperm or eggs – initially 'hide' in the embryo, near the heart and away from the gonads. By the time they later migrate through the embryo to the gonads, these have already become ovaries or testes. If the germ cells enter a testis, they are destined to rest for many years until they receive a wake-up call from the surge of hormones that go through a boy's body at puberty. Only then will they start to make sperm, and the boy start to become a man.

While genes are crucial to the development of sex and gender, environmental forces can be equally important in determining how accurately and how well genetic instructions are carried out. The story of the drug thalidomide and its capacity to cause major deformities in babies is a well-known example of how external influences can play havoc with normal body development.

Drugs and pollutants can likewise mess with the process of sex differentiation in embryos. In 1998, scientists from the Norwegian Polar Institute and the University of Oslo revealed that they had discovered seven pseudo-hermaphrodite polar bears. They were all genetic females with vaginas, and some had given birth to cubs, but they also had small penises. One of the researchers, Andrew Derocher, said there might be a perfectly natural explanation. Adrenal or ovarian tumours in females of many mammal species, for example, occasionally can cause fetal sex organs to develop abnormally by exposing them to hormone imbalances at critical times. A much more likely cause, however, is contamination of the bears' environment and food with chemical pollutants. Compounds such as polychlorinated biphenyls (PCBs), which were once widely used in equipment such as electrical transformers, are known to accumulate in body fat and to mimic the effects of sex hormones, at least in laboratory rats.

In mid-1999 a disturbing study underscored how the threat from environmental contaminants begins before birth. Indeed, that may be when the dangers are greatest. For the first time, the research team – led by Warren Foster, of the Center for Women's Health at Cedars-Sinai Medical Center – was able to show that unborn children can be exposed to traces of contaminants from pesticides and industrial chemicals in the amniotic fluid of their mother's womb. Some of these contaminants are of special interest because they are compounds known to be able to disrupt human hormone activity. The study analysed the amniotic fluid of 53 Los Angeles women who were 16–20 weeks pregnant.[6] Almost a third of the samples contained measurable levels of DDE, a waste product of DDT. That notorious pesticide has long been banned from use in North America but is still used in some developing countries. DDE is known to bind to testosterone receptors on cell surfaces. While these receptors prefer the real thing, they will accept DDE as a substitute. So in high enough concentrations, DDE can get in the way of testosterone doing its job. The contaminated amniotic fluid samples contained DDE concentrations ranging from 0.1 to 0.63 nanograms a millilitre.

The highest readings raise a red flag because they are nearly equal to the amount of testosterone normally found in female fetuses and about half the level normally found in male fetuses, according to Claude Hughes, who directs the Center for Women's Health. 'The key factor in assessing the significance of compounds that act like hormones is how their concentrations relate to the naturally occurring hormones,' Hughes said. In this case, the levels of DDE seem high enough to raise concern, but we still don't know whether they are high enough to interfere with the normal action of male sex hormones – particularly testosterone – in the developing testes and thus affect sperm production later in life, or with the development of sex-related body structures. It's not just a question of dose but the timing of the exposure that is critical in determining its impact, Hughes pointed out. In the first few months of gestation, a fetus's organs are forming and their detail is becoming organised. 'And up to three to six months after birth, brain organisation is still occurring in important ways and there is evidence to suggest that sex hormones are being produced in some rather dynamic ways before they become quiet during the baby's first year of life.'

Such findings heighten concerns about chemical exposure and the integrity of the sex-determining process in men worldwide. 'Each year several hundred new compounds are added to the 70,000 compounds and 4 million mixtures already in commercial use,' warns Steven M. Schrader, of the US National Institute for Occupational Safety & Health. We barely have a clue how some of these compounds may interact in the environment and affect living things. So it is hardly surprising that this vast, unplanned, biological experiment can have some nasty side-effects. DDT, for example, was used extensively last century because it killed insects but was thought to be safe for other animals; its persistence in the environment saw it spread everywhere, from the tropics to polar regions, and threaten the survival of birds including penguins and falcons by thinning their eggshells.

But the important side-effect that concerns us in the context of maleness is the apparent damage DDT causes to men's reproductive systems. Evidence now links many widely used pesticides to reports of declining sperm counts in Western men, rising rates of testicular and breast cancer and bizarre 'gender-bending' in animals as diverse as fish and turtles. While the links with human disease and a decline in male fertility remain unclear and in some cases controversial, studies of wildlife in polluted areas increasingly suggest that even brief exposure before birth to pesticides and industrial chemicals can trigger major changes. Whole stretches of some British rivers produce only female fish; male alligators in a Florida lake are born with shrunken genitals, and some turtle and bird species in this lake have developed weird reproductive problems. Other studies suggest that pesticides such as 2,4,5-T, dieldrin, DDT, endosulfan and 2,4-D, along with industrial compounds used as plasticisers, surfactants and at least one food additive, may cause these lifelong changes in sex-hormone production in animals exposed to them at critical times in their embryonic development.

Experiments carried out by a team headed by Louis Guillette, a conservation reproductive endocrinologist at the University of Florida, have suggested that many pesticides mimic the action of estrogen, in both people and alligators. This could explain why the alligator population in Lake Apopka, near Orlando, has suffered severe reproductive problems since a relatively small spill of dicophol, a pesticide used in the citrus industry, in 1980. The lake's alligator population subsequently crashed: most eggs did not hatch, most females had elevated estrogen levels, and most males not only produced low levels of male sex hormones but also had penises 25–30 per cent smaller than normal. John Sumpter, of Brunel University, has found that stretches of some British rivers feature only female fish where the water is polluted with pesticides and industrial chemicals. The problem has parallels with the disastrous consequences of the use of the prescribed synthetic hormone diethylstilbestrol (DES) from the mid-1940s until 1971 (DES was also once used as a growth promotant in cattle). As many as 5 million American women took the drug: those who were pregnant at the time gave birth to apparently normal children, but later in life some of those children were found to be sterile or to have developed cancers of their reproductive organs. The organs most affected by DES and similar chemicals include the ovaries, fallopian tubes, uterus, cervix, vagina and breasts of females, and the testes, prostate and seminal vesicles in males.

DES taught medical scientists some important lessons about the possible toxic effects of estrogen, helping to pave the way for greater alertness to the potential health effects of estrogen-like compounds in the environment. There is growing global concern, for example, that over the past 50 years or so more and more men and boys have been suffering from abnormalities of their reproductive systems. While the statistical evidence is complex, there seems no doubt that testicular cancer, hypospadias (the failure of the urethra to form a tube correctly, leaving a hole somewhere along its length) and undescended testes have become more common. Testicular cancer is one of the most common malignancies in young men. Its incidence in Denmark increased three to four times between the 1940s and 1980s, and smaller rises have been seen in Finland, the US and Scotland. Its incidence in Scotland increased by 15.7 per cent in the 1980s alone. In Britain, the incidence of male genital abnormalities has been increasing as well, with hospital records indicating that the number of boys treated for undescended testes doubled between the 1950s and

1970s. Britain experienced a similar rise in hypospadias, as did Hungary, Sweden, Norway and Denmark (but no such trend was recorded in Finland, Spain, Czechoslovakia, New Zealand or Australia).

A growing number of artificial and naturally occurring compounds in the environment are being found to have estrogenic activity. They range from the so-called phyto-estrogens that occur naturally in plants (such as soy beans) to those in some pesticides and industrial compounds. They are found virtually everywhere and many are in daily use in our homes and workplaces, as Tiaan de Jager and M.S. Bornman reported to the Eleventh World Congress on In Vitro Fertilisation and Human Reproductive Genetics.[7] 'Male reproductive health has received remarkably little attention considering that sub-fertility affects 5 per cent or more of all men,' their report says. 'It is now evident that several aspects of male reproductive health have changed dramatically for the worse over the past 30–50 years. Elimination of agents with hormone-disrupting properties from the environment is probably not a realistic approach to prevent the problem, owing to the immense mass of agents already in the environment and their persistence. The goal that can be reached is to prevent humans from taking up large amounts of these substances. Measures must also be taken to stop the production and diffusion of hormone disrupters. However, environmental effects should not be considered independent from other factors such as lifestyle and genital diseases, with which they probably act synergistically.'

All in all, it seems that long-term 'natural' evolutionary forces have been making maleness a more and more hazardous and tenuous state of affairs. Worse still, on top of that trend has come this new and potentially even more hazardous human-made threat to men's ability to become fathers. And as we'll see further on, the sperm already have a tough enough time simply doing their age-old job.

5

GENDER:
Vive la différence! But what is it?

David Reimer was seven months old, one of healthy twin brothers, when a dreadful accident happened. He had just been circumcised and the surgeon was using an electrical current to cauterise the wound and stop it bleeding. It was a standard procedure, but this time something went horribly wrong. The current was too strong and it severely burned the entire penis, which soon died and fell off. How David's parents, doctors and counsellors responded to this calamity was initially viewed as a classic case study in understanding gender and the power of medical technology to manipulate it. But how David eventually reacted to his treatment has made it a humbling illustration of the flaws in that science.

The year was 1963. At the time, many experts in human biology and psychology had come to believe that nurture was more important than nature in determining gender. In effect, babies were seen as a kind of slate on which their genetic and physical sex at birth could be rewritten if necessary, with the help of hormonal treatments, surgery and psychotherapy. Just nip and tuck, add testosterone or estrogen, a course of counselling and you could raise a child to look, live and think in a male or female role – a role different from the one nature had decreed in that individual's genes. This is, of course, grossly oversimplifying the argument, but in essence that's what it amounted to: the mind would fall into line with the body and the role expectations of others. And it was no doubt a great source of hope and comfort for parents unhappy about their children facing the prospect of a life with an ambiguous gender – those who were born intersexual or, like David, suffered genital traumas.

David's parents were young rural Canadians and 'understandably desperate to know what could be done' for their damaged little boy, according to sex researchers John Money and Anke Ehrhardt, in their classic book on gender, *Man & woman, boy & girl*, first published in 1966.[1] The search took David's parents to a plastic surgeon, who recommended a drastic remedy: that the damaged little boy be transformed into a girl. 'The parents agonised their way to a decision, implementing it with a change of name, clothing and hair style when the baby was 17 months old,' the book records. Four months later, Money and colleagues first saw the toddler's parents in Baltimore, at the Johns Hopkins University psychohormonal research unit, to advise and counsel them at the time of the first surgery. 'In particular, they were given confidence that their child [could] be expected to differentiate a female gender identity, in agreement with the sex of her rearing.'[2] The unit's successful experience with the gender reassignment of hermaphrodites was cited. Money himself was an influential figure in the field, credited with introducing the concept of gender into psychology and social science in 1955. He was also responsible, according to his book's cover notes, 'for the now universally accepted idea that there is not one criterion of sex, but several, ranging from genetic sex to gender role as male or female'. Ambiguity, however, did not fit the criteria.

Under Money's guidance, David (identified as 'John' in publications) became Brenda ('Joan' in the literature). The boy with no penis now lost his testes as well: he was castrated and had genital reconstruction, with a further operation to fashion a vagina left until 'she' was full-grown. At puberty, Brenda's growth spurt and feminisation would be managed by hormone replacement therapy with estrogen. As an article in *Time* magazine reported in 1973, when the treatment was publicised: 'This dramatic case . . . casts doubt on the theory that major sex differences, psychological as well as anatomical, are immutably set by the genes at conception.'

In their book, Money and Ehrhardt record how Brenda's progress was followed for the next six years. Her mother at first eased the child into her new gender by dressing Brenda in 'little pink slacks and frilly blouses . . . and letting her hair grow'. Before long, Brenda had only dresses to wear, only nightdresses for bed, bracelets for her wrists and ribbons for her hair. By four and a half, young Brenda was said to have 'a clear preference for dresses over slacks and to take pride in her long hair'. She was 'neater' than her twin brother and 'in contrast with him, disliked to be dirty'. Her mother encouraged Brenda to be dainty and feminine, and said Brenda responded with enthusiasm, copying her in domestic duties while her brother copied his father's behaviour. Brenda's mother won praise from the psychologists for her 'success' in explaining to both her children the relative merits or being male and female, especially after an occasion when the children were aged five and bathing together. An incident was sparked when Brenda's brother bragged about having an erect penis. Brenda's mother described what took place: '. . . he managed to get a hard-on, and he was standing there and saying, look what I got, proud as a peacock and she [Brenda] got so mad she slapped him – she didn't like it – right on his little penis. I think she was a little jealous. So then I went and I told her you wait and see, women can have babies and boys can't.'

Brenda's reaction was thought to be an example of 'normal' penis envy and hence a positive sign that the child was thinking in a female way. And when it came to Christmas, the twins' present requests seemed to confirm that the strategy was working. Brenda wanted dolls, a doll-house and a doll's stroller, while her brother wanted a garage with cars, fuel pumps and tools. Both were rehearsing their future gender roles, it was noted approvingly. At the book's last recorded encounter with the twins, just before they turned six, they were clearly expressing different goals, according to their mother: 'I found that my son, he chose very masculine things like a fireman or a policeman or something like that. He wanted to do what daddy does, work where daddy does, and carry a lunch kit, and drive a car. And she didn't want any of those things. I asked her, and she said she wanted to be a doctor or a teacher. And I asked her, well, did she have plans that maybe some day she'd get married, like mommy? She'd get married some day – she wasn't too worried about that. She didn't think about that too much, but she wanted to be a doctor. But none of the things that she ever wanted to be were like a policeman or a fireman, and that sort of thing never appealed to her. So I felt in a way that was a good sign . . .'

As things turned out, that certainly wasn't the case. Indeed, the bathtub incident was a more accurate glimpse into the turmoil brewing in Brenda's mind. There were other clues as well. The mother worried, for example, that she could never quite manage to teach her daughter to be less rough and loud or more polite. Money's own final observation hints at other disquiets: Brenda had 'many tomboyish traits, such as abundant physical energy, a high level of activity, stubbornness, and being often the dominant one in a girls' group'. From that point on, the doctors lost touch with the case because the family stopped coming to see them. Money was able to conclude, however, that David/Brenda's case demonstrated 'that gender dimorphic patterns of rearing have an extraordinary influence on shaping a child's psychosexual differentiation and the ultimate outcome of a female or male gender identity'. Nurture could impose itself on nature, even over-ride it.

But they were wrong about Brenda. Tragically wrong. If they had observed their charge for a few more years, they would have realised it. Indeed, when other researchers followed up the case in the 1990s, they found that David's case better illustrated the old saying that boys will be boys. Milton Diamond of the University of Hawaii and Keith Sigmundson of the Canadian Ministry of Health found that Brenda had long since given up a female role, had undergone another sex change and was living happily as a man.[3] What's more, he had first come to make this decision without knowing the truth about his sex at birth or about his accident.

Diamond, a sexologist who has followed the case since the 1970s, reported that despite consistently being treated as a girl since very early childhood, Brenda was never comfortable with the role. Even as a toddler she felt 'different' and recalled trying to throw off the frilly dresses. And despite the story of the Christmas dolls, Brenda actually preferred boys' toys. In one memorable case, she went into a store to buy an umbrella and came out with a toy machine-gun. 'I suspected I was a boy since the second grade,' David recalled. His doctors had insisted that these were normal 'tomboy' feelings for a girl, he told Diamond and Sigmundson in interviews in 1994 and 1995.

Other children teased Brenda about her boyish looks and behaviour. David's doubts grew strong between the ages of 9 and 11: 'There were little things from early on. I began to see how different I felt and was, from what I was supposed to be. But I didn't know what it meant. I thought I was a freak or something . . . I looked at myself and said I don't like this type of clothing. I don't like the types of toys I [am] always being given. I like hanging around with the guys and climbing trees and stuff like that and girls don't like any of that stuff. I looked in the mirror and [saw] my shoulders [were] so wide, I mean there [was] nothing feminine about me. I [was] skinny, but other than that, nothing. But that [was] how I figured it out. [I figured I was a guy] but I didn't want to admit it. I figured I didn't want to wind up opening a can of worms.' His doctors and counsellors would not entertain his doubts and pressed him to behave in a more feminine way. He at last rebelled at 14, after two years of estrogen therapy, deciding that he must either kill himself or live as a male. After tearfully confronting his father, David was told the truth about his past. 'All of a sudden everything clicked. For the first time things made sense and I understood who and what I was.'

He eventually found new doctors, had a mastectomy, treatment with male hormones and surgery to create a small penis for him. His family rejected advice to move and start a new life in a new town. They decided instead to stay put and be open about what had happened. Despite some uncomfortable reactions, David's school friends largely took the change in their stride and stuck by him. David felt more accepted by his peers than he ever had as Brenda. At 25, he met a woman who already had children and they got married. He was still happily married, with three adopted children, when he collaborated with the author of a recent book about his case, *As Nature Made Him*, by John Colapinto.[4] He revealed that much of his penis had no sensation, nor did the areas of scarring where the grafts had been taken. He was able to have sexual intercourse with ejaculation, but his surgeons were never able to reconstruct a fully closed urethra for him, meaning that he had to sit to urinate from an opening at the base of his penis.

When they published their 1997 report, Diamond and Sigmundson pointed out that 'John', while at that time wanting to remain anonymous, strongly wanted his case history to be made available to the medical community to reduce the likelihood of others suffering his psychic trauma. Diamond believes the case has important implications for those charged with the care of babies born with ambiguous genitals. David was treated in the belief that it is easier to make a good vagina than a good penis, that a child's identity reflects its upbringing and that as a man David would find it devastating not to have a penis. That clinical advice was relatively standard in medical texts of the time and reflected the current thinking of many physicians, Diamond pointed out. Yet David's story and an extensive review of the medical literature has shown that not a single person born with unequivocally male genitals and chromosomes has ever easily and fully accepted an imposed life as a female, regardless of surgical and medical interventions.

In an accompanying editorial on Diamond and Sigmundson's article, William Reiner, a surgeon and psychiatrist from Johns Hopkins Hospital, commented: 'Past clinical decisions about gender identity and sex reassignment when genitalia are greatly abnormal have by necessity occurred in a relative vacuum because of inadequate scientific data. Clinical decisions have been constructed largely on the predicted adequacy of the genitalia for adult sexual function. Clinical decisions must ultimately be based not on anatomical predictions, nor on the "correctness" of sexual function, for this is neither a question of morality nor of social consequence, but on that path most appropriate to the likeliest psychosexual development pattern of the child. In other words, the organ that appears to be critical to psychosexual development and adaptation is not the external genitalia, but the brain.'

Today, some intersexual lobbyists argue that children of ambiguous sex should not be subjected to any medical intervention until they near puberty and can better take part in the choice about whether they will live as a man or a woman, or continue as they were born. But as one expert working in the field told me: 'That's all very well and I can see the sense of what they're saying, but try telling the parents that – they're very anxious to have the uncertainty resolved as soon as possible.' That sentiment is understandable and you cannot help but empathise with it. After all, the idea that people are either male or female is deeply entrenched in culture, a concept reinforced right from the moment of birth when the cry of 'It's a boy!' or 'It's a girl!' is heard. We don't make allowance for an 'other' option. I was in a group of men recently, for example, when one announced the birth of a baby in his family. 'What did you get?' asked another. 'One with plumbing or without?'

As we've seen, sex is a lot more complicated than that: it doesn't always come in neat pink-or-blue, inny-or-outy packages. The existence of intersexuals reflects the fact that it is not a simple either/or issue. The biology of sex determination means that usually the outcome is a person with genes and a body in agreement with each other, male or female. Usually, but not always. There *is* a third option: a true hermaphrodite, who has one testis and one ovary, or sometimes a merged organ known as an ovo-testis. And a fourth option: pseudo-hermaphrodites whose genitals are ambiguous, or whose genes and bodies are mismatch. And there are further variations.

Biology is far from being the end of the story, either – the overlay of human culture is so rich and flexible that it becomes impossible to set a distinct boundary between nature and nurture, or between male and female. Indeed, the interaction of genes and culture is so complex in humans that science is nowhere near understanding it. It's reasonably clear, though, that there's no fixed, biological 'true sex'. Instead, individuals have an overwhelming trend towards male or female, and this is qualified by a wide range of other genetic, physical and mental states.

For that reason, I'm going to dare to be different in this chapter. What usually happens at this point in popular and academic debate about sex is that it turns to the *differences* between men and women. I'm going to focus instead on the *similarities*. If you've read this far, you will have realised that nailing down sex and gender differences is a lot trickier than it looks. I sought help on the Internet, for example, from an international discussion group for experts in andrology – those involved in studying males and their health. I explained that I was writing this book and was finding it hard to answer a simple question, 'How do you define a man?'. The many e-mail responses I received ranged from a punctilious 'XY', to a highly detailed dictionary definition of the word 'man' and its etymology (it predates the twelfth century).

An Australian andrologist replied cautiously: 'A less etymological, contemporary definition would be a human being born with biological features of, and expressing self-defined gender role of, a male adult and accepted as such by their community at large.' Another, from a sexual dysfunction clinic in Cairo, warned: 'Any definition that is based upon gender role or types of behaviour expected from a man would be too subjective and judgmental as gender roles differ not only from culture to culture but also within the same culture and have been continuously changing throughout history. Definitions based on fertility would again be inaccurate as well as insulting to infertile couples.' That seemed fair enough: European noblemen once wore long curly wigs, powdered their faces and put peacocks to shame with their finery; today, they usually wear conformist plain dark suits. And a man is no less worthy of being called a man if he can't have children.

A South African correspondent invoked religion, stating that man is 'the first spirit created in the image of God' and had been given two tasks in life, to 'reproduce and reign over the earth. For this God has given him a reproductive and hormonal system fit for the first task and a strong muscular body to complete the second task.' A prominent American urologist sympathised with my struggle for definition: 'One reason finding an answer is so difficult is that the question can be answered from two perspectives, one referring to "man" in only the biological sense, and one referring to "man" in the sociological or anthropological sense. Sort of physics vs. metaphysics, if you know what I mean. Which do you mean or do you mean both? If you mean both, do you mean to consider them separately, or consider them together, as they occur (or fail to occur) in nature. The question is complex enough, let alone an answer!'

The response that seemed to best summarise the scientific consensus came from Donna Vogel, a senior researcher in reproductive science with the US National Institutes of Health. 'You have your choice,' she wrote. '**Genetic male**: traditionally, having XY chromosomes, but we now know that some XX individuals with a specific portion of the Y DNA develop as males. **Gonadal male**: having testes. Occasionally they are within the abdominal cavity so not visible. Some individuals with abnormalities of sexual development have mixed gonads or incompletely developed gonads, but if they make enough testosterone, the individual usually develops as a . . . **Phenotypic male**: someone who has male external genitalia and a masculine appearing body and hair pattern. Again, there are syndromes of incomplete male development yielding a spectrum of maleness through ambiguity all the way to a condition of resistance to androgens where XY "males" with high testosterone levels develop as phenotypic females because their cells do not recognise the androgen. **Sociobehavioral male**: individuals who view themselves as male and act accordingly. This is what many people in the field now refer to as "gender" rather than "sex".'

Those 'sociobehavioural' roles muddy the picture even more if you're trying to define men by how they express their sexuality. Many men don't only have sex with women, for example: they may have it exclusively or occasionally with other men, with both men and women, with several people simultaneously, with themselves, with no-one at all and even with other species. They also change their behaviour over time: an individual man might have many serial sex partners in his youth, followed by years of monogamy, then monogamy punctuated by the occasional affair, followed by years of abstinence if his steady partner dies.

Now, if the mere concept of 'man' is so bedevilled by subtleties of genetics, anatomy, perception and culture, it's harder still to say what distinguishes men from women. Scientifically, the essential difference between males and females of any kind is simple: males have small sex cells and females have large ones. A rooster's sperm are microscopic, for example, but a hen's eggs are relatively huge. Males basically only contribute their DNA to conception, females put in DNA plus a lot more by way of food reserves. That's it. So I'm not going to rattle off a long list of human sex differences merely to prove a point. I'm going to credit you with common sense and assume that you *know* what men and women are. It's not science, but it's obvious. I'm also going to assume that you're observant enough to have spotted that men and women (however you define them) are different.

We are reminded all the time about those differences – separate clothes, separate names, separate toilets, separate magazines, separate sports, separate roles and even separate laws. We can tell pretty quickly whether someone is a man or woman without having to think about it, and we find it unsettling when their sex is uncertain. Some of the cues we use to decide someone's gender are unquestionably biological – breasts, hips, muscles, facial hair and pitch of voice are obvious ones. They make us feel confident that we know a guy from a girl. We should remember, though, that our confidence is more often based on cues that have little to do with biology – how we cut our hair, what clothes or cosmetics we wear and how we act are largely the products of culture. When that confidence is shaken, it can deeply disturb some people: witness the 1999 American film *Boys Don't Cry* – based on the grisly true-life story of Brandon Teena, a Nebraska female-to-male trans-sexual who was beaten, raped and murdered in 1993 for 'lying' about his sexuality.

As anthropologist Margaret Mead once explained, a child can't simply decide that it belongs to its own sex. It must also decide *how* male or female it is. Children hear men 'branded' as feminine, women 'condemned' as masculine and yet others described as real men or true women. Different attributes and character traits are gender-labelled as well, so that sensitivity and stoicism take on female and male meanings.

And what those extraordinary XY mares from the last chapter make blindingly obvious is that looks can be deceptive: genes, bodies and behaviour don't always match. On the basis of sex chromosomes alone, those horses were male. According to their outward appearance, they were female. But judged on their behav-iour and the parts of their bodies devoted to reproduction, they were neither definitively male nor female. Similar anomalies have been found in a prominent bloodline of cocker spaniels that produces XY bitches.

In fact, XY females are now known to occur across a great range of mammal species, from rodents to humans. It is estimated that one person in 20,000 is sex-reversed (many of whom remain unaware of their condition until later in life when they seek help for fertility problems). But that doesn't mean the other 19,999 are unequivocally either male or female. Sex-reversal is just one of many midway zones within a spectrum of human sex and gender, grouped together by the convenient umbrella term 'intersexual'. The Intersex Society of North America (ISNA) asserts, for example, that 1 person in 500 has sex chromosomes that are neither XX nor XY. There are no definitive statistics on this, but if you add the other variants it's a reasonable guess that perhaps 1 person in 100 is intersexual in the broadest sense. In other words, it's not a common condition but neither is it especially rare; the birth of non-identical twins occurs less often.

However, intersexuality is not so obvious as twins or red hair – you can't usually see the disparity between genes, body and mind. I vividly remember when I was a boy seeing one of the 'human freaks' on Sideshow Alley at Sydney's venerable Royal Easter Show. This performer went by the stage name of Anna John Lee and was billed as half-man and half-woman. On reflection, the freakiest thing about this exhibit was the thought that anyone might take it seriously. Its major credibility problem was that the dividing line between the halves went neatly down his/her middle vertically. The performer would show that the John side was dressed in a man's trousers and shirt, with a man's short haircut (and half a moustache, if I recall correctly). With a 180-degree turn, the Anna side would reveal a shapely leg in a fishnet stocking, and a skimpy spangled costume bursting with an ample breast; beneath a long blond wig was a beautiful female face in profile, fully made-up with lipstick, eyeshadow, mascara, foundation and a plucked eyebrow. The beguiling thought that such a person could exist was what persuaded me to part with my pocket money, but the reality was an anatomical impossibility.

Elizabeth's story

Elizabeth is a male-to-female transsexual who works at a publicly funded gender advisory and support service in Sydney. Here she tells how she was born as a male in 1950 in England, but by the time her family emigrated to Australia in 1958, she had already begun to realise that within her male body was a female mind.

'About that time I was pretty much aware that I felt like I should have been a girl. I wanted to be a girl and I wanted to play and socialise with the girls. But I didn't do any of that. I pretty much stuck to the male roles and did what I was supposed to do as a male – played all the right sports, all the right games and hated girls at whatever the appropriate age was that you're supposed to hate girls before you start to like them.

'I very much conformed to the world's expectations of how I should be and how I should live my life. That continued through my education and through a number of jobs. I had a normal male sex drive and was attracted to women. I got married when I was 22 and we had three children.

'But I had been cross-dressing since I was eight. I did it whenever I could in the privacy of my own bedroom. I went to extraordinary lengths for many years to conceal from anyone connected with me that I cross-dressed. I actually revealed it to my wife prior to us getting married. That was a very traumatic moment. But I probably didn't go into the idea that I really felt I should be a woman. She marched me off to a psychiatrist, who saw me four times and pronounced me cured.

'Other than cross-dressing, I endured that denial of myself until my late thirties and then I think I quite genuinely reached a mid-life crisis. I thought: "My god, I'm halfway through my life and I'm not living my life as myself." Probably that was the trigger for me to realise that I needed to do something about it and, for want of a better cliché, to be true to myself.

'That was the start of probably the most difficult part of my life and – ultimately the most rewarding and spiritually uplifting. I found myself exiting an identity that I didn't feel comfortable with, but it was an identity I'd known for some 38 years and I found myself travelling into this kind of void.

'My perception of myself as a woman had often been projected onto individual people, like Doris Day when I was a kid and Dusty Springfield when I was a teenager. I had all these female icons I wanted to be. When I made that transition I found that I wasn't those people, but I'd left behind the only person I knew.

'For much of that time I felt suicidal. The destination I was aiming for seemed an impossible one to reach. I was a six-foot-tall, fairly hefty, white, middle-class male. I couldn't really be a woman, I just physically couldn't do it. But I realised one day that that there was another side to the coin. When I flipped that coin I was able to start celebrating what I had and stop lamenting what I didn't have.

'My daughter was the first person I came out to. There was

lots of crying but she was really good about it – she said she couldn't understand why anyone would want to be a man anyway. It was more difficult for my two sons. I used to be a very active father. They're still uncomfortable about being in public with me.

'I left my job as a teacher and moved cities and started living as a woman – it was about going somewhere else to become someone else. My marriage folded, although my wife and I had close and fairly amicable contact for about three years after I'd begun the process. But she needed a husband and I couldn't be that for her any more.

'I began hormone treatment in 1991 and I had sex reassignment surgery in Thailand on 5 January 2000, so I guess I'm truly a new woman of the new millennium. Physically I am now as close to being a woman as I'm able to achieve, having been born a genetic male.

'I don't miss my penis. I carried it for 49 years of my life and now I can't really remember it. After starting the hormone treatment I stopped getting erections anyway, so for the last decade it was just something I peed through.

'Sex as a woman is very different. It doesn't need to end with a bang as it does when you're male. In fact, it doesn't really need to end at all, which is very pleasant. I now identify as a lesbian and I have a partner. I'm still attracted to women: my sexuality has never changed – it was always my gender identity that was at odds with me physically.'

Intersexuals justifiably complain that many people seem to imagine them as being something akin to Anna John Lee – two distinct beings of opposite sexes fused into one body, or having both male and female genitals. 'Genitals develop from a common precursor, and therefore intermediate morphology is common, but the popular idea of "two sets" of genitals (male and female) is not possible,' explains ISNA in its material. 'Intersexual genitals may look nearly female, with a large clitoris, or with some degree of posterior labial fusion. They may look nearly male, with a small penis, or with hypospadias. They may be truly "right in the middle", with a phallus that can be considered either a large clitoris or a small penis, with a structure that might be a split, empty scrotum, or outer labia, and with a small vagina that opens into the urethra rather than into the perineum.'

That wondrous variety of genital anatomy reflects the way our embryos grow – the reproductive tissues have bi-potential that, for a range of reasons, doesn't always fully express itself one way or the other. Of course, thanks to our practice of wearing clothes and having sex in private, most humans never get to see each other's genitals. And we certainly can't see internal organs. So our gender is perceived by others according to the way we look and behave, and we carry in our minds many stereotyped images about it. Margaret Mead has pointed out that in any given group of people it is possible to arrange the men and women so that between a 'most masculine group' and a 'most feminine group' there will be others who fall in the middle – displaying fewer of the pronounced physical features linked to one sex or the other. You get the same outcome whether you judge only by the secondary sex characteristics (body hair, fat layers and so on) or only by the primary sex characteristics (such as breasts and hip-to-waist ratio). Overweight men can have large breasts, just as some women are as flat-chested as any man.

What's more, there's little obvious link between your degree of maleness or femaleness and your success in making babies. As Mead astutely observes, a square-jawed, muscular fellow may have no children, while the weedy little guy with a soft, feminine face may father a football team. Arrange your sample in a different way, though, and an alternative picture emerges: 'When the meek little Caspar Milquetoast is placed side by side not with a prizefighter, but with the meekest female version of himself, he might be seen to be much more masculine than she. The plump man with soft breast-tissue, double chin and protruding buttocks, whom one only has to put in a bonnet to make him like a woman, when put beside the equally plump woman will be seen not to have such ambiguous outlines after all,' Mead observed.[5]

I was taken aback when I first learnt that humans and peas have some genes in common. I'd never thought of myself as being related to a pea. But once I got used to the idea that I was a far distant cousin to a tasty little green legume, I found it rather charming. I'm not sure I feel so warmly about the fact that I'm also related to bacteria or that about 50 per cent of my genes are identical to those of a worm. But them's the evolutionary breaks – all life on Earth has a common origin, it seems. The more recent the link, the more genes you share. That's why I have over 90 per cent of my genes in common with a rat, as do you, dear reader. Chimpanzees are closer still, being 98.4 per cent genetically identical to humans. That number highlights our near kinship with chimps, but the 1.6 per cent difference is actually a vast gulf in its practical effect. If there are about 30,000 genes in the human genome (that's the current estimate), it means chimps have about 500 genes that are not identical to those of people. Obviously, those genes must include some that code for appalling table manners, hairier bodies, stockier legs, longer arms, flatter noses, more rubbery lips, higher pain tolerance, a stubby tail, knuckles that can be walked on, a humbler voicebox, lesser brains, much larger testes and much greater upper-body strength in males, as well as smaller breasts, narrower pelvis and a radically different sexual cycle in females . . . the list is long and its import is great. Despite their closeness to us, chimps are not people. They did not invent agriculture, football or television. It's hard to imagine that they have any concept of the Big Bang, any knowledge of dinosaurs, any inkling of when the next solar eclipse will occur, who Adolf Hitler was or why spiders don't get stuck in their own webs. Even if chimp sperm could fertilise a human egg – and it is a possibility – 6 million or so years of evolution separate us from our common ancestor and modern humans are in a very different league.

Conversely, the 500 human genes that chimps don't have must be the ones that help to confer on us our uniqueness as a species. Somewhere in that lot is the special something that sets us apart from apes, rats, worms and peas, and makes it possible for us to talk to someone on the other side of the planet by telephone, send spaceships to Mars and make Ken dolls.

We're also unique as individuals, because we reproduce sexually and mix our genes in new combinations every time human egg meets human sperm. We are not peas in a pod (excepting identical twins), yet we all have a great deal in common. Every one of us is 99.9 per cent genetically identical, so on average we differ from each other in only about 30 genes (that's just a ballpark figure, to illustrate the point). But if you do as Margaret Mead suggests and put a jockey next to a basketballer, it's obvious that people can differ from each other quite markedly, based on the effects of that small number of genes.

The genetic differences between races of people are smaller still. Indeed, there's more variation between individuals within any race than there is between races – a Briton is more like a Maori than a jockey is like a basketballer. So racial variation is determined by a relatively small number of genes, less than the 30 or so that separate individuals. Yet those different genes can still create dramatic variations in surface features. With my Anglo-pale skin, coarse wavy hair, round eyes and large straight nose, I still look very different from the Asian man at my local bakery, with his brown-ochre skin, sleek black hair, almond eyes and flattish snub nose.

Now, as we saw in the previous chapter, the genetic differences between men and women are smaller still. Indeed, just one gene – SRY – holds the key to all of the physical differences that later emerge. No SRY means no testes. No testes means no testosterone. No testosterone means a baby girl. Of course, as I explained, many other genes are involved in fine-tuning the development of male and female anatomy. But SRY has to be there and functioning first of all for a sexless embryo eventually to become a boy and then a man.

Biologically, that's surely the single most important difference between the sexes. To be sure, it's a gap of great significance. But it serves to emphasise a profound truth – that men and women fundamentally have far more in common with each other than they have differences. Those differences are real and they are very important, especially when it comes to making babies, but perhaps we shouldn't make as much of them as we do. Molecular biology teaches us that discriminating against someone on the basis of their race is not just ethically dubious but also scientifically unsound. If the aim of racism is to exclude outsiders, people who are least like you and your kin, then discriminating against jockeys and basketballers makes more sense than singling out people because they are black, white or tan. So perhaps we have a new lesson to learn: that men and women are essentially the same, merely different melodies played on the same instrument. And armed with this new insight into ourselves, we may see afresh the injustice of discriminating against someone on the basis of their sex or gender. Perhaps it is also time to reconsider how we pigeon-hole people on the basis of what *we* think their gender is, rather than what *they* think.

One ingenious study in the 1970s, for example, involved showing a mixed-sex group of university students a videotape of a nine-month-old infant playing with toys. The child was dressed in gender-neutral clothes but half the students were told they were watching a girl and the other half were told the child was a boy. In situations where the child's behaviour was ambiguous the students watching the 'boy' rated 'his' behaviour as angry, while those watching the 'girl' saw 'her' as being afraid. In a related experiment, other researchers asked mothers to play with infants of a similar age to their own children. Half the infants were dressed in gender-appropriate clothing and the other half were cross-dressed. 'When the baby was presented as a boy, mothers responded with physical actions; when presented as a girl, mothers responded with soothing and comforting actions,' Gilda Morelli, of the Department of Psychology at Boston College in the US, summarised.[6] A third study involved male and female students being asked to wait in a room and told that if a sleeping baby in the adjoining room cried, they were to alert the researcher. Half the subjects were told it was a boy and half that it was a girl (in fact, the crying baby was merely a recording). Female students were much faster to respond if the 'girl' was crying than those who thought it was a boy (male students were generally slower to respond than female students, regardless of the perceived gender of the baby). Little wonder that most of us grow up so clearly 'knowing' how to behave according to our gender identity, when our behaviour is subtly influenced into gender roles by other people from the very beginnings of our lives.

The gender identity we each adopt is tailored to gender roles that each human society makes it possible to have – as with sex, there's no biologically fixed 'true gender' and many categories other than man and woman have been invented. Modern Western societies, for example, have an androgynous layer in their gender fabric that is often occupied by male entertainers, who may be homosexual, intersexual, transvestite, transsexual or just plain making a dollar out of dressing up as a woman. Boys played the parts of women in Shakespeare's day, and countless 'drag' shows and cross-dressing acts have been enthusiastically performed and watched over the years. Boy George, David Bowie and Prince reached fame and fortune with the help of androgynous dressing. Australia's Dame Edna Everage – the alter ego of performer Barry Humphries – is as popular as actor Paul Hogan's macho character of Crocodile Dundee.

In some Polynesian cultures, boys and men may adopt women's roles in their youth, or all their lives. In the bar of the famous Aggie Grey's Hotel in Western Samoa, for example, I recently watched with interest as a group of equally fascinated American men crowded around a glamorous *fa'afafine*. The word translates simply as 'like a woman', and this person certainly was: slim, tall, finely featured and wearing lovely Western-style women's evening clothes and accessories – 'she' was sophisticated and beautiful, but apparently male beneath the feminine exterior and behaviour. In a remote Samoan village, I saw another *fa'afafine* who was rather chubby and plain, simply wearing the usual unisex T-shirt, sandals and wraparound *lavalava*. He was distinguishable as a *fa'afafine* mainly because his hair was grown long and tied back in a woman's style, and because he was sitting cross-legged with a group of women sharing their domestic chores. That social role is accepted as part of the normal spectrum of life in Samoa, and parents whose sons are *fa'afafine* often say they are blessed because their son can do both 'men's' and 'women's' work. The now-extinct Juaneño people who once lived on the coast of south-western California are known, along with some other Native American groups, to have socially approved of transvestism and homosexuality. A boy with such tendencies was encouraged to develop and display them. Male transvestites were appreciated as hard workers and often married, according to my *Encyclopaedia Britannica*. Its entry on the social control of sexual behaviour notes: 'Societies differ remarkably in what they consider socially desirable and undesirable in terms of sexual behaviour and consequently differ in what they attempt to prevent or promote. What is normative behaviour in one society may be a deviation or crime in another. One can go through the literature and discover that virtually any sexual act, even child–adult relations or necrophilia, has somewhere at some time been acceptable behaviour.'

So gender identity is responsive to human culture and to individual needs or desires. The people you pass on the street may be concealing a different genetic, physical or mental sexuality from the gender identity they project to the world, especially if there are good reasons for doing so. A famous case emerged in 1980 when a woman named Stella Walsh was shot dead in the parking lot of a discount store in Cleveland, Ohio – an innocent victim of cross-fire from an armed robbery that occurred while she was shopping. Walsh was already well known as an athlete: under her given name, Stanislawa Walasiewicz, she competed for Poland and won a gold medal in the 100 metres sprint at the 1932 Olympic Games, and the silver medal in that event in 1936 in the controversial Games held at Berlin. She later took up US citizenship and changed her name. She retired having set 11 world records and won 41 US championships in sprinting, discus and long jump. The question of sexual identity first touched her life indirectly, when she was beaten by US sprinter Helen Stephens in the 100-metre event in 1936. Members of the Polish media questioned whether Stephens really was a woman, and the issue was decided in the affirmative by a physical examination. (The journalists' doubts were legitimate: Hermann Ratjen entered the women's high jump event for Germany at these Games – later claiming he did so under duress from Nazi officials – but he was beaten by three women.) It was only when a stray bullet took Walsh's life all those years later, however, that it emerged that the wrong sprinter had been quizzed. An autopsy revealed that Stella Walsh had mosaic male and female sex chromosomes and ambiguous genitals. Widespread publicity ensued and a friend revealed how Walsh had long suffered emotional problems related to her androgynous condition. Her athletics records were formally challenged as well, but the challenge was dismissed on the basis of insufficient evidence that Walsh was a man, and her name is honoured in the US National Track and Field Hall of Fame in Indianapolis.

Not that the International Olympic Committee (IOC) has shown much reticence in tussling with such subtleties in the modern era. It has insisted that entrants in women's events undergo highly intrusive gender tests to obtain a 'certificate of femininity' before they can compete. Chromosome testing of female athletes was introduced to the Olympic Games in 1968, supposedly to weed out men who might try by stealth to compete in women's competitions. This was despite the fact that sex-reversal in human beings had been scientifically confirmed a decade earlier. At first the tests were based on the premise that sex chromosomes would decide the matter – if you had a Y chromosome, you were a man. Even at the time, the distinction was dubious at best. From today's viewpoint, it is ridiculous: we know that genetic males can lack the SRY gene or fail to respond to testosterone in the womb and thus develop female bodies, but under the IOC rules of 1968 they could not have competed as women.

'I first heard of this in 1969 and I said, "It can't be true. Nobody can be so stupid,"' geneticist Albert de la Chapelle, of the University of Helsinki, told *Discover* magazine in 1992. 'There should be no test at all.' As an authority on human sexual development, he fought the IOC on the gender-testing issue, personally arguing the case for Spain's best hurdler in the mid-1980s, Maria Jose Martinez Patino. She failed a chromosome test in 1985 at the World University Games in Japan, but refused to heed the advice of Spanish athletic officials that she retire quietly from competition. Patino suffered greatly for her stand once it became publicly known. She lost a scholarship, her place of residence, her records and her coach. Patino was indeed a genetic male, but she had androgen insensitivity syndrome. In a sense, she was even more 'womanly' than most women, since her body could not develop masculine physical traits no matter how much testosterone she produced or was given. Her failure to menstruate had been put down to her heavy training regimen and lack of body fat. De la Chapelle successfully swayed the IOC in her case and she was allowed to compete again as a woman, complete with a 'certificate of femininity' that exempted her from further testing. Yet if Stella Walsh had been sex-tested she probably would have been barred from Olympic competition, even though her performances were in line with those of her female contemporaries and not those of the men.

The IOC's medical code still states (at the time of writing) that 'all competitors taking part in women's events in the competition . . . or as a female competitor of a mixed team . . . shall be subject to gender verification'. Entrants in men's events are not 'verified' for gender. But after its meeting in Seoul in June 1999, the IOC revealed that it had decided 'to refrain, on an experimental basis, from performing gender tests at the 2000 Games in Sydney. The IOC will nonetheless reserve the right to conduct such tests, if necessary.' The announcement was buried in the last paragraph of a brief press release about random drug testing, and gave no further explanation about why this decision had been taken. The answer seems obvious. It also seems inevitable that at some time in the future, another exceptional intersexual athlete such as Stella Walsh will emerge in top-level competition. It will be intriguing to see how sport administrators, other athletes and the public react when that happens.

It's also a reminder that the battles of recent generations over gender discrimination have yet to be fully played out.

'While the notion of a sex test to find men disguised as women may seem a reasonable idea, the trouble is that it misses some hereditary disorders where women may have chromosomal abnormalities that cause them to "fail" a test, while men with chromosomal abnormalities could theoretically "pass" the test,' states the Women & Sport Unit of the Australian Sports Commission (ASC). 'If a female athlete "fails" a test, then she undergoes a physiological examination. A negative test can cause incredible distress to women whose gender is suddenly called into question and there are many documented cases where women's lives have undergone massive change because of this public scrutiny. One such woman was Polish sprinter Eva Klobukowska who, at the European Championships in Budapest in 1966, passed a gynaecological examination. One year later, after the introduction of sex chromatin testing, she was found to have one chromosome too many to be declared a woman for the purposes of athletic competition. Despite having a rare XXY condition that gave her no advantage over other athletes, she was forced to return her Olympic and other medals, and retired from competition surrounded by controversy.' Of the thousands of women tested at the Atlanta Games, about 1 in 400 tested 'male', although all were cleared by subsequent physical examinations. 'Why use a test that is inaccurate, does not really test what officials are trying to test for and has the potential to subject some women who "fail" the test to unwarranted stress when the number of men who would be attempting to compete as women in international competition would be negligible?' the ASC asks.

Many scientists, doctors, administrators and athletes have opposed gender testing in sport on technical and ethical grounds. Other critics say the tests are discriminatory, unreliable, invasive and ultimately based on value judgements about what a woman is. Norwegian medical officers refused to perform them at the 1994 Winter Games in Lillehammer. The chief medical officer for the Sydney 2000 Games organisers, Dr Danny Stiel, told me in late 1999 that none of his staff had expressed such concerns. Until the event was exempted he had been expecting to test between 3000 and 3500 women entrants the next year. He also noted that the IOC had reserved 'the right to conduct such tests, if necessary' and he expected some entrants would have to undergo a potentially rigorous battery of tests, ranging from sophisticated genetic and hormone analysis of cell and blood samples to ultrasound examinations of internal organs.

As it turned out, not a single sporting federation or national Olympic committee taking part in the Sydney Games asked the IOC to perform a gender test, so none were done. Dr Stiel later stated: 'I'm not terribly surprised', he said, 'since most of the major international federations don't do it anymore anyway.' The IOC's experiment thus seems to have produced an unmistakeable result – that none of the participating nations and sporting bodies want gender tests, except perhaps in the most exceptional circumstances. History suggests that abuses are few and that gender testing is tainted with bias, inadequate knowledge and injustice. As one medical expert with a close interest in the issue (who would not be named), told me: 'I don't think there will be gender testing at future Games unless some abuse is made public or some new test emerges that is absolutely foolproof.'

The discoverer of the SRY gene, Andrew Sinclair, concedes that in sport the distinction between men and women is important: 'Clearly, males have a larger body mass and greater muscle strength and so there should be separate categories, but you don't define these categories by chromosomes or genes. Someone with androgen insensitivity syndrome has XY chromosomes, the SRY gene and testes, yet they have a typical woman's body and even less body hair than most women. Most people would accept that they are women. If we accept people as women, that should be enough.' And how have Sinclair's discoveries affected his own view of gender? 'These days I don't think so much in black and white about male and female. Now I think of it all as being on a spectrum.'

There are many intersexual states along that spectrum. The list includes (with thanks to the American Society of Andrology and ISNA):

- **True hermaphroditism.** Individuals have both testicular and ovarian tissue. External genitals are usually ambiguous, although relatively normal male or female appearance is possible. Most true hermaphrodites are raised as males because of the appearance of their genitals, even though more than half have XX sex chromosomes. Many XX hermaphrodites don't have the SRY gene, while those with XY chromosomes may have the SRY gene misplaced.
- **Klinefelter syndrome.** These people inherit an extra X chromosome from one of their parents (they have 47 chromosomes altogether and an XXY sex-chromosome pattern). The effects are variable, but they are usually raised as males. Their testes are usually small, hard and produce no sperm and often low testosterone levels, so at puberty they don't develop adult male

physical traits (body hair, muscle, deep voice, larger penis and testes) as strongly as other boys. This syndrome is the most common cause of testicular failure, with an incidence of 1 in 1000 males.

- **Turner syndrome.** These people lack an X chromosome (so they have 45 chromosomes altogether and an XO sex chromosome pattern). They are clearly female in appearance, but their ovaries are usually little more than 'streaks' of ovarian tissue.
- **XX males.** Individuals are genetic females with male bodies. This happens when an SRY gene translocates from the Y to another chromosome, usually the X. They may have undescended testes and hypospadias and usually have small testes, which produce no sperm and low testosterone levels.
- **XY gonadal dysgenesis.** These men fail to develop normal male gonads, so they may have a 'streak' of testicular tissue on one or both sides, with varying degrees of function. The cause is thought to be a deletion or mutation affecting the SRY gene.
- **Female pseudo-hermaphroditism.** These people have ovaries and an XX sex-chromosome pattern but their external genitals are virilised during their early development by exposure to excess androgen, most commonly from their own adrenal gland. In rare cases, the androgen source is the mother.
- **Male pseudo-hermaphroditism.** These individuals have an ambiguous sex-despite having an XY chromosome pattern, symmetrical testes, along with various degrees of incomplete virilisation.
- **5 alpha-reductase deficiency.** Male pseudo-hermaphroditism can result from a deficiency of 5 alpha-reductase, the enzyme that helps to masculinise the external genitals in a fetus. The

testes make normal amounts of testosterone, but the sperm-carrying ducts end blindly, so if the testes do make sperm they do not reach the ejaculate. At puberty, the ambiguous genitals become more virilised, the penis grows and male patterns of body hair and muscle growth occur, along with development of a muscular male body shape.

- **Androgen insensitivity syndrome.** A genetic condition in which the body's cells cannot respond to male hormones. These people are genetic males with testes, but at birth their genitals look female (the testes are usually retained in the abdomen and the vagina is often short, with no cervix). At puberty, the testes make enough estrogen to produce breasts and the individual clearly has a woman's appearance with scant body hair, but she will not menstruate and is infertile.
- **Partial androgen insensitivity syndrome.** The same cause as AIS but the effect is incomplete, resulting in genitals with a wide range of ambiguity along the male–female spectrum. The phallus, for example, can range from a large clitoris to a small penis.
- **Hypospadias or micropenis.** Occur as isolated events. Hypospadias is the failure of the urethra to completely develop within the shaft of the penis, so the opening through which urination occurs can be anywhere from near the tip of the penis to its base. It is thought to occur in 8 out of every 1000 boys. Micropenis is a fully formed penis that is very small.

Despite all these variations, we persist in seeing sex and gender as clearly divided into pink and blue. It may be an illusion, and it may not be fully logical to maintain that illusion, but perception is reality. In doing so we seem to be in tune with the majority of human communities. On the whole, we're not comfortable with ambiguity in sex and gender, so like Samantha in the television series 'Bewitched' we crinkle our noses and blink it away. It can also be argued, of course, that things are intended to be this way – not in the theological but in the evolutionary sense. That is, there may be good biological reasons why we avoid gender ambiguity and create cultural institutions that discourage it. If such reasons exist, then according to the theory of natural selection it would need to be one that increases our 'fitness' – our ability to survive and reproduce.

That's not such a far-fetched idea. After all, we know from research into many other species that fitness can be increased by making sex and gender pliable to many different life strategies. Mushrooms take the prize, with their number of possible genders running into the tens. One type of tiny slime mould has 13 known genders. Remember the fish that switch their sex according to what other fish around them are doing? But it's clearly not that way with humans. If we want to reproduce, we need to know for sure what sex our potential mates are, because our life strategy involves such a large investment in forming social groups, bonding with a partner and parenting. So a clearly defined gender identity may serve as an honest signal of your reproductive biology, and all that goes with it.

'We can debate all kinds of fine variations in behaviour; we can find enormous overlap between male and female behaviour,' comments US science writer Deborah Blum.[7] 'But, barring genetic disorders or hormonal malfunctions, we get a clearly male or female body and a strong sense of gender identity. Our genes do not offer the option of sliding between male and female according to the environment. At some stage in evolutionary time, our species opted for a certain rigidity.' Kim Wallen, a psychologist at the Yerkes Regional Primate Research Center in Atlanta, says this predisposition to be one sex or the other has the effect of opening a path of least resistance. Wallen's view is that while less rigidity is possible, it requires a great deal of trouble and energy to achieve it: 'The path of least resistance in our species is that males don't give birth and females do.'

Why do we so strongly tend to have that rigidity, despite the many exceptions? 'Gender identity, like biological sex, is almost completely binary,' says the veteran US developmental psychologist, Eleanor Maccoby. 'Hermaphrodites do exist, and for them the assignment of a gender category is not straightforward. And some transsexual people believe that their gender is not the same as their biological sex . . . For the overwhelming majority of people, however, their own gender and that of other people falls into one of two categories: male or female. While the basis for being labelled at birth as a male or female is of course biological, the labelling itself is social. Adults of a society decide which sex category a child belongs to, and from then on the child is named appropriately for this category, dressed appropriately, referred to by whatever binary linguistic labels (he, she; his, hers) the culture provides. That a child should come to understand his or her own gender identity at an early age – as well as the gender identities of others – is no surprise. It is an overdetermined matter.'

Bearing in mind the new understanding that has emerged from modern genetics about the slim biological gap between the sexes, it is hard to disagree with Maccoby. Indeed, the rigid male/female gender roles that I recall from my boyhood in the 1950s – roles made especially inelastic by the harsh realities of

World War II – quickly crumbled under the onslaught of the youth-based social revolution that swept much of the world in the 1960s. They stayed elastic and seem to be even more so now. The global spread of feminism, growing scientific enlightenment and the need for all human cultures to be flexible in this era of great social and technological change make it unlikely, in the foreseeable future, that the developed world will revert to the narrow vision of gender as a world coloured only in pink and blue.

However you define it, though, the essence of being male does involve a unique capacity to produce a special little something to help start a new life. Now let's turn our attention to those microscopic, wriggling things that only male bodies make – and, man, how they make them!

6

SPERM: Amazing journey of a tadpole hero

THE NUMBERS ARE simply mind-boggling. We're talking sperm here. Buckets of them. From the first rumblings of the hormonal storm that heralds a boy's puberty until the fateful day he drops dead, his testes blindly push on, making sperm in prodigious quantities. Men are a bit weird in that respect. Males in most animal species make sperm for well-defined and often short breeding seasons. The golden hamster, for example, is sterile for months on end each year and its sperm production only kicks in when the longer days of spring are sprung and mating time arrives. A male walrus is potent for only three months a year. A male emperor penguin is thought to save up all its sperm for one – just one – orgasm a year. For other species, sperm production may be triggered by the availability of a certain seasonal food, a social cue or some subtle chemical signal from females or from other males. But none of that applies to men. Their year-round breeding potential means that they churn out these tiny tadpoles non-stop, day and night, as if there were no tomorrow.

To appreciate just how many times a man could become a father – in theory at least – try on some of the arithmetic for size. A normal healthy man makes as many as 1500 sperm a *second*. That's 90,000 a minute, 5.4 million an hour, 130 million a day, almost 50 billion a year. Or put it this way: at that rate, it would take no more than a fortnight for that one man to make a sperm for every fertile woman on the planet. For the economists among us, someone has calculated that the United Kingdom's gross national product in sperm is 636,324 trillion a year – an extreme example of a market hopelessly mismatched in supply and demand.

When I try to work out the global output of human sperm, my calculator gives up and displays an error message. But if my back-of-the-envelope sums are correct, the world's men presently produce up to 286,000,000,000,000,000 sperm a day. If you could stop the little blighters from wriggling and align every one of those sperm end-to-end, the line would stretch for many millions of kilometres – enough to encircle the Equator thousands of times, or to reach further than the Sun. Or, if you were serious about colonising other worlds, it would be enough for the starship *Enterprise* to beam thousands of human sperm a day to every far-flung star system in the Milky Way.

You could also measure men's reproductive efforts by looking at their output of semen, the sperm-bearing milky fluid that a man ejaculates during sex. Each man produces on average about 2 millilitres of semen a day – about half a teaspoonful – so the total global production of semen is about 4.5 million litres a day. A year's worth would keep Niagara Falls gushing at its peak summer rate for about 10 minutes.

A man's sperm production rate declines a little with age, but let's say, for argument's sake, that this relentless assembly line typically kicks off at age 12 and continues without a break at the same rate until he is 72. In those 60 years our fecund fellow will personally make a grand total of about 3 trillion sperm. And since fewer than 20 of those are ever likely to be on the short-list to fertilise a human egg, each individual sperm has less chance of success than you do of being hit by a meteorite or winning a Nobel Prize. Yep, we're looking at the biggest bunch of losers on the planet.

But that's a harsh judgment. As we have seen, once a species sets sail on the high seas of sexual reproduction, the uncertainties involved grow enormously. By making sperm continuously, a man can at least be sure that he always has some fresh and ready when the proverbial ship happens to pass in the night. And by making lots of it, he can also greatly increase the chances that just one of his tiny DNA packages will successfully dock with one egg. Each ejaculation will yield an average of about 200 million sperm (but the 'normal' range is wide, with some men producing many more and others many less). That may sound impressive but male dogs, which have far fewer mating opportunities than humans, take even fewer chances and ejaculate up to 2 billion sperm each time. Even that pales into insignificance beside stallions, which can flood a mare's reproductive tract with a staggering 25 billion sperm in one copulation. But boars are ranked as the gold medal winners for sperm production among the mammals, producing an average of 600 million an hour, or over 100 times more sperm than a man.

Put aside the question of why so many useless sperm are made and focus for now on the one successful tadpole that emerges from this wriggling pack and succeeds in its task. In fact, the story of how a single sperm comes into being and manages the brief but perilous journey from its safe harbour to its intended port is extraordinary and surprisingly complex. In humans, the whole sequence of events involves the sperm travelling a straight-line distance not much more than the span of this open book, yet it is a highly complex mission fraught with great hazards and obstacles. It requires a blind determination and a vast amount of luck, and it is truly one of the great tales of human biology. So let's tell it.

A delightful analogy of the sperm's wondrous feat appeared in a textbook called *Essential Reproduction*, written by two British academics at the University of Cambridge, Martin Johnson and Barry Everitt.[1] They likened the journey to travelling 'from Edinburgh to Paris by a combination of active transport by train, extensive drifting by water, a high-risk parachute crossing of the Channel and a pretty heavy spell of uphill walking over the Ardennes'. The whole route must be carefully conditioned by hormones to ensure not only a safe and tranquil passage but also to maintain friendly relations between France and England, they add. The tiny voyager must then be able to detect and respond to the changing terrain and social conditions en route, to ensure that it is in a fit state to converse with the Parisian egg. As if all that was not enough, the whole trip is complicated even further by being a marathon race against millions of competitors and almost hopeless odds. Not even being first to arrive is a guarantee of success; the winning sperm may reach the rendezvous only to find that the elusive egg has come and gone. *C'est la vie!*

Let's stay with the travel analogy to make the tale easier to follow. First, we need to set the scene, because making sperm is a co-operative effort that depends heavily on a large support crew working in subtle ways in the background. The captain of this crew is found, naturally enough, high up on the bridge of the vessel: it is the hypothalamus, a vital part of the brain that sits roughly in the centre of the head above the inner regions of the nose. Captain Hypothalamus is a real time-and-motion man, helping to regulate the body's water balance, temperature control, heartbeat, breathing rate and sleep cycle. While he may take his sailing orders from unseen admirals behind the scenes – the genes – he is the one who directly controls the timing of when sperm production begins and the rate at which it continues. The hypothalamus contains a special group of cells that make a compound called gonadotrophin-releasing hormone (GnRH). In a boy, those cells are switched off until he reaches puberty; it is not known what signal activates them, but once switched on they keep making and releasing regular pulses of GnRH until he dies.

Once the hypothalamus orders the dispatch of a new batch of GnRH, the chain of command moves down to the pituitary, which is a kind of master gland responsible for making the sex hormones. It hangs on a narrow stalk beneath the hypothalamus, a bit like an upside-down golf ball on a tee. First Officer Pituitary is specially attuned to the captain's GnRH signal: when his receptors detect it he swings into action, making sex hormones and releasing them into the bloodstream. These chemicals are shunted quickly below decks to the engine-room of sperm production, the scrotum – a wrinkly air-cooled external pouch containing two sperm-making production plants, the testes. As our sperm arithmetic makes plain, one testis would be more than enough to do the job. But evolution has sensibly equipped men with a back-up, as it has with the kidneys and other vital organs, in case of accident or disease.

When the hormone-laced blood enters the testes, two engineers by the name of Leydig and Sertoli receive the message and go to work. These two guys are actually groups of specialised cells. Leydig cells make the classic male hormone, testosterone, using cholesterol as their raw material (a reminder that, despite its bad name in heart disease, cholesterol is a vital ingredient of human sex and of many other bodily functions). Another hormone fires the Sertoli cells into action on a number of fronts. They produce several key substances involved in sperm production. One is androgen binding protein, which maintains high local concentrations of testosterone in the testes. Another is inhibin, which sends feedback to the pituitary about how the rate of sperm production is going. Sertoli cells also produce transferrin, which carries nutrients into the germ cells, the tiny seeds from which all sperm start their lives. In this chain of command they are the able seamen (pun intended).

Germ cells are unique in the human body. Their name has nothing to do with the way the word 'germ' is used in the everyday sense, meaning a disease-causing bug. No, these fellows earn their title because they are the guardians of the very essence or kernel of life. They are different to all the other cells in the body and have only one function: to transmit DNA from one generation to the next through sex. Strictly speaking, all the other cells of the body – the somatic cells – are there only to give the germ cells the best possible chance of succeeding. Germ cells have another special attribute: whereas somatic cells are programmed to grow old and die, germ cells have the potential to reset their biological clocks and achieve immortality.

The germ cells are found on the inner linings of the dense network of tiny fluid-filled tubes that make up most of the bulk of the testes. These seminiferous tubules are looped and coiled up like cooked spaghetti, each being about 0.5 millimetres wide and up to a metre long. Within them, and with support from the Sertoli cells, germ cells go through an intricately orchestrated series of changes and divisions that lead to the creation of microscopic ball-like objects known as round spermatids. These are a sort of proto-sperm, equipped with only half the usual number of chromosomes. As they mature, they move inwards towards the fluid-filled centre of the tubules.

Spermatids become sperm in one of the most complex and dramatic processes of change to take place in an adult's body. Many important details remain a mystery, especially how genes control the transformation. But we do know that the entire journey takes about 60 days from when the first hormonal signal from the pituitary prompts Sertoli cells to start nourishing a nearby spermatid. First, the nucleus of the germ cell gradually elongates and takes on the familiar flattened tadpole-head shape of the sperm. Sperm heads can vary greatly in size and shape in different animals: the heads of rat sperm are hook-shaped, those of bull sperm are flat and oval, while some marsupials have truly bizarre sperm, with heads sporting strange attachments that make them look like inflated rubber gloves. Once the head is formed it grows a sort of cap, known as the acrosome, which is full of enzymes. Meanwhile, at the opposite end of the spermatid the tail forms, a long slender bundle of movable filaments. At its base a little sheath of breathing apparatus appears – this will effectively become the sperm's scuba tanks and snorkel during its cross-Channel swim.

The result is an immature human sperm, a semi-independent critter just 60-millionths of a metre long and equipped with a sleek, flexible tail. Its design reveals a long evolutionary lineage. For example, the basic arrangement of some of the moving parts of the tail is essentially similar to the whip-like flagella used by primitive algae to move around, notes Jim Cummins, a spermatologist at Murdoch University in Western Australia. Because the design links between the sperm of species are so strong, scientists have been able to study them closely in non-humans; much of what we know about sperm movement is based on studies of marine animals, especially sea urchins, whose sperm is almost identical to human sperm in shape, size and swimming patterns. Ponder that ancient and surprising sexual link next time you see one of these spiny marine creatures.

Before it is ready to leave the body, the juvenile sperm must spend another fortnight going through its final maturation. It does this while being carried to, and then held in, a long coiled tube known as the epididymis, which is the exit route from the testis. Remember the famous scene in the Woody Allen movie *Everything You Always Wanted to Know About Sex*, in which the sperm are depicted as a squad of parachute commandos lined up inside the belly of a roaring aircraft, ready to leap blindly into the wild blue yonder? The epididymis is like that plane. It's one of a pair of crescent-shaped structures attached to and draped over the testes (if you happen to have a testis handy and are in private you can actually feel the soft spongy epididymis on its outer surface, but be gentle). Unlike Allen's commandos, however, while the sperm is in storage here it can't move on its own – its tail is chemically suppressed from wriggling almost up until the point of ejaculation.

Perhaps this is to make it more manageable and less likely to bolt from the stable. It was long thought that sperm were simply stored and aged in this organ. But we now know they go through important maturing steps within it, and that a sperm is incapable of fertilising an egg when it first enters the head of the epididymis.

As the sperm complete their growth here, they are bathed in a special fluid containing salts, water, proteins and hormones. The epididymis also acts like an isolation ward: it has elaborate barriers that protect the maturing sperm from the body's immune system, which would otherwise detect and attack them as 'foreign' invaders. The sperm move along this production line through a combination of being pushed from behind by the pressure of the masses of new sperm and by muscle contractions. They finally go into storage in the tail of the epididymis, at the entrance to the off-white, rather featureless tube better known as the vas deferens (which is cut to sterilise a man in a vasectomy operation).

At last our lucky sperm is ready for its big adventure. First, let's put the final leg of the journey into the context of global human sex. It is estimated that about 100 million acts of heterosexual intercourse (sorry, we're briefly back into arithmetic again) take place somewhere on the planet every day, or about 1100 every second. While that number sounds formidable, you must remember that this tally is amassed by some 2 billion potential couples (leaving out those too young, too old, celibates and so on), so our sperm initially has only a 1 in 50 chance of being involved in an orgasm that just might lead to conception. Many billions of sperm (most in fact) never even get the chance to see active duty – they either grow too old and are absorbed by their maker's body, or they seep out in his urine or are ejaculated during masturbation or some other non-reproductive sexual act. Even then, less than 1 per cent of all the sperm released in heterosexual intercourse actually result in a conception, and less than half of those conceptions result in the birth of a child. So from a daily tally of 286,000 trillion sperm produced, a mere 400,000 babies are born, meaning that only 1 sperm out of every 715 billion succeeds in creating a new life. Now you can see just why the intrepid little sperm we are following is one of the extremely fortunate few.

Anyway, let's return to where its maker is at last about to send our traveller on its way. The sperm is now fully developed physically, its on-board fuel tanks are ready and primed, its environmental sensors are switched on, its tail is at the ready to whip it into action and its owner is fully aroused and about to have sex. The sperm's first problem is how and when to leave the man's body. Happily, both problems are being taken care of by the brain. How a man becomes aroused is described later in the book, so for now let's just assume that the 'when' has been sorted out and the sperm's maker has reached the point of orgasm and is ready to ejaculate.

First, electrical signals are sent by the brain to the muscle tissue that surrounds the storage ducts in the epididymis. Those muscles contract and narrow the duct to propel its contents forward, something like what happens when you squeeze toothpaste from a tube. At the same time tiny hair-like structures, known as cilia, which line some of the ducts, sweep forward in waves, giving the sperm an extra shove along. As the sperm move through the various ducts, they are bathed in concentrated fluids of salts and sugars to top up their reserves and help them survive.

Next, they enter the ejaculatory duct, the two tubes that empty into the urethra about halfway through the prostate gland. Here the sperm are mixed with thick gluggy fluid from the prostate. The nearby seminal vesicles contribute about 60 per cent of the fluids that make up semen, but it is the sperm and prostatic fluid that emerge first in ejaculation. Seminal fluid is a veritable broth of chemicals, containing water, sugar, citric acid, salts and prostaglandins. The last-named are compounds that can trigger muscle contractions (doctors use prostaglandins to induce labour in women), and the sugar will become the sperm's main fuel source. One last ingredient remains to be added to this brew and it comes from a pair of 1-centimetre-diameter pea-shaped structures known as the bulbo-urethral glands, or Cowper's glands. They sit just beneath the urethra, emptying into it right at the base of the inner part of the penis. They feature a network of small tubes and sacs containing a clear but thick mucus-like, protein-rich fluid. Just before the beginning of orgasm, the Cowper's glands squirt out small amounts of their fluid – sometimes called pre-cum – which is thought to flush the urethra, lubricate the head of the penis to make its entry into the vagina easier and to generally make conditions more hospitable once there.

Now comes the dramatic moment of the parachute jump, one of the more extraordinary moments in life. A signal from the brain dictates when all is ready and a muscular-walled sac near the base of the penis begins sudden rhythmic contractions to expel this marvellous man-soup. The seminal vesicle fluid follows close behind. (Other mammalian species blend the broth in very different ways and in greatly varying quantities. Boars, for example, are true to prolific form and ejaculate about half a litre of semen.

Some rodents and primates quickly follow the sperm with a much larger ejaculation of gluggy mucus-like material that effectively plugs the female's vagina: these copulatory plugs presumably stop their own sperm from leaking out and competing sperm from other males from getting in.)

For all the effort that goes into making human semen, though, there's precious little to show, a mere teaspoonful at most. The speed at which it shoots out is unknown – one estimate puts it at 18 kilometres per hour – but some men claim to be able to squirt semen a metre or more into the air when they masturbate. Suffice to say that it is fired from the penis with some force to start our sperm on the most arduous part of its journey, that 'pretty heavy spell of uphill walking over the Ardennes'.

And remember, to get here, it has already:

- undergone a total transformation from a nondescript cell to free-swimming independence;
- travelled for a metre along a seminiferous tubule;
- been expelled into a maze of tiny ducts and carried up to another 6 metres through tightly coiled tubes within the epididymis;
- wound its way another 45 centimetres along the vas deferens;
- been vigorously propelled perhaps another 30 centimetres from the prostate to the tip of the penis.

That's a total distance of almost 8 metres. If you could scale up a sperm to the size of an adult man, the trip so far has taken it the equivalent of 240 kilometres before it briefly encounters the chill air of the world beyond its maker. Now it faces a very hostile environment and although it is a sort of semi-independent life form in its own right, it is very fragile and has a potential lifespan of a few days at most.

The first serious problem the sperm must deal with is, in fact, plain old air. Exposure to air, or more specifically to too much oxygen, is decidedly unfriendly to sperm – in fact, to all living cells. That may sound strange, given that we depend on oxygen for our lives, but the body dilutes it so well that between the time we inhale oxygen and the time it reaches the inside of a typical cell to be burned as fuel, the level of this vital gas has been reduced by about 80 times. Life probably evolved at first without much air or oxygen at all, in what are known as anaerobic conditions, and they are pretty much the conditions in which our sperm has developed and in which it will conduct the last part of its journey. But ejaculation from the penis puts it into potential contact with some air in the vagina. A whimsical article in a pharmacology journal, by an author designated simply as B. Max, details exactly what a stressful problem that can be for sperm.[2] A high-altitude balloonist, for example, will die from oxygen deprivation within 2 minutes of exposure to the 'thin' air 9000 metres above the Earth. But deep within a man's genitals or within a woman's inner reproductive tract, the oxygen levels are even lower – the equivalent of being above the stratosphere. So for our sperm the experience of being ejaculated into the vagina is a bit like the stresses a balloonist would face by plummeting suddenly from an altitude of 60 kilometres, down to sea level and back up beyond the stratosphere again. Happily, human sperm have a flexible breathing and fuel-burning system, enabling them to adapt rapidly to these violent environmental changes. We may marvel that giant whales can dive to extraordinary depths of the ocean, but we forget that tiny little human sperm do something similar every minute of the day.

Some simply don't survive the trauma, but the rest – protected by their thick cloud of semen – now face an even worse hazard. Inside the vagina may be a very pleasant place to be for a penis, but conditions there rate as simply appalling for sperm. It is a dark and heavily defended labyrinth bathed in acid, which is designed to stop and kill tiny intruders, such as bacteria. Within minutes of ejaculation, the scene is littered with millions of sperm corpses as the invading army succumbs to this chemical warfare. But the ejaculation process has also activated the sperm's tail and our hero, having survived this acid bath, is now thrashing blindly upstream through a sea of mucus, a second barrier that will trap even more of its fellow swimmers. As one of the strong vanguard, our sperm soon arrives at the distant end of the vagina. Here there's a new problem to be overcome: the vagina is a dead-end alley terminated by a slippery wall of soft flesh on all sides. To progress further, the travellers must somehow clamber up these walls to seek out the small hole that marks the entrance to the cervix and the womb beyond.

If the two people making love have been especially passionate, it has been suggested, these lucky sperm may get a lift. Special cameras have revealed how a woman's orgasm (which occurs only in a minority of acts of sexual intercourse) results briefly in powerful muscular contractions inside her reproductive tract. Remarkable filmed recordings of this event – such as those broadcast in the late-1990s BBC television series, *The Human Body* – show clearly how the elongated head of the cervix repeatedly dips down into a pool of semen during her orgasm, looking like a miniature elephant's trunk being lowered for a drink. There's no good evidence, though, that the cervix actively draws or sucks in the semen. The film is missing a vital organ that would otherwise be occupying this site in real life – the penis. It seems equally possible that the dipping head of the cervix simply provides an extra sensory stimulus to the head of the penis to maximise its arousal.

But let's assume for dramatic purposes that our sperm manages to hitch a ride on this flesh elevator, wriggles through the narrow entrance and begins another potentially deadly struggle to swim through yet more mucus along the walls of the womb, which is about the size and shape of a pear. In the hours after ejaculation, it is thought that gentle contractions within the womb may help to push the sperm in the right direction. Eventually its blind slithering takes the sperm to its last staging point, the entrance to a fallopian tube. It is one of only a few thousand of the original 200-million-strong army to have got this far.

Even so, the odds are heavily stacked against there actually being an egg in the fallopian tube. A woman releases only about 400 eggs in her lifetime from the ovaries at the top of this narrow passageway, and each egg dies within about 24 hours of being released. So only on about 12 days a year is it possible for her to become pregnant. But this happens to be one of those days, and the final task for the meagre band of surviving sperm is to track down that egg in the maze of feathery folds of pink tissue and viscous fluids within the tube. The egg is big in relation to the sperm – about 100 times larger in volume – but even so it may be hidden within the folds. A flow of mucus and beating cilia seem determined to push the sperm the wrong way, almost as if willing it to fail.

But we now know that the mucus is arranged in long strings that may actually channel the sperm to steer them the right way. Picture them as swimmers in a pool with marked lanes to keep them going straight, or like ten-pin bowling balls that always reach the far end of their lane because the side gutters are conduits for even the most wayward ball. One recent study has even suggested that the egg sends out a siren call to the sperm. Dina Ralt, at the Weizmann Institute of Science, did laboratory experiments that seem to show human sperm, given a choice of hospitable liquids, will swim towards follicular fluid, the watery liquid that surrounds a maturing egg.[3] If so, it is the first evidence of sperm–egg communication in humans. The researchers suggest that this may act as a final hurdle to weed out the weaker sperm, or it may be the egg's way of choosing the most suitable sperm, based on criteria we don't yet understand. It has been proved that the sperm of several species, such as sea-squirts and some fish, are indeed actively attracted to their eggs. Such a trick may be needed because those species broadcast their eggs and sperm into the surrounding water and the two need all the help they can get to increase the odds of meeting up. Other scientists remain sceptical of the evidence that such a thing occurs in humans because, as we saw, mucus in the fallopian tube gives sperm very little room to manoeuvre – unlike the relatively unconstrained swimming conditions in a laboratory dish.

In any case, our sperm has now crossed the Ardennes and is at last pounding the pavements of central Paris in hot pursuit of its *amour*. (Perhaps we should remember here the vast age difference between the two. Eggs are formed in the female embryo, a few months after conception; they go into a kind of suspended animation in the ovaries until their release. If a woman is say, 30 years old, so are all her eggs. As we've seen, though, sperm are mere toy boys, just a few months old at the time when the two cross paths.)

The sperm may or may not 'know' that the egg is at the rendezvous but all the signposts seem to direct it straight there. And in the home straight it has a few remarkable tricks left up its sleeve. Let's say our chosen sperm puts in a burst of speed and slips ahead of the few other remaining travellers. Drifting down from the ovary at the top of the fallopian tube are traces of a hormone, progesterone, that prepares the inner lining of the womb to help a fertilised egg implant itself. For our sperm, though, a taste of that hormone sparks an incredible change in its behaviour, aptly known as hyperactivation.

All of a sudden it becomes greatly energised, as if jolted by a bolt of electricity. Its energy output has been calculated to skyrocket by as much as a thousand times. It now whips its tail far more dramatically and vigorously than ever before and its swimming motion becomes decidedly ungainly, with its head thrashing from side to side. It turns the last bend and literally crashes into its quarry. Now you may have the impression that the egg is basically like a ball – it looks that way when you see those striking images of fertilisation taking place. But the reality is very different. The egg is actually surrounded by several layers of defences and support systems. The outer layer is a thick jelly, known as the cumulus. Beneath that is the corona, made up of several layers of cells radiating out like wheel spokes. Beneath that is a tough protein coat, the zona pellucida, with a surface pitted like the moon. Then there's a gap and at last, in the inner sanctum, is the egg. Now it's plain to see why our sperm has become turbo-charged – it literally has to shove and headbang its way through all these barriers.

It first cleaves its way into the jelly and then, pushing and squirming with all its might, slips between the cells of the corona and bangs headfirst into the zona. In one last amazing stunt, the cap on its head begins to dissolve, leaking out the little package of enzymes – stowed there way back in the testis as part of its original supply kit. They act like a kind of chemical blowtorch, softening the zona just enough to let the sperm bind fast to it. Then it gives one more mighty shove to push its head through this last barrier and cross the narrow gap, to at last make direct contact with the egg. And that's it. That special touch – the ultimate lover's kiss – triggers a speedy reaction. The egg's coat alters in such a way as to stop other sperm from entering (in most cases at least). The door is shut and all those that have come so far only to be pipped at the post are repelled and soon perish. For them, it is a lonely and futile death far from home. For the winning sperm, though, a brave new life is about to begin. Its brief but spectacular independence is now over and the egg decisively takes control. The sperm's tail stops thrashing and falls still. It is often said that only the sperm head, with its vital chromosomal cargo, enters the egg. But that is not so in humans, or in most other species that we know about. David Mortimer, a reproductive biologist who has studied sperm for many years, recounts how impressed his students are when he shows them a film of rat fertilisation revealing what really happens when sperm and egg dock: 'The sperm touches the egg cell and its motor just switches off. The tail stops moving straight away.' The egg draws the sperm's head in and pauses, leaving the limp tail hanging out. 'Then you see the egg draw in the tail; slurp! It's just like a strand of spaghetti being sucked in.'

Fertilisation has been studied for more than a century, but the more we learn about it the more we realise how complex it is. Now is the most exciting time in this field of science, with a whole new array of research tools unleashing a stream of insights into this strange, wondrous and incomparable event. To Victor D. Vacquier, of the University of California in San Diego, fertilisation 'remains one of the least understood fundamental biological processes'.[4] He calls it 'the bridge between generations', and it is exactly that. All the trials and tribulations the sperm goes through to enable this moment to occur are trivial compared to the far more remarkable and magical journey of which it is just one very small part. Just think: when a man's sperm finally fuses with a woman's egg they form a new link in an incredible unbroken chain that goes back billions of years, through countless ancestral species, to the very beginning of life itself. It may happen 10 times a second, every minute of every day, but each one is indeed a breathtaking miracle.

7

FERTILITY: Vanishing surnames and downward motility

IT MAY BE stating the obvious, but human sperm are tiny – too tiny for the unaided eye to see. They're about 60 microns (a micron is one millionth of a metre) long – that's about 1000 times smaller than the width of one of the hairs on your head. So even if their existence was somehow guessed at in ancient times (and there's very little evidence to suggest that), we can be sure that no one knew they existed until strong magnifying lenses were invented a few centuries ago. We also know that the first person to see human sperm through a microscope didn't have a clue what he was looking at – in fact, he thought he was the first to sight the cause of an unpleasant venereal disease. Even so, he deserves to be better known for what, with hindsight, was a scientific scoop, especially since he rarely gets credit for it. Worse, the credit often goes – even in many respected publications – to the wrong man.

To set the record straight, the man who discovered sperm was

Johan Ham. He was born to Rutgera Otters and Dirrick Ham in 1654 in the Dutch city of Arnhem, and he died there in 1725. Young Johan matriculated in philosophy at Leiden University and later studied medicine. There's no record of whether he ever got a medical degree but we do know he became an alderman in Arnhem and later a diplomat. Ham also had the good fortune to know the extraordinary Antony van Leeuwenhoek, a Delft merchant who in middle age became fascinated with making and using microscopes. Van Leeuwenhoek built single-lens microscopes that were simple by today's standards, but were the best of their time, very effective and able to magnify objects up to 200 times. More important, van Leeuwenhoek was an acute observer with an enthusiastic and inquiring mind, and was the first to really grasp the exciting potential of this new device. Despite his lack of formal scientific training, he pioneered a whole raft of scientific studies into the Lilliputian world of life previously hidden from human eyes and thought. In what Isaac Asimov has called 'a triumph for the democracy of science', van Leeuwenhoek was later elected as a fellow of the lofty Royal Society in London in recognition of his important work.

Van Leeuwenhoek is sometimes credited with inventing the microscope, and he often gets credit for the discovery of sperm. Neither claim is correct. He was a fine scientist, there's no doubt about it, but his own letters record that in November 1677, Ham brought him a specimen of semen collected from a man with gonorrhoea. The donor's identity is unknown, but he probably would have been grateful to assume his rather dubious place in posterity anonymously. Ham reported that he saw tiny animals with wriggling tails in the specimen and thought they might be the bugs that caused the disease. As British scientist Brian J. Ford points out, that in itself was a radical idea, given the basic state of medical knowledge about infection at the time: 'You must remember that this was 100 years before Pasteur.' Ford studied van Leeuwenhoek's work closely after rediscovering in the early 1980s some of his original preserved microscopy specimens, along with letters and other records in the archives of the Royal Society. It was an extraordinary find.

Van Leeuwenhoek had earlier peeked briefly at his own semen through his lens, seeing 'globules' of some kind, but found the whole idea of investigating sex ethically distasteful and had not persisted. Ham's discovery (he was also the first to see the sperm of a rooster) prompted the great microscopist to look again. Coyly, van Leeuwenhoek did not record exactly how he obtained the sample from himself, but it was probably after having sex with his wife, not by masturbation: 'Whatever he did, he emphasised that he didn't do anything "impure",' Ford comments wryly. Within the semen he saw many 'animalcules' a tiny fraction of the size of a grain of sand and with thin, undulating, transparent tails, which he described in a brief letter the following month to the Royal Society. His eye was certainly keen. He spotted crystals in the semen, for example: these were later identified as spermine phosphate, a compound which, it has only recently been suggested, acts to protect the DNA in sperm from damage by oxygen. He was even able to make out subtle details of his 'animalcules', including the sausage-like section behind the head that we now know as the midpiece of sperm. Since van Leeuwenhoek did not have gonorrhoea, he had clearly dispatched the idea that these were the germs that caused the disease. But he did not seem at first to attach any great significance to what he had seen – that they were germs of human life. Indeed, it was many years before anyone understood exactly what sperm were, but the scientific study of male reproduction can certainly trace its origins directly back to Ham and van Leeuwenhoek.

Today we know vastly more about the sperm, about how it is made and what it does and does not do. One of the key insights has been that human spermatogenesis (the process of sperm-making) is far less impressive than might be surmised from the great numbers involved. Men are actually extremely poor sperm-makers when judged by the standards of other animals. As Sherman Silber, of the Infertility Center of St Louis, told the Eleventh World Congress on In Vitro Fertilisation and Human Reproductive Genetics in May 1999: 'The human male has just about the worst spermatogenesis of any species on the planet. Most animals produce about 25 million sperm per day per gram of testicular tissue, whereas the human produces only 4–6 million per day per gram of testicular tissue. We are satisfied that a man is fertile when he has greater than 20 per cent normal sperm morphology, but for most animals it would be inconceivable to find more than a few abnormal sperm in the entire ejaculate.'[1]

A recent study by an international team of reproductive biologists looked at 15 different variables in the way testes work, comparing those of humans with those of males in many other well-studied mammals.[2] Men scored worst or next to worst in 13 of those 15 measures. Scale up a male rat's body to human size, for example, and its testes would jointly weigh close to a kilogram, as opposed to the paltry 40 grams a man is equipped with. Male mice and rats devote 10 times more body mass and energy than men to maintaining their testes. Male chimps produce far more sperm. Male orang-utans are far more consistent in producing normal healthy sperm. Other male primates produce three or four times more sperm than men for each unit of testicular mass. In short, human testes are remarkably inefficient: they are small and make relatively few sperm, of which a high proportion are abnormal. Only male gorillas seem to be sitting somewhere near men at the bottom of the fertility league table. Any livestock producer would wince if his stud animals were such lousy sperm producers. Yet the Earth's population is exploding. How do we explain this paradox?

It's important to realise that statistics and averages can be misleading. Individual men vary greatly, for example, in their sperm output at different times – by as much as two or threefold on different days, spermatologist Jim Cummins points out. If a man abstains from sex for a few days, he'll ejaculate significantly more semen than if he ejaculates each day. A week's abstinence can boost his sperm count by up to four times. Semen quality can even vary according to the time of day, an Italian study of 54 men attending a clinic suggested.[3] It found that semen collected in the afternoon contained more, and healthier, sperm than samples collected in the morning. The authors speculated that better motility in the afternoon might have something to do with daily variations in some seminal fluid components, such as hormones and nutrients. (They even suggested that infertile couples try having sex in the afternoons to capitalise on the small advantage. By happy coincidence – or perhaps by an evolved synchrony – women are most likely to ovulate between about 3 p.m. and 7 p.m.) Many sperm are also released before they are fully mature, and men who produce a high proportion of immature sperm are often infertile. While hormone therapy can improve the quality and maturity of sperm produced by some infertile men, the causes and genetics of the condition are largely unknown.

As well, it's very common for even healthy young men to produce a substantial proportion of abnormal sperm. It may surprise many readers to learn here that no scientific benchmark exists for what is a 'normal' level of sperm production. We can certainly measure averages but we still cannot say for sure, for example, how many viable sperm a man should produce, or whether that number is stable over time and place. The World Health Organisation simply sets a guideline for normal sperm concentration as being more than 20 million in each millilitre (million/ml) of seminal fluid, although these days routine semen analysis also measures sperm shapes, sizes and motility.

'British researchers Robin Baker and Mark Bellis have argued that the relatively large proportion of abnormal sperm made by men may have a positive purpose,' Cummins says. 'Their "kamikaze sperm" hypothesis suggests that the abnormal sperm are used to combat a rival's sperm. But other studies have shown no links between numbers of abnormal sperm and mating patterns in other mammals. If their hypothesis was correct, species with the most intense sperm competition would have the most abnormal sperm; if anything, the reverse is true. As well, barriers in the reproductive tract – such as cervical mucus – actively deter sperm that are abnormal or move weakly. That means such sperm take little or no part in fertilisation.'

As reproductive biologist Roger Short has said: 'It is sobering to realise that we still have no idea what a 'normal' sperm looks like. The so-called abnormalities that we see under the microscope are mostly in the shape of the sperm head or in its motility. This tells us nothing about its DNA blueprint.'[4] Like some other scientists, Short is scathingly critical of Baker and Bellis's kamikaze sperm hypothesis, set out in popular form in Baker's best-selling book *Sperm Wars.*[5] Briefly, Baker argues that human females are far more promiscuous than is generally assumed and that many abnormal sperm are in fact purposely designed to act as blockers and killers of competing sperm from other men. Sperm heads vary in size and the relatively few large-headed sperm are the 'egg-getters' that actually have the capacity to fertilise an ovum, Baker claims.

Baker's assertion that women are so promiscuous – and apparently so brilliant at concealing the practice – that they have heavily skewed male reproductive biology towards such radical sperm competition lacks evidence when put to the test of either science or common knowledge. It also seems downright offensive to most women, I would have thought. Short points out that the theory ignores the fact that he and others have studied those large-headed sperm and found that they are also abnormal, having a double set of chromosomes that makes them incapable of producing a normal embryo. Furthermore, there's simply no scientific evidence that sperm from competing males can kill each other. Short has also shown that where sperm competition – promiscuity by one sex or other – exists, males invariably have larger testes. Geese mate for life and have tiny testes, while the more promiscuous turkeys have very large testes. Male chimps have 60-gram testes, for example, while gorillas average a mere 18 grams. Men have 20-gram testes. At worst, our biology puts us among the serial monogamists, not serious sperm competitors. So let's put the kamikaze theory aside and refocus on the question of why men are so infertile.

It's important to know that not all sperm-producers are created equal. Jim Cummins suggests that we can learn some important lessons on that score from genealogy. In societies where surnames pass down through the generations from father to son, for example, those names can be a rough guide to paternity. The available records suggest they go extinct surprisingly rapidly. While 300 British families today claim to be descended from William the Conqueror, only one can prove an unbroken descent through the male line. 'All 5000 feudal knighthoods listed in the *Domesday Book* of 1086–87 are now extinct, and the average duration of a hereditary title in the Middle Ages was only three generations,' Cummins and colleagues say in their study. 'In general, male-inherited surnames last only about 200 years. In the English nobility the practice of double-barrelling names was used as a device to retain inheritance for a daughter in a family with no sons, provided she could find a partner willing to add her name to his (or abandon his own). One spin-off of the low level of fecundity among the aristocracy was a massive increase in the wealth of the Church, through bequests from spinsters and widows. At one point it owned about a third of England – although this was enhanced by the tradition of younger sons entering the priesthood coupled, of course, with an official insistence on celibacy.' Another long-term analysis of English genealogical records between 1359 and 1986 showed that a surprisingly high 1 family in 3 produced no male heirs who had children.

So, some men may leave many descendants while the family lines of a large proportion of others peter out fast. In other words, some men are far more fertile than others. The more-fertile fathers tend to have more-fertile sons, while men with low fertility tend to have sons with low fertility. Another clue comes from an intriguing analysis of the official Census of Australia's population in 1912. Importantly, this was a peacetime period before the advent of widespread and effective contraception, so it gives worthwhile insights into the natural variability of fertility between individuals. That analysis, by the famous biologist R.A. Fisher, revealed that half the Australians born in 1912 were descended from 11 per cent of the men and 14 per cent of the women from the preceding generation.[6] In that generation, a whopping 60 per cent of all children died unmarried and 11 per cent of marriages were sterile. Clearly, fertility and infertility have a strong genetic basis. Fisher estimated that genetic factors account for almost half the variation in human reproduction and those individual fertility differences are very important in driving human evolution.

How has it come about that most men have evolved to be duds, not studs? It seems very unlikely to be an evolutionary accident. Evolving, after all, is a way that living things solve problems, not create them. Some evolutionary biologists argue that we ought to expect human sperm counts to be low and in decline. It's a complex argument, but in a nutshell the reasoning is that we are more likely to make a relatively low investment in reproduction as our lifespans increase and our culture becomes more complex. A monogamous couple might have the biological potential to have 20 children, but if they do they'll soon be eaten out of house and home. Much better to have fewer kids, teach and care for them well and see them thrive. That scenario raises the fascinating possibility that one of the drivers in the evolution of men has been that a high proportion of women have followed a 'duds-preferred' policy.

It's hard to imagine how women could judge – short of

demanding a medically certified sperm count – that a potential mate had low fertility. As we will see later, the criteria men and women use to assess mate attractiveness can be very subtle, and all kinds of cues are subconsciously detected and evaluated. It's not unreasonable to wonder whether highly fertile men give off some kind of '*parfum de* stud' or behavioural 'I'm prolific' signal. The explanation could be even simpler, though. It's a fair bet that in pre-industrial times people living in smaller, more closed communities were well aware of the reproductive potential of individual families (that's certainly the case in many contemporary hunter-gatherer societies). Given that fertility is heritable – a fact long-known to animal breeders – the sons of highly fertile men would be obvious. They would plainly be the men to avoid for women who preferred, for any number of reasons, a relatively small number of pregnancies widely spaced in time. Sexual selection of that kind, practised by women over thousands of generations, would likely favour a trend towards men with inefficient testes.

There's one more important evolutionary issue to consider. Earlier I explained that men and women have contrasting reproductive strategies. All a woman's eggs are formed before birth in the safety of her mother's womb and rest in her ovaries until they are ready to be released. But once a male goes through puberty, he constantly makes vast numbers of fresh sperm. The testes are more vulnerable (they're certainly more susceptible to injury and insult: as any man will tell you, they're not terribly well placed for straddling fences, crossing your legs quickly or taking a winter dip in the sea) than the ovaries to external influences, such as cosmic radiation, that may interfere with all those intricate germ-cell divisions going on inside them. Other kinds of cells that divide rapidly, like bone marrow, are protected deep within the body.

Sperm-making occurs at an extremely high metabolic rate – up to 1500 new sperm a second – and so the process is even more directly vulnerable to disruption by toxins and traumas within the testes. Men who flood their bodies with the poisonous and cancerous by-products of cigarette smoking, for example, most certainly are poorer sperm producers than non-smokers. Some reproductive biologists argue that the testes may in fact be 'designed' to produce a high mutation rate – that most of the genetic variability in human populations emerges from the testes being unstable reproductive hot-houses. A high mutation rate naturally means that many deleterious mutations will occur, that many unfit sperm are made. If so, it makes sense for the female reproductive system to be a severe sperm critic. The testes may be positioned outside the body and air-cooled simply to reduce the metabolic rate of production enough to ensure that sufficient healthy sperm emerge (testes that don't descend and are retained in the abdomen are also vulnerable to cancer).

We can only conclude that the cultural, biological and evolutionary forces influencing the sperm-making process are far more complex than have so far been realised. But the process itself is also far more subtle than we thought. So let's return to the important question we put aside in the last chapter: why do men make so many useless sperm?

Jack Cohen, an internationally known reproductive biologist, has calculated that the number of sperm made in relation to the number that succeed in fertilisation is about the same as the number of all human beings who have ever lived in relation to those who have walked on the moon. It's a tiny, tiny fraction. So what gives? Rest assured, men aren't unique in having such a high sperm redundancy rate. Our long-time companion species, the dog, is about equally inefficient and a bull is far worse – it produces 16 times as many sperm as a man does to achieve each fertilisation. Our closest cousin, the chimpanzee, produces 10 times as many as a man, while gorillas and orang-utans produce about 5 times less than a man. But other species are far more miserly. Around 1 out of every 10 sperm ejaculated by a fruit fly, for example, will be a successful fertiliser. Remember that for men, the equivalent ratio is about 1 in 150,000,000,000.

In a recent article, Cohen canvassed his views on why sperm redundancy is generally so high in most males.[7] Simply making a greater number of sperm doesn't increase the genetic variability of your offspring. Although each human sperm is genetically unique, only one can fertilise each egg, so the variation among those that succeed remains pretty much the same no matter how many extras you make. He sees the three most plausible reasons for this profligate over-production as follows:

- In species where females are promiscuous and sperm competition occurs, sperm-rich males will tend to leave more offspring, whose descendants in turn leave even more offspring, to the detriment of sperm-poor males and their descendants.
- Sperm populations are heterogeneous – the quality of each sperm is highly variable. Males may thus need to make lots of sperm to ensure that their semen contains a few good ones amid a larger number of duds. Cohen likens it to computer-chip making, where stringent quality control means that thousands are rejected for each one that passes muster.

- Females may use the extra sperm – and/or semen – for nourishing themselves or their unborn young. In that case, all those extra sperm are effectively a lover's gift, a box of candy offered by males to boost their chances of being favoured as mates.

There's good evidence, Cohen argues, that the second choice – heterogeneity – is the most likely be correct. But if that's so, why would so many faulty sperm be made? Why would the vast majority, in effect, be meant to fail? Cohen believes that meiosis – the fiendishly complex cell divisions that let the genes we inherit from our parents mix and recombine when chunks of chromosomes are swapped in a process known as crossing-over – goes wrong in a systematic way. The more crossovers that occur during the process, the more the 'mistakes' build up and the smaller the number of 'good' sperm emerge. Cohen suspects that only a few hundred 'good' sperm are likely to be found among the many millions in a typical human ejaculation. If so, it would make sense that the good ones pass easily through the daunting maze of defences a female uses for quality control.

Cohen's research team decided to test this proposition in experiments on rabbits from the early 1970s to the early 1980s. It took them three years, working with two or more rabbits a week, to work out how to recover viable sperm from a mated doe's egg duct. Eventually, they mated a buck white rabbit named Chalky with a white doe, waited a while, then flushed some of Chalky's sperm from her oviduct. Then they mixed those sperm with semen from a brown buck named Don and re-inseminated the whole mixture into another doe. Chalky's contribution to this blend was a mere 60 sperm, while Don's numbered an estimated 12.5 million. The result was striking: despite the apparently high odds against it, there was no mistaking that the subsequent litter consisted of six brown kittens and one white one. Clearly, among the 60 sperm from Chalky that reached the first doe's oviduct was at least one good 'un. Equally clearly, it was so good that both the does 'let' it pass through their reproductive tracts while rejecting many millions of others.

Members of Cohen's group later showed that a doe's body is primed to launch a ferocious attack on sperm entering her reproductive tract. Her immune system detects their presence and pours in so many defences (white blood cells and antibodies) that her vagina becomes inflamed with pus-like fluid within 30 minutes of mating. The sperm are engulfed in it. A woman, too, shows antibody reactions in her vagina when sexually aroused (although less dramatically), and many white blood cells emerge from the surface of her cervix when it is stimulated by sperm. As difficult as it is for sperm to reach her eggs when she is ovulating, the path is even more hostile – thanks to thick mucus barriers – for most of the rest of her menstrual cycle. In both women and rabbits, the immune response seems to be much weaker after intercourse with a vasectomised male, suggesting that it is sperm specifically that trigger the reaction. Cohen's belief is that females somehow discriminate heavily in favour of 'good' sperm, possibly by a sorting process based on detecting proteins on the surface of the sperm. The flops may well be marked for destruction with a 'defect' tag long before they even leave the male's body and so never stand a chance.

In short, the sperm-making process may be as complex and inefficient as it is prolific. But that doesn't really matter, because for the serious business of fertilising eggs there's probably a fiercely effective failsafe system to weed out all those dud sperm. If you take the best-made chips from the end of the production line and send them back once more through the quality control department, they pass muster again. No mystery there. The rabbit experiments suggest that the sperm's journey is not really like a marathon after all, since at least one of Chalky's good sperm – far from being exhausted at the finish – was clearly able to turn around and run the race a second time. Instead of all that arduous swimming, parachuting and hiking, it may be that a few hand-picked competitors make the journey from Edinburgh to Paris in the equivalent of an express VIP motorcade.

Other scientists disagree with Cohen's conclusions. While no one can yet say what proportion of all the sperm a man makes and ejaculates is 'good', David Mortimer says that if he had to speculate, he'd 'have no trouble believing that it's a quarter or even half'. Real-life human experience with assisted reproduction techniques such as intra-cytoplasmic sperm injection (ICSI), in particular, does suggest that the quota of sperm able to fertilise an egg is much higher than Cohen believes. As Jim Cummins puts it: 'With ICSI we now know that you can get an embryo with pretty much any rubbishy sperm – it may not survive, of course, but will certainly grow for a while.'

And there's other evidence that weight of sperm numbers does make a difference to male fertility, but only up to a point, according to a recent study led by a Danish researcher, Jens Peter E. Bonde.[8] His team recruited 430 childless couples who volunteered to stop using contraception; they were then monitored for up to six menstrual cycles, or until pregnancy was confirmed. All the men gave a semen sample at the start of the study and the women kept a daily record of their sexual activity and menstruation. In all, there were 256 pregnancies. About 65 per cent of the men whose sperm counts were 40 million/ml or more impregnated their partners, while just over half those with lower sperm count did so (there were 28 pregnancies to couples where the man's sperm count was below the WHO infertility guideline of 20 million/ml). The study found that as a man's sperm count rose, so did the likelihood of a pregnancy in his partner. The more 'normal' sperm each man had, the more likely he was to become a father, independent of his sperm count. But once sperm counts passed 40 million/ml the odds of a pregnancy occurring improved no further. If Cohen was right, surely the odds would keep rising in line with sperm concentrations? After all, the more sperm a man makes, the more 'good' sperm it should contain. So we're still in the dark on that question.

A man may have a low sperm count for any number of reasons. He may have inherited a fertility problem from his father, something may have gone wrong with his development before birth, he may have had a later injury or disease, or have been exposed to something harmful in his environment. A topic often debated in this context is whether wearing tight underwear or tight trousers lowers sperm counts. Even the ancients had their doubts about the wisdom of men wearing tight clothing. Archeologist Timothy Taylor points out that Hippocrates recorded that the fiercesome Scythian nomads were 'the most impotent of men', observing that wearing trousers and the 'constant jolting of their horses' made them unfit for intercourse. Some modern-day racing drivers reportedly have similar troubles.

A US study in the late 1980s added to the concern: volunteers who wore tight briefs for many months ended up with lower sperm counts than those of a control group who wore loose-fitting boxers. Sperm counts can certainly decline when the testes are overheated; some fertility clinics advise prospective fathers to avoid hot baths. But a more recent study threw cold water on the theory that tight jocks alone can raise scrotal temperatures enough to have much effect on fertility. In that study, 21 healthy adult male volunteers wore close-fitting jockstrap-like supports each day for a year. Although the men's average scrotal temperatures increased slightly, they kept producing normal amounts of healthy sperm.

Steven M. Schrader, of the US National Institute for Occupational Safety & Health, notes that the modern industrial workplace certainly can be hazardous for male fertility. As early as 1961, animal toxicologists reported that the pesticide dibromochloropropane (DBCP) made rodent testes shrink. But that report went essentially unnoticed until the 1970s, when workers exposed to this pesticide became infertile and in some cases sterile, Schrader says. Since then, more human male reproductive toxicants have been identified, including lead, further pesticides and organic solvents. Some have been shown to cut sperm production directly. Workers exposed to DBCP, for example, had average sperm counts of 46 million/ml, compared to 79 million/ml in unexposed men. When their exposure ceased, men with low sperm counts partially recovered (but those who had become sterile stayed that way). In another example, workers exposed to ethylene dibromide (EDB) were found to have relatively high numbers of sperm with tapered heads, sperm that were slow swimmers, lower sperm counts and reduced semen output.

All that said, most readers of this book will be aware of the ongoing controversy and concern about the disturbing claims that men's sperm counts worldwide have been falling markedly over the past 50 years or so. The debate began in 1992, when a Danish team led by Elizabeth Carlsen and including the prominent fertility researcher Niels Skakkebaek, reported on the results of a meta-analysis of 61 studies of sperm counts in various countries at various times. The studies involved a total of almost 15,000 men.[9] The team concluded that sperm counts had plummeted from a global average of about 113 million/ml to 66 million/ml between 1938 and 1990 – that's a drop of about 1 million sperm, or 1 per cent, a year. If they were right and if the trend continued, men would be out of the sperm business within 50 years. Yikes!

Skakkebaek later said he became interested in the issue in the late 1980s, when 'wondering why it was so difficult for sperm banks to establish a core of donors. In some areas of Denmark, they were having to recruit 10 potential donors to find one with good semen quality.' So he felt there was a groundswell to support the data (along with some evidence of increasing sperm abnormalities and male reproductive disorders). Astonishment greeted the report on two grounds: first, the alarming speed and scale of the apparent decline called into question the very future of our species; second, many fertility researchers simply did not believe it could be correct – it seemed inexplicable that sperm counts could take such a sharp nosedive without being noticed sooner and without an obvious reason. Debate on the issue then followed a familiar pattern in science: the methodology of the study was challenged, a string of new reports ensued to both confirm and contradict the original findings, other studies pointed to possible causes and then also came under challenge, and the rest of us non-scientists were left worried, puzzled and wondering who and what to believe. A subsequent study of 1350 Parisian men seemed to confirm the trend: it reported that the subjects' sperm counts declined from 89 million/ml to 60 million/ml between 1973 and 1992, a fall of 2.1 per cent a year – and similar rates of decline have been reported from Canada, Sweden, Greece, Italy and Belgium, among others. Something fundamentally harmful seemed to be happening to men's sperm production, raising the very worrying prospect of people losing the ability to conceive babies naturally, of IVF clinics mushrooming into existence in every suburb of every city.

So is it true? Frustratingly, the answer is no clearer today. Based on the evidence so far, it's simply not possible to say with certainty whether human sperm counts really are declining worldwide, whether they have a roller-coaster variability over time (perhaps in response to social conditions or climate), or even whether such a decline will cause birth rates to fall as well. There's contrary evidence from countries such as Finland, where sperm counts are steady, and parts of the US, where they seem to be on the rise. It seems equally possible that we face an appalling evolutionary dead-end or that it won't make a scrap's worth of difference in the long run. As usual, the truth probably lies somewhere in between.

Making sense of this issue is very difficult because we're only equipped with a small part of the story. Indeed, we're plain ignorant of even some of the most basic facts about male reproduction. You'll recall that we don't even know what 'normal' sperm are, let alone what 'normal' sperm counts should be. Neither do we have good information on how sperm counts vary from region to region.

But from what you've read so far in this chapter alone, you'll realise that measuring sperm-count trends can be confounded by the way samples are collected, when they're collected, how they're collected, who they're collected from and so on. The Carlsen study, for example, did not take into account such variable factors as the age of the subjects, how long they had abstained from sex before giving semen samples, and laboratory methods used to prepare and count their sperm – each of which can strongly influence any measured trend. Clearly, it's in large part an argument about statistics.

Jack Cohen's group found what it believed was a significant mathematical flaw in the original Carlsen analysis: the WHO moved the male-fertility goalposts in the middle of the time period in question. The analysis compared the sperm concentrations of 'normal' men but in 1967 the WHO changed its definition of normal, dropping the cut-off point for infertility from 60 million/ml to 20 million/ml. Thus, the Danish group didn't compare apples with apples: after 1967, they included men whose sperm counts were in the 20 million/ml to 60 million/ml range, Cohen argues, and so dragged down the average among the 'normal' men in the more recent studies.

The Statistical Assessment Service, a US non-profit research organisation devoted to the accurate use of scientific and quantitative information in public policy debate, has cited another criticism of the Carlsen study, that 'if valid conclusions are to be drawn from a compilation of assorted studies, roughly comparable numbers of men would have had to be tested in the early, middle, and late years under consideration'. In fact, 48 of the 61 studies were from after 1970; less than 600 of the subjects were tested before 1950 and more than 13,000 were tested after 1970. And when the later studies are examined by themselves, they show an actual increase in sperm counts between 1970 and 1990.

A prominent critic of the Carlsen study, a US fertility specialist from Columbia University, Harry Fisch, stirred the pot even more in 1996 when he and colleagues reported that sperm counts can vary dramatically not just between individuals but between men in different regions as well.[10] Fisch found that men in Los Angeles, for example, produce an average 73 million/ml, whereas those in New York produced 132 million/ml (which seems to scotch the notion that if you can make it there, you can make it anywhere!). Other studies have since found that sperm counts can vary over much smaller geographic ranges, even within different parts of London.

Fisch found that the vast majority of men included in the Carlsen study before 1970 were from the US and that most of them were from New York. But after 1970, only half the men included were from the US and only a quarter of them were New Yorkers. Perhaps the declining trend was a statistical glitch, simply highlighting differences in place, not time. Because we know so little about the potential regional and ethnic variations that may exist in normal sperm counts, their potential to confound sperm analyses simply cannot be ignored. Tracking trends can depend not just on when you start and stop counting sperm, but where you count them as well.

The argument soon came to the boil again, with more public alarm, when a reanalysis of the Carlsen study by American researchers seemed to confirm its findings. The reanalysis made more sophisticated statistical corrections for things such as the subjects' ages and abstinence, and concluded that the decline might be even greater than previously thought. It indicated an average annual rate of decrease of 1.5 million/ml in samples collected from US men. For Europeans, the rate of decline seemed to be twice as high.

Shanna Swan, who headed the reanalysis group, reportedly told Reuters newsagency at the time: 'Overall, in Europe and the United States there is a strong and significant decline.' She added: 'The question now is not if average sperm counts are dropping, but why.' No uncertainty there.

But there were still problems with the numbers when you looked closer. The evidence from non-Western countries, including Brazil, Hong Kong, India, Israel, Kuwait, Nigeria and Thailand, was that the trend was slightly positive – sperm counts there seemed to be increasing. But because those data were taken from only 13 studies, all of which were published after 1978, that trend was not deemed statistically significant. Swan's group also confined itself to reviewing studies published in the English language and excluded several non-English studies that were included in Carlsen's original analysis. It is surprising that translations couldn't be made. Two of the excluded studies, written in German and Danish, apparently recorded sperm-count values that were low relative to later European studies. If they had been included, would the apparent European drop-off in sperm counts have seemed so severe? Nor was Fisch impressed by Swan's apparent confirmation of the Carlsen study, reportedly telling one journalist: 'If you keep on analysing bad data, no matter what model you use, it's still bad data. While the statistics look robust, they're not . . .' Cohen says the WHO fertility benchmark change 'had produced the illusion of decline in numbers. Sperm numbers may be declining but the work which initiated the story does not in fact support it!'

The whole debate probably sheds as much light on scientific process itself as it does on sperm counts. The way scientists gather and communicate facts and ideas to each other is often puzzling to the rest of us. Equally, the sharply contrasting approach of the mass media – mostly blind and uncritical acceptance that the claims are true, and reported in alarmist terms – leaves many scientists shaking their heads. As Swan and Skakkebaek have said, if sperm counts are dropping it's not necessarily a cause for concern in itself, but it may be a warning flag about other emerging problems in male fertility. Yet, as one sceptical editorial in a US newspaper wryly observed: 'Sound science is incremental and plodding, a cumulative process of observing, challenging, checking and revising – not a one-night stand based on a single study. More research on the effect of so-called environmental estrogens is needed before taking drastic regulatory measures. Given the uncertainties and scientific caveats surrounding the case of the disappearing sperm, it's safe to say that reports of the End of Manhood have been greatly exaggerated.'[11]

The sperm-count issue should become clearer over the next five years or so, as a string of international studies bears fruit. At the very least the controversy will have helped to spur more research into this fundamental question and we should soon have a much better grasp of the differences in place and time that affect sperm production. Longer-term monitoring studies will be able to take those differences into account and make it easier to tell if there really is a problem. For now, all we can say is that there's no cause for panic. Not a single nation or region in the world has reported an average sperm count below the WHO infertility level. Men in most countries are still averaging well above the 40 million/ml level, beyond which there seems little real gain in actual fertility. The only evidence we have of decline in birth rates is easily explained by (and most likely attributable to) contraception, better family planning and voluntary postponement of births. No sharp jump in global infertility rates has been reported. Indeed, there is no evidence that the alleged sperm drought has led to reduced fertility anywhere. As they say, watch this space.

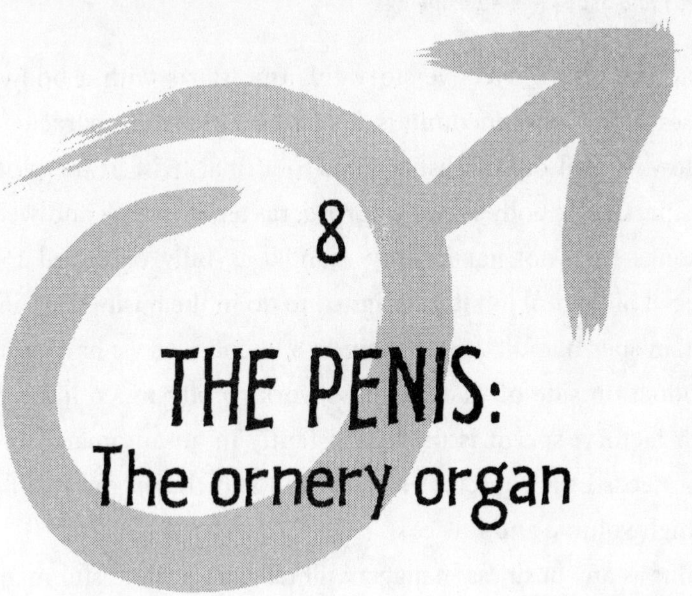

8

THE PENIS:
The ornery organ

'When men from another community or tribe arrive for ceremonies, they usually first perform a penis-offering ritual with their hosts. Each visitor approaches each of the seated hosts in turn and lifts the latter's arm. He presses his penis against the host's hand . . . and then draws the penis firmly along the hand. A man with a grievance against the visitor refuses to raise his hand for the ritual. At this sign of hostility, the visitor at once presents his penis to each of his classificatory "brothers" among the hosts. Should none of the "brothers" take it, the outsider must be ready to fight or flee; he now knows that public opinion is solidly against him. But a "brother" who touches the visitor's penis consents to sponsor him and must stand and plead his case. If the appeal fails, he must also fight beside the outsider.'

Mervyn Meggitt, Desert People[1]

LIKE ANY GOOD detective story this one starts with a body, then poses a mystery, encounters a cast of colourful characters and follows a trail of tantalising clues to a final twist in the plot. But this particular body is not a corpse; rather, it is alive and well and belongs to a normal healthy man. It is fully equipped for the special biological job it is designed to do in the business of life – to obtain sperm and transfer them to a woman. As we have seen, the production side of that business works pretty much like a high-tech factory: sperm is made constantly in an automated process that needs little conscious supervision and churns out its product at high volume and low cost.

But as any business manager will tell you, a successful manufacturing enterprise depends just as much on an efficient delivery system. Our mystery, then, is why the chosen delivery vehicle for our subject's sperm – his penis – is so volatile and fickle. As we'll see in the next chapter, for surprisingly many men it simply refuses to perform its task at all. Indeed, if there could be such a thing as a penis obedience school, there'd be a permanent line of new recruits queuing down the street. While a man's ability to mass-produce sperm aspires to the Henry Ford model, the penis often seems more like one of those infernal contraptions designed by Heath Robinson.

Getting a penis ready to successfully perform its unique reproductive role depends intimately on its physical, electrical and chemical connections with the rest of the body, but most of all on the subtle inner workings of that vastly more complex and enigmatic organ, the brain. Some animals, such as frogs, avoid the issue by not having a penis at all. Others have sidestepped mating itself by cunning devices: some male salamanders drop little packets of sperm and leave a chemical scent trail from them, to be followed by females, who then pick up the packets with specially adapted genitals. Most birds – except ducks, swans, geese and several flightless birds such as the emu and kiwi – simply have an opening (known as the cloaca) in both sexes, and the male aligns with the female's to transfer sperm.

The significance of the penis in men's self-image is difficult to overstate, although it plainly doesn't enjoy a similar status in female culture. No other part of a man's naked body so clearly signals his physical gender, especially if he shaves off his beard. There's no mistaking the presence or absence of a penis. It can be a proud flag of a man's virility, a cause of embarrassment and shame, a misleading symbol of his fertility, a barometer of his mood, age, status or health, an ever-ready source of pleasure and, of course, a rich wellspring of bawdy humour.

And here's where the list of colourful characters enters our tale. To appreciate the prominent place the penis occupies in the way we think about sex, you only need to eavesdrop on men's locker-room talk to realise how strongly it has made its mark in the English language. In the weighty thesaurus on my desk, for example, almost three pages are devoted to some 40 categories of body parts. Tellingly, the section dealing with genitals is by far the largest category, including 123 words or expressions: within that tally, words referring to male genitalia outnumber those for female genitalia by two to one. Of the 67 male-related entries, just 14 refer to the testes while 53 refer to the penis, despite the testes being far more important players in reproduction.

It's a graphic list, notable not just for its variety but for the imagery that has been identified with this vital organ and for the contradictorily coy, crude and creative ways in which we discuss sexual matters. There are many monosyllabic names – cock, dick, dong, fat, horn, hose, prick, rod, schlong, tonk, tool and wang – that hint at its solo status in a body that otherwise features many paired parts. Sometimes actual names are employed, such as Big Ben, John Thomas, Johnson, Oscar, Percy, Peter and Willy, that lend it individuality and a male identity. Some liken it to objects with similar shapes: banana, carrot, cucumber, salami, sausage and weiner. Others hint whimsically at its perceived role or function – as a joystick, pork sword, trouser browser, lap lizard, love pump, one-eyed trouser snake and cherry-picker. Others again attribute personality and character to it: the penis is Mister Happy, the purple-headed warrior, the bishop, Wicked Willy, the little guy or the old fellow.

The penis is arguably the most infamous human body part, but some individual penises have also achieved exceptional notoriety. I well remember when I was young the shock and dismay when a prominent local politician was publicly disgraced by allegations that he had shown his penis to his female office assistant. Therein lies the flasher's power to shock, as Paula Jones claimed Bill Clinton did to her in 1991. She alleged that he exposed himself to her, a claim he denied. Unfortunately for him, similar controversies dogged his presidency, making his arguably the single most discussed penis in the world in the 1990s. In recent times, perhaps only the severed and reattached penis of another American, John Wayne Bobbitt, eclipsed that of Clinton in terms of its dramatic impact. Bobbitt's desperate wife, Lorena, suffered years of abuse by her husband before she cut off his penis – a shocking symbolic removal of his physical power over her.

Napoleon Bonaparte's penis also achieved enduring notoriety by virtue of having been cut off after its owner's death in 1821. In November 1992, Dr Stanley Bierman of the University of California, Los Angeles, reported that the great general's member was stealthily claimed by Vignali, the priest who administered the last rites.[2] The mummified memento was passed on through several descendants until in 1924 it came into the hands of a Dr A.S. Rosenbach, who put it in a case of blue leather and velvet. In 1927 it was put on public show at the Museum of French Art. A newspaper report at the time commented: 'Maudlin sentimentalizers sniffled; shallow women giggled and pointed. In a glass case they saw something looking like a maltreated strip of buckskin shoelace or shrivelled eel.' It passed through several more owners until it was acquired in 1969 by Dr John K. Lattimer, a prominent American urologist with an interest in unusual artefacts. One of Lattimer's reported reasons for buying the penis was to keep it out of 'unscrupulous' hands and to ensure it was treated with 'dignity'.

Then there is the question of penis design – spartan, basic and functional, but not exactly a masterpiece of universal aesthetic appeal. As two British doctors, Tim Webb and Sarah Brewer, rather severely put it in their entertaining *Bluff Your Way in Sex*: 'It is one of the Creator's better jokes that the straggling fleshy afterthought which hangs from a man like a knotted rubber blow-hole on a half-dead Boxing Day balloon, is the tool by which he shall reproduce his own kind.'[3] Of course, because it is so intimately involved in sex it's easy to overlook the fact that a penis has another basic function, urination. As any man will attest, having a 'spout' makes it a lot simpler and more manageable to urinate. He can do so standing up, lying on his side or squatting and can direct the stream of urine clear of himself and, as even young boys soon discover, aim it at a target as well. Obviously, however, the ability to pee high up a wall, to carry out a precision drowning of an ant colony or to create interesting patterns in snow and sand is not so beneficial that evolution has seen fit to similarly equip females.

But when you look a little closer at this unorthodox organ, its outwardly simple and basic form conceals a wealth of complexity. Penises in fact come in all shapes and sizes throughout the animal kingdom. Wherever internal fertilisation of a female's eggs is required – in other words, where her body must be penetrated to deliver sperm – there's a penis to suit the job. Despite that job being essentially the same in each species, zoologists have found that penis design varies enormously. Some monkeys, for example, have penises with flanges that look like little wings, those of kangaroos are forked and double-headed, and snakes and lizards have two penises, while a tomcat's is studded with spines that make it look distinctly unlike an organ of pleasure. Some are hydraulically operated, some are erectile, some are permanently rigid and some are fully retractable.

In the insect world this amazing variety is even more evident, with a whole range of hooks, grapplers, corers, extensions, springs and even barbs on show: seen close up, many seem more suited to the Spanish Inquisition than to the dating scene. The European rabbit flea is the unlikely holder of the title for having the most elaborate of all, while the oriental cockroach is noteworthy for a penis that unfolds a series of hinged parts like a Swiss Army knife. One unsavoury species of mosquito even has a long sharp penis that enables it to rip open female pupae and effectively copulate with the unborn.[4]

Goran Arnqvist of the University of Umea, in Sweden, has made a rare study of the sex lives and penises of literally hundreds of insect species, in an effort to discern why such variety of shape and design exists. The 'lock-and-key' theory holds that all this diversity has a unique purpose – to ensure that only males and females of the same species can mate successfully. Pigs seem to be a perfect example, with an anti-clockwise 'corkscrew' penis so precisely fitting the coiled bore of the sow's reproductive tract that the happy couple remain literally locked together during their lengthy copulation. But Arnqvist's work suggests that penis diversity is more like the wonderful complexity of bird plumage patterns: it is largely the result of female preferences, or sexual selection.

Arnqvist showed that in species where females mate with many partners it is not just sperm competition between males that puts a selective pressure on the design of their bodies, there is penis competition as well. It follows that an improvement in penis design can give an individual greater success at inseminating females. Arnqvist set out to prove this by comparing the penises of many pairs of insect species; each was chosen to feature one species with females that mate only once a lifetime and a closely related species in which females take many male partners. They included mayflies, butterflies, flies and beetles. The outcome was striking: in species where females mate only once, the males' genitals are far more mundane and uniform than those of males in the more promiscuous species. In contrast, there was little variation in the non-sexual body parts of the males.

That shot down the lock-and-key theory. If it had been correct, a female with only one chance of finding the right mate would have to get it right first time, so uniquely shaped male genitals for each species would help to provide that certainty. But Arnqvist clearly showed that the opposite was true: the chocolate-box of variety in the penises of the multiple-mate species revealed that those males were being redesigned to seek a competitive sexual edge.

Male damselflies, for example, feature a little bottlebrush-like structure on their penis tip that does the dastardly deed of scouring his mate's genital tract to clear out any other male's sperm. The spines on a tomcat's penis may somehow stimulate ovulation in the female, giving his sperm a better chance of arriving on cue for an egg. But what most of these pioneering penises do remains unknown. Some may be like the peacock's tail, an elaborate advertisement of macho vigour and rude health. 'There doesn't always have to be a reason for female choice, but once it starts, once this component of male genitalia has been preferred over that one, it can have a runaway effect on evolution,' wrote Darryl Gwynne, of the University of Toronto, in an editorial concerning Arnqvist's study in the journal *Nature*. We'll return to that matter later, but for now let's stay with the issue of form and function.

The human penis may pale in comparison with the complexity seen among insects, but it is actually a deceptively canny piece of design. For starters, it needs to be rigid to do its job of deeply penetrating the vagina, but a permanent erection would surely be too susceptible to injury. 'Fracture' of the penis is uncommon but it does happen often enough for about 200 cases to have been reported. The most common causes are blunt trauma during sexual intercourse, masturbation, or an unlucky fall. Victims often report a characteristic 'cracking sound' at the moment of fracture, followed by an immediate loss of erection, severe pain and swelling. Sometimes the fracture is bad enough to leave the penis greatly misshapen or to make urination impossible.

Clearly, for human males a penis that stayed permanently rigid would be a liability and the consequences of a calamitous injury to it could be severe – no more fatherhood, no more pleasurable sex and perhaps even death from disease or despair. The fact that such accidents are so rare strongly suggests that its normal flaccid state keeps the penis well protected.

One way to get around the need for reliable rigidity would be to include a bone. As it happens, among their near relatives in the animal world, humans really are the odd men out in this respect. All other male primates – including our nearest relatives, the chimpanzees – have a penis bone, a baculum. It is one of only a few bones in the bodies of mammals that are not directly joined to the rest of the body skeleton (another example being kneecaps). It generally floats freely, unattached even to muscles, like a loose pencil lead within the penises of its possessors. This may make the baculum less likely to fracture in the event of injury. All male insect-eating mammals, such as shrews and hedgehogs, have penis bones, as do male bats, rodents and the meat-eating carnivores, including cats and dogs. The walrus is infamous for having a baculum the size of a baseball bat; it is said that seal hunters once prized them for use as clubs to kill their prey.

Exactly why so many animals have a penis bone is unclear, although during the thrusting of intercourse it may act a little like a piston to increase internal pressure within the soft parts of the penis. The fact that the baculum is present in so many different kinds of mammals suggests it appeared quite early in the evolution of this group, making their absence in men strange. And exactly when our more recent human ancestors lost the penis bone, as it seems likely they did, is another mystery.

No fossil baculum has been reported from a Neanderthal man, for example (although Neanderthals seem to have known about them in other mammals – an archeological site in Croatia yielded a bear baculum carved with designs). It seems more than coincidence, however, that a species with such an exceptional brain and exceptional upright posture should also have such an exceptional, boneless penis. Perhaps the baculum became more exposed and so more of a liability once our ancient forebears stood up on two legs. We can only guess.

What we do know is that for all our brains and culture our animal origins have bequeathed to us a penis that needs to be made rigid at the right time and to the right size to deliver its precious payload of sperm effectively. So evolution compromised: it gave the penis an ability to exist and function perfectly well in two contrasting states. All it takes to inflate the thing is a few tablespoons of blood, but its failure to do so reliably causes no end of trouble. Conversely, its apparent readiness to display its abilities at times when its services are not required can be mortifying to adolescent boys. Both experiences confirm an essential truth about the penis: while it may at times seem to have a mind of its own, it is what goes on in its owner's mind that really counts.

Yet, as Diane Kelly, of Cornell University, has found, we're still ignorant about some of the most basic details of how the penis works, let alone how it links to what goes on in our brains. Kelly has recently carried out the first technical studies of the biomechanics of the penis. She gained much insight at first from an unlikely source – road-kills of armadillos in Florida. The males of these bizarre animals are unusually well endowed, with a penis that may be up to one-third the length of their body. That extraordinary length is probably related to the logistics of reaching the female's vagina, which is well hidden beneath her armoured shell.

As Kelly put it in a recent *Discover* magazine report on her work, the penis represents one solution to 'the mechanical problem of how to make something that's floppy stiff'.[5] To do so, nature devised what is basically a spongy cylinder with inflatable chambers. There's nothing mysterious about that. But the insights into the practicalities of penis rigidity Kelly gleaned from armadillos turned out to be quite unexpected.

Penises rely on pressurised liquids to keep their ends up and this is something they share with many soft-bodied animals, such as worms. Worms are equipped with a strong but flexible external skin to spread the pressure evenly along the length of their body, to prevent one part ballooning out or another part kinking when they bend. The skin is reinforced all over with spirals of fibres, arranged much like the famous double-helix structure of DNA. Modern garden hoses often feature that kind of design for precisely the same reasons. It had been assumed that the reinforcement system employed by the penis was similar. Kelly found, however, that the collagen fibres on the surface of the penis form a criss-cross pattern, more like a tartan (now you know what's under a kilt!) or the weave of a sock. One parallel set of fibres runs lengthwise along the penis from base to tip, while another is aligned at right angles, encircling the organ. That arrangement helps to keep the penis stiff on its lengthwise axis. As the *Discover* article neatly put it: 'Apparently no one had argued that a penis is not a worm. A worm, though, if it's going to get anywhere, needs to be really bendable. A penis, for reasons that do not need explaining, must be rigid. It has one place it needs to go, and wriggling is not how it gets there.'

A subtle balance of hydraulic forces, based on an interplay of inflow and outflow of blood, helps to maintain the erect penis's internal pressure. Mechanically, its innards are a delicate but fairly straightforward work of plumbing based on three masses of loose tissue. Those masses are honeycombed with spaces (which are collapsed when the organ is in its usual flaccid state), containing smooth muscles, fibrous tissues and blood vessels. When arousal happens, the smooth muscles relax and blood flows into the spaces to elevate and increase the penis's size by about half, a neat trick in the larger scheme of human body parts. One main artery feeds blood into two of these masses, called corpora cavernosa, which are identical, running along its sides, and are surrounded by a membrane. The third mass, the corpus spongiosum, lies beneath them and surrounds the urethra (the tube that carries urine and semen) and extends to form the head of the penis, known as the glans.

Normally, only about a teaspoon of blood flows through the penis at very low pressure each minute, enough to keep its tissues supplied with nutrients and oxygen when it is deflated. Other organs have a blood throughflow that is much higher – the kidneys, for example, have about a hundred times as much blood flowing through them. The penis's bloodflow rate is controlled by the smooth muscles that line the erectile tissue. Normally, those muscles are contracted, but when arousal happens a cascade of chemical reactions makes them relax. As blood flows into the penis at a greater rate, the expanding erectile tissue constricts funnel-shaped valves in the veins that drain the penis, thereby slowing the outflow. Reinforcements in the corpus spongiosum protect the urethra from collapsing as the pressure grows; otherwise semen could not pass through it easily. But it is the outer skin of collagen fibres that deters bends and kinks and lets the inflated penis hold its vital shape with integrity, despite the creative gymnastics that can feature in the human sexual repertoire.

The next trail of scientific inquiry in the great penis mystery is the vital issue of size. And, yes, it really *does* matter. And it matters every bit as much for humans as it does for armadillos. Despite the cliché that it matters most to men, there's ample evidence to the contrary. Sure, men are impressed – obsessed in some cases – with penis size. The bigger the better. Jared Diamond, of the University of California, Los Angeles, argues that the human penis may be an example of one of two evolutionary traits, the runaway selection model or the (aptly named) handicap principle.[6] He asserts that it is unusually large when measured against those of our near relatives in the animal world, pointing out that a gorilla's erect penis length is only a little over 30 millimetres (there goes the mystique of King Kong). An orang-utan does little better at just 38 millimetres. Both apes, however, have larger body sizes than men, who boast penises of about 130 millimetres on average – in imperial measurements, that's just over 5 inches (penis-measuring in humans, while popular among teenage boys, is for obvious reasons a difficult exercise so the data are relatively poor and the real average may vary 20 per cent either way).

Other experts argue that chimpanzees and the closely related bonobos, however, have penises that rival those of men in relation to their body sizes. Frans de Waal, whose many years of study of the bonobo have brought to light the intriguing sex lives of these endearing animals, is in no doubt: Desmond Morris and Jared Diamond are wrong and it is the male bonobo, not man, that deserves 'the prize for the longest penis' in the ape world. Even so, it is safe to assume that men certainly are up there on the winner's podium for at least a bronze or silver medal.

Diamond argues that the human penis is not likely to be big by chance. A large penis doesn't help a male perform better: it does not it make it easier to pursue a greater variety of copulatory positions or longer duration of intercourse, for orang-utans 'out-perform' humans in all those positions while hanging from a tree branch. For Diamond, the human penis is a puzzle – why should an 'ancestral' ape penis that can be supposed to be much smaller have grown so large since we parted company with our cousins? 'That evolutionary problem is posed by the fourfold expansion in human penis size beyond its inferred ancestral size over the course of the last seven to nine million years. Such an expansion cries out for a historical, functional interpretation . . . we have to ask what selective forces drove the historical expansion of the human penis and maintain its large size today.'

Diamond's answer, put simply, is that somewhere back in the mists of human origins some males happened to be born with penises larger than average. This innovation somehow became the preferred model for females, so those males enjoyed greater success in sex and passed on their large-penis genes to their male offspring. They likewise prospered, and before long the other guys in the prehistoric locker-rooms could only look on in envy as the choosy females of the species ensured that this secret weapon – like the peacock's tail – swamped the gene pool. This is the runaway selection theory.

Alternatively, if the large penis is an example of the handicap principle in operation, it is essentially a brag by its possessor that he can divert precious energy away from making much more useful brains and brawn yet still be a prime mate. 'In effect, a man is boasting, "I'm already so smart and superior that I don't need to devote more ounces of protoplasm to my brain, but I can instead afford the handicap of packing the ounces uselessly into my penis",' Diamond says. He goes on to wonder whether this signal is, in fact, aimed at other men, since they seem so much more interested in penises (the familiar sideways glance at the urinal) than women tend to be. Perhaps it is a mixture of both handicap principle and runaway selection. In fact the animal world is replete with examples of body ornaments – the lion's mane, the parrot's crest and so on – that serve the dual purpose of attracting mates and deterring same-sex competitors.

There are other possible explanations for large penises in humans. Our more recent ancestors' strong reliance on visual and behavioural cues could simply have made it useful for males to possess a penis that would obviously signal to females the sincerity or otherwise of their romantic overtures. After all, there's no mistaking what is on the mind of an approaching man with an erection. A larger penis would make the signal all the more obvious and increase its effectiveness – a billboard is a heck of a lot more visible than a leaflet.

Asked to speculate on the size question, Goran Arnqvist says he believes that the evolution of penis shape, structure and size in humans is no different from that of any other species, but it is of course impossible to do controlled experiments with humans to decide the matter. Some of our ancestors, he suggests, may have had a mating system in which females were not inclined to monogamy but were polyandrous (mating with several males, as chimpanzees do). 'Large penises may very well have been associated with high post-mating fertilization success in polyandrous human females in our evolutionary past. This could have been brought about in a variety of different ways, all leading to the same results: enlargement of the penis. These different mechanisms (such as higher success in sperm competition due to deposition of the ejaculate closer to the uterine cervix, or higher rates of sperm resorption due to female climax) are, as far as I'm concerned, impossible to distinguish between in humans. We're having troubles separating between these mechanisms in insects, where we can conduct controlled experiments.'

It also seems reasonable to ask why so many men in so many cultures – in fact, the majority of men alive today – conceal such a crucial organ of display beneath their clothes. Or does that simply highlight yet again how we as a species have been able to take charge of our biological legacies and divert them for our own cultural purposes? Will there be any long-term effect on penis size if it is no longer displayed – buried beneath underpants, trousers, kilts, grass skirts or whatever? If we keep concealing it, will men become more like gorillas in that respect? There's good reason to think not.

John Langdon, of the University of Indianapolis, believes the answer to the size question is much simpler and one of more basic mechanics: 'If penis size reflects sexual selection, then we need to ask why females would prefer a large penis in the first place. Often sexual selection arguments at this point say, "It doesn't matter, as long as the preference became established". That is not a satisfying answer. Another line of reasoning, beginning with Desmond Morris, is that penis size provides sexual pleasure for the female. I would counter that the more important feature here is not size, but fit. Why is the human penis large? Because the human vagina is deep. Selection favours placing sperm closer to the cervix. That requires a long penis; and that, in turn, requires a large diameter for mechanical strength. The important question is why the vagina is so deep.'

Langdon believes the solution lies in the detail of a 1983 paper in the *Journal of Human Evolution*, which concluded that the depth of the vagina is a secondary consequence of our upright posture.[7] When our ancestors rose up to walk on two legs, the vagina became concealed from view and was physically placed farther out of reach. So males with longer and broader penises would have gained a reproductive edge by being best able to ejaculate their sperm close to the egg. Not so much survival of the fittest, but survival of the best fit.

That also seems to hold true for whales, whose penises shame even the best-hung animal of any other kind for sheer size. As with testes, the right whale tops the list: its 17-metre-long body boasts the largest known penis in the animal world, measuring an average of 2.3 metres. Those who have observed right whales mating have been awestruck not just by the size of the penis but by the way males use it. Stephen Burnell has seen many right whale couples lying side by side on the sea surface to mate. The male's penis is normally retracted within its body, bent back in an S-shape, but it emerges briefly for copulation. This is no rigid penis like a man's; rather it is fibrous, narrow, highly muscular and flexible. Since the whale cannot see where to insert it, the penis goes hunting by itself. On emerging, it powerfully writhes around like a snake, and it 'literally searches out the genital slit as if it has a mind of its own', Burnell says.

The penises of right and bowhead whales are over 14 per cent of their body length, those of humpback and grey whales are over 11 per cent and those of other whale species range from 10.8 per cent down to 7.5 per cent (for men, penis length is about 6 per cent of body height). An obscure but fascinating scientific report published in 1986 by the International Whaling Commission lists penis and testes sizes for all 10 species of baleen whales (the filter-feeders).[8] The theory of sexual selection suggests that in species where females often mate with more than one male, the males are not highly aggressive towards each other but they have relatively large testes and long penises. In species where females tend to copulate with only one male, however, male–male interactions are generally highly aggressive. They try to monopolise a female and prevent other males mating with her: these males have relatively small testes and shorter penises. Humpback whales and pygmy right whales, although poorly studied, seem to fit that description. Following that reasoning, the fact that men have a relatively large penis and moderate-sized testes may suggest we emerged from a line of apes that had a bet each way.

All that said, its seems reasonably clear that the sting in the tail of the penis mystery is that, one way or the other, a man's definitive organ has in effect been designed by women. Perhaps that explains why so many men in so many cultures have been clearly dissatisfied with the thing. Poor old penis: they have shortened it, lengthened it, scarred it, tattooed it, padded it, pierced it with bars and rings and even inserted little balls beneath its skin to give it a bizarre lumpy texture. Men in at least 20 South-East Asian cultures insert bells, balls, pins, rings, or marbles made of ground shells under the skin of the genitals; in some cases it is said that the greater the number of insertions, the better a man's prospects of marriage. Dyak men of Borneo are famous for favouring a *palang* (a smooth bar with rounded ends made of bone or metal) to pierce the glans of their penises, a practice that became more widespread outside Borneo in the late twentieth century with the increased interest in body-piercing in many Western societies.

Men in some Highlands tribes in New Guinea adorn their penises with a large sheath, sometimes of extravagant length – a penis sheath 60 centimetres (2 feet) long is unremarkable – and featuring curves, curls, elaborate decorations of feathers and fur. They are often painted bright red or yellow, to make sure that they stand out. Jared Diamond has observed: 'Each man owns several models, varying in size, ornamentation and angle of erection, and each day he selects a model to wear according to his mood, much as each morning we select a shirt to wear.' Men of the Ketengban tribe in the Star Mountains told him that they felt 'naked and immodest' without their sheaths. 'That answer surprised me, with my Western perspective, because the Ketengbans were otherwise completely naked and left even their testes exposed.' Diamond claims that the sheaths represent what a man would like to be endowed with if the evolution of the penis was not limited in size, for practical reasons, by the human vagina.

That limitation hasn't stopped men in some cultures, however, from deliberately enlarging their penises by stretching them or hanging weights from them. Men of the semi-nomadic pastoralist Karamojong people of northern Uganda, for example, have elongated their penises in this way to as much as three times their original size, yet the attention-grabbing result is usually tied up in a knot to keep it manageable – another reminder that there are practical limits to penis size. I have not been able to learn how this practice affects the function, potency or sensitivity of the penis, or whether such men fare better or worse sexually than other men. But it seems pertinent that the advent of cosmetic penile enlargement surgery has attracted much interest in Western men over the past decade or so. One such operation involves severing the tissue that tethers the internal part of the penis, sacrificing some directional control but allowing it to protrude more obviously from the body and thus look longer. Implants of the patient's own fat are also used to make the penis physically thicker. In Australia and New Guinea, several traditional peoples long ago figured out how to achieve a similar effect by subincision, in which the underside of the penis shaft is cut open lengthwise to make it spread and widen. If the urethra is cut as well, urine and semen will spill out from the base of the penis, suggesting that subincision may have, or once had, a birth-control function.

British biologist Robin Baker has suggested that the firm, broad head of the erect human penis evolved through reproductive competition between men. He argues that males in some species produce a thick semen plug to block a female's vagina, and those same males tend to have narrow-headed penises that are thrust vigorously before ejaculating, to 'batter' their way into, or to slip past the edge of, a competitor's semen plug before depositing their own semen. Since human semen is only a soft plug, a broad penis head thus seems well suited to pushing through such a plug and dragging it out of the vagina when the penis repeatedly withdraws during copulation, as Baker sees it. But if human sex is as much about pleasure as reproduction, it's not just penis length that matters, but breadth as well. After all, the vast majority of human copulation is not for procreation. So it seems equally possible that a fat-headed penis evolved to bring greater pleasure to the act.

Pleasure may be the reason for subincision, too. Anthropologists report that women in those communities which practise subincision prefer to have sex with a subincised man because they both like it better that way. That was certainly asserted by the people of the Walbiri tribe of the deserts of Central Australia, the subjects of the quote at the start of this chapter. Mervyn Meggitt, who conducted field studies among these remarkable people between 1953 and 1960, records that all the Walbiri men he encountered had been both circumcised and later subincised, which meant that they had to squat to urinate. They told Meggitt that a key reason for enduring the pain and inconvenience of subincision was hedonistic: 'Men and women both stated that the marked lateral extension of the erect penis, which is directly due to the slitting of the urethra, greatly increases their enjoyment of coitus. Indeed, some women said flatly that, for this reason, they would not consider marrying a man who was not subincised.'

The operation, traditionally done with a sharp stone blade when boys were about 17, was also occasionally repeated later in life. 'Sometimes, when a youth is subincised, other men present may take the opportunity to have their own incisions enlarged. They invite their brothers-in-law to perform the operation. In this way, a man's incision may be progressively lengthened until it reaches the scrotum.' By Walbiri custom, subincision was also supposed to be immediately performed on a youth if he was discovered to be having a sexual liaison, which suggests that birth control was at least part of the reason for the operation. Meggitt records that one such young man who tried to avoid the operation was solidly clubbed on the back of the neck by his elder brother and subincised before he regained consciousness. Many Walbiri men also underwent piercing of the nasal septum and cicatrisation, or ritual scarring, of their chests. They explained that this was to help them look 'flash' to women, but it was also an important mark of the bravery they were expected to display as men. 'It is clear that a man who has been forcibly subincised suffers a great loss of personal prestige, and other men never forget his cowardice,' Meggitt says. 'In any dispute his opponents are entitled to remind him of this in order to put him at a disadvantage.'

Raven Rowanchilde, of the University of Toronto, has suggested that sexual selection can explain why so many societies have been disposed towards modifying the penis, just as it may explain the organ's basic design and size. She speculates that men have endured the discomfort and pain of these penile redesigns to boost their appeal as mates. That certainly seems plausible in the light of comments by women that they prefer the stimulus provided by the various scars, bars and baubles of some modifications. Yet where is the evidence that women prefer a penis that has undergone the single most common and widespread penile modification – circumcision? Sexual taboos being what they are, it's at least possible that such a preference exists but is not talked about publicly. However, there's little or no folklore to suggest it does: we don't hear many jokes hinting at it, we don't read articles proclaiming the glories of circumcision in women's magazines (despite their general willingness to publicise any other sexual subject) and, in my research for this book, I was unable to find a single credible scientific source that even hinted at solid evidence of a universal female preference for the removal of the foreskin. I was easily able to find plenty of persuasive material from anti-circumcision activists, several of whom assert that a circumcised penis is likely to have drier, thicker and tougher skin than an uncircumcised one and is thus likely to be more abrasive to the vagina. If that is true, why would women prefer a penis likely to make sex less pleasurable, even painful?

Circumcision has deep historic, and perhaps even prehistoric, origins. The ancient Egyptians recorded it, and the practice is also known to date back many centuries among Moslems, Jews and Aborigines. There's also no doubt that circumcision has long carried great cultural or religious significance to its advocates. Indeed, Australian prehistorian David Horton defines circumcision simply as: 'One of the steps on the way to becoming a man in most parts of Australia.'[9] But it has even wider significance as a rite of passage and as a sign of special group membership for some Aborigines. He adds: 'It is seen as being a highly significant marker of cultural difference both by people who do and do not circumcise. For those who do, it is a very important step along the path from boyhood to adulthood. It is also important in later life, since involvement in the circumcision ceremony is based on kinship, and the relationships resulting from roles played in the ceremony add dimension to kinship obligations (e.g. it might impose the responsibility of later finding a wife for the initiated boy).'

Circumcision removes the foreskin, or prepuce, covering the penis's head, or glans. The foreskin folds in on itself to make a double protective hood for the glans and is lined with mucous membranes. Despite claims that it is merely a redundant tag of flesh, opponents of the practice argue that the foreskin is in fact a highly specialised piece of tissue that serves many useful purposes.

Hardline critics assert that circumcision is nothing short of genital mutilation and a socially approved form of assault.

The National Organization to Halt the Routine Mutilation of Men (NOHARMM), in the US, argues that the foreskin keeps the tip of the penis soft, moist and sensitive; it contains many hundreds of nerve endings that enhance sexual pleasure; it enables the penis skin to comfortably reach full stretch during erection; and that its mucous membranes make intercourse less traumatic (and so reduces the chance of vaginal and penile abrasions that may provide entry points for germs). Cutting it off in infancy exposes the glans to chafing – especially against a urine-soaked nappy – and gradually leads to the thickening of its skin and hence loss of sensitivity. Post-operative scarring on the shaft of the penis can also make it less sensitive and, at worst, leave it unsightly, misshapen or deformed. NOHARMM also cites research suggesting that the average adult-male foreskin laid flat would have a total surface area of about 100 square centimetres (15 square inches), and that its removal thus constitutes the loss of about half of the penile skin and at least a thousand delicate nerve endings. All in all, a man may pay a heavy price in loss of pleasure.

Debate about the relative merits of circumcision goes back a long way, notes Edward O. Laumann, who heads the department of sociology at the University of Chicago.[10] In the fifth century BC, the Greek historian Herodotus recorded why the Egyptians did it: 'They practice circumcision for the sake of cleanliness, considering it better to be clean than comely.' Jews copied circumcision from the Egyptians, but it was banned – under punishment of death – by the ancient Greeks. In a sort of prelude to the understandable but odd fringe movement today for men to try to 'reverse' their circumcisions by stretching their penile skin, some Jews apparently tried to conform to Greek law by doing likewise with a special weight known as the *pondus Judaeus*.

In Victorian times, circumcision was credited with all manner of moral and medical benefits, from curing epilepsy to the prevention of masturbation – a view espoused by John Harvey Kellogg, better known for his association with breakfast cereal. Ironically, Laumann's research group has found evidence that circumcision may actually encourage the very thing Kellogg and others were trying to deter: 'Contrary to the Victorian notion that circumcision weakens the sex drive and prevents masturbation, we found that circumcised men actually engage in a somewhat more elaborate repertoire of sexual practices than uncircumcised men do. In particular, among whites the likelihood of a circumcised man masturbating at least once a month was 1.76 times that of an uncircumcised man; the lifetime odds of a circumcised white male receiving oral sex were similarly elevated.'

Seeking more frequent or more arousing penile stimulation certainly fits the claim that a circumcised penis loses sensitivity during vaginal sex. But there may be an up-side to this as well. Laumann's group has also found evidence that circumcised men aged 45 to 60 seem to suffer fewer sexual problems, including impotence, anxiety about sexual performance and loss of enjoyment in sex. He speculates that circumcised men might by then have had more practice with 'alternative routes to stimulation and have more options for expressing their sexuality should they encounter difficulties'.

As sounder health reasons for the removal of the foreskin became known during this century, it came to be increasingly performed as a routine medical procedure on newborn boys. For example, I am the youngest of four brothers born in England between 1944 and 1952. My eldest brother and I are both circumcised because we were born in hospital, where the surgery was routine, whereas my other two brothers were born at home and were not circumcised, apparently because midwives did not do so. However, conflicting scientific views led to different circumcision trends on either side of the Atlantic after World War II.

In Britain, circumcision rates fell after an influential 1949 report by a physician, Douglas Gairdner, questioned the medical value of the operation on newborns and suggested that it might cause harm; by the mid-1980s, the British circumcision rate for newborn boys was less than 10 per cent. But in the US, another 1949 report, again by a physician, Eugene Hand, suggested that circumcised men were less likely to be infected with venereal disease, and it led to a surge in circumcision rates. The operation's popularity in the US seems to have peaked in the 1960s when up to 90 per cent of all newborn boys were circumcised. But as doubts about the medical validity of the operation emerged, its popularity there also declined sharply. Even so, circumcision was still the most commonly performed surgical procedure in the US in 1992, when six out of 10 newborn boys had the operation.

It was also popular in Australia and Canada in the post-war era. Many of my Australian men friends of the 'baby boomer' generation are circumcised, but almost to a man they have decided not to have their sons similarly treated: less than 20 per cent of Australian boys are now circumcised at birth. British, Canadian and Australian medical associations during the 1990s all published papers advising against routine circumcision of newborns.

Malcolm Potts and Roger Short argue that while female circumcision seems to have arisen solely as a crude physical assertion of male power over female reproduction, male circumcision may have originated as a preventative health measure.[11] For the ancient Egyptians, for example, circumcision 'may have been a wise precaution in a desert environment to prevent sand getting under the prepuce and setting up an inflammatory reaction. When Australian troops were sent to fight in the desert during World War II, many who were uncircumcised developed an acute inflammation of the glans penis (balanitis) and had to be circumcised.' American troops fighting in comparable conditions were often routinely circumcised for the same reason. Potts and Short point as well to recent studies suggesting a lower incidence of HIV infection among circumcised men in Africa, and of other sexually transmitted diseases elsewhere.

But in the light of today's understanding of public health and hygiene, and the availability of antibiotic drugs, the supposed benefits of circumcision now carry less weight with the medical establishment. The latest word on that score was from the American Academy of Pediatrics (AAP), a taskforce of which reviewed 40 years of research into circumcision before issuing new recommendations on 1 March 1999. The AAP said any benefits circumcision provided were not significant enough to recommend it as a routine procedure. 'Circumcision is not essential to a child's well-being at birth, even though it does have some potential medical benefits,' said the taskforce head, Carole Lannon, clinical associate professor of pediatrics and internal medicine at the University of North Carolina. 'These benefits are not compelling enough to warrant the AAP to recommend routine newborn circumcision. We encourage parents to discuss the benefits and risks of circumcision with their pediatrician and then make an informed decision about what is in the best interest of their child.'

The policy statement concluded, however, that it is legitimate for parents to take into account cultural, religious and ethnic traditions, in addition to medical factors, when making this decision. For the first time, the AAP recommended also that it is essential to provide pain relief for circumcision. In hindsight, it seems remarkable that doctors did not previously believe that pain relief was necessary for an operation on an infant organ so clearly designed to be sensitive.

The recommendations supersede those issued by the AAP in 1989, which concluded that newborn male circumcision did have potential medical advantages, based on research exploring links between circumcision, urinary tract infections and sexually transmitted diseases, particularly AIDS. The 1989 recommendations were widely interpreted – rightly or wrongly – as being a continuing imprimatur for the operation. But more recent studies have shown that although the relative risk of developing a urinary tract infection in the first year of life *is* higher for uncircumcised boys, their absolute risk of developing such an infection is low – at most, a 1 in 100 chance.

There is strong evidence, however, that the risk of an uncircumcised man developing a disease with far more serious consequences – penile cancer – is more than three times higher than that of a circumcised man. But then again, this cancer is extremely rare, with no more than 1 case diagnosed a year for each 100,000 men in the US. And penile cancer rates vary widely from region to region, in ways that seem to bear little relation to circumcision rates. On that basis alone, it is likely that other medical or environmental factors are more important than circumcision in the development of penile cancer. The AAP also points out that a man's circumcision status is of only minor relevance to his risk of catching syphilis or HIV; his sexual behaviour is far more important. In short, being circumcised is a trivial protection if you don't use a condom.

Meanwhile, there's much new evidence that circumcising newborn boys without anesthetic causes them pain and stress (as measured by changes in heart rate, blood pressure, oxygen saturation and hormone levels) and that the experience may cause them to react more strongly to the pain of later immunisations than those who are uncircumcised.

Circumcision is generally a safe procedure. Statistically, complications occur at a rate of between 1 in 200 and 1 in 500 with babies – and problems are most often minor, usually mild bleeding and local infection. The rare exceptions, of course, can have tragic consequences.

An estimated 15 per cent of all men (or about 450 million individuals) today have been circumcised. Why has it been so widely done? It seems on balance that, for whatever practical reasons it may have begun, it is more likely to have continued because of its appeal to men, not to women. There's widespread evidence from very different and geographically distant cultures of the overwhelming involvement of adult men in regulating and performing the operation on younger males.

In that sense, it has more in common with female circumcision than at first seems the case. Many traditional circumcision ceremonies among widely dispersed cultures are imbued with the idea that through this practice the boy or youth is being ritually 'killed' and reborn into a new social class, giving the circumciser a symbolic power of life and death over him. His subsequent admission to the ranks of manhood or a special group, with all the social bonds and rights that can entail, surely gives the circumciser a measure of power over the novice's reproductive potential as well. It is telling, for example, that Walbiri tradition demanded that a boy be circumcised at puberty, that he could not marry without being circumcised, and that his circumciser (as in some other Aboriginal tribes) assumed the duty of later finding a wife for his charge. There are no clear-cut scientific answers here, but male circum-cision has all the hallmarks of men trying to gain social power by exerting control over lower-status males.

And here's a final twist in the tale. The fact that millions of men who have had their penises 'modified' in many ways can still enjoy a rich and satisfying – if not fully natural – sex life shows not just that the penis is complex and resilient but that there's much, much more to male sexuality than just this one organ. Despite what many men may think, the penis is just a bit player in what defines their gender and in how they experience sex and being male.

9

IMPOTENCE: What lowers the flag

'Smoking, smoking, smoking!'

James Barada, urologist

One of the many witticisms that sped briefly along the well-worn smutty joke trail at my all-male secondary school went like this: *Question* – What's the lightest part of the human body? *Answer* – The penis, because you can lift it with just your imagination.

Well, yes and no. When you're a healthy young man, getting an erection can seem that effortless. A twinkling eye here, a dash of fantasy there, a quick surge of excitement and within seconds, to paraphrase the old sea shanty, it's hooray and up he rises. But later in life, a man may find to his dismay that no amount of imagination will budge the thing: it resolutely dangles in the general direction of his feet.

Now that impotence is emerging from the closet in many societies, it is timely to look afresh at why, despite its canny design, the penis can and does fail to work sometimes. Although we still have a lot to learn about erections, we do know that they are second nature to men from the very earliest stages of their lives. And now that we can peer into the womb, we know they start even before a boy is born. Some parents are surprised to find that their sons are born with an erection, or have one soon after birth. And it doesn't usually take long for a male infant to discover that the little thing down there feels good to play with, even more so when it stiffens and becomes more sensitive.

Later in life, most men are aware that their penises sometimes become erect when they are asleep – usually for no apparent reason. In fact, the phenomenon is so common and predictable that therapists can use nocturnal erections as an early line of inquiry into whether a man's impotence has a physical or psychological origin. A man who is unable to get an erection during sex yet clearly does so routinely while asleep is unlikely to have a physical problem. Sleep studies show that the average healthy man has four or five of these erections a night, each lasting about 15 minutes. That's a total of about an hour a day. Or look at it this way: if a man does this nightly for 70 years (although nocturnal erections happen less often as he ages), he will spend a total of more than 25,000 hours – almost 3 years of his life – with his penis erect. So perhaps it's even lighter than that old joke suggests, since you can lift it without even the effort of imagination while you're fast asleep.

Impotence is defined as the inability to maintain an erection that is rigid enough and lasts long enough to permit sexual intercourse. It has nothing much to do with infertility, although many people still confuse the two. This confusion is a good reason why the medical world has come to use the term 'erectile dysfunction', or ED for short, to describe impotence. The word 'impotence' also conveys a range of negative meanings, all emphasising a loss of power, ability, force or effectiveness. My dictionary gives one meaning as being a male 'wholly lacking in sexual power'. Clearly, that's not the sort of label many men would choose to be tagged with, nor does it accurately or specifically describe the inability to achieve a reliable erection for intercourse. Sexual power in men and women has many sources and finds many ways to express itself. So although 'erectile dysfunction' is clinical and lacks the colour of everyday language (such as the 'floppy', 'half-master' and 'brewer's droop'), I'll use ED here instead of 'impotence' for its greater precision of meaning.

All men experience failed erections at some time in their lives, particularly when they are tired, distracted, ill, under stress or affected by alcohol. But ED is different, in that it's not a briefly passing thing. If it has a physical cause, it can be permanent. And even if the cause is psychological there's no certainty that normal erections will return, even with the help of therapy.

While it's not common, ED certainly isn't rare. It is estimated, for example, that up to 20 million men in the US alone are afflicted with it (with perhaps another 10 million having partial erection problems). In a population of about 133 million men, that means ED affects more than one man in every seven. Globally, as the new millennium gets under way, about 50 million men are estimated to be affected. Of course, the rate of ED is not static through all age groups – it becomes increasingly common with age. At 40 years old, about 5 per cent of men have ED, increasing to 15–25 per cent at age 65 and older. Up to half of all men over 75 are affected. Because these rates depend to some extent on lifestyle factors, they vary from place to place; the US figures reflect one of the unwanted realities of an affluent society.

Despite a widely held perception that psychological problems – or waning sex drive – are largely to blame, 8 out of 10 cases of ED are due mainly to physical problems, according to Irwin Goldstein, a professor of urology at Boston University School of Medicine. The effects of aging, alcoholism, diabetes (up to half of diabetic men have ED), hardening of the arteries and the side-effects of some drugs are known risks. Indeed, there's growing evidence that ED is not so much age-related as health-related, and that it's more common in old age largely because that's when a man's health generally declines. Thus, it is also linked to affluence because affluent men not only live longer but have the health problems that come with the consumption of too much fatty food, tobacco and alcohol, and lack of exercise.

ED is usually the result of another problem, so in that sense it is a symptom, not a disease. Of course, this also means it can be an early warning sign of a more serious medical problem. It has a wide variety of causes, some common and some very rare. Among the most common are the so-called vascular diseases – those to do with the 'plumbing' side of erections. Hardening of the arteries, smoking and diabetes can reduce blood flow to the penis to below the level needed to sustain an erection. Asked what he considered to be the main cause of ED, James Barada, an American urologist involved in formulating treatment guidelines for the condition, answered with three words: 'Smoking, smoking, smoking!'.

Diabetes can also damage the nerve endings in the penis, so that they do not respond normally to sexual stimulus. Likewise, ED can result from other 'wiring' problems related to nerve damage from injuries to the spinal cord or brain, or from neurological diseases such as Parkinson's, Alzheimer's and multiple sclerosis. Sometimes it is an unavoidable or accidental side-effect of nerve damage resulting from surgery or radiation to the prostate gland, bladder, rectum or large intestine.

♂ Herman's story

Herman, a 62-year-old South African business executive, has a strong sex drive, and a lively sexual relationship with his wife of 30 years has always been very important to him. Things changed suddenly 5 years ago when a routine medical examination revealed cancer in his prostate gland. Here he reflects on the subsequent decline of his sexual powers and pleasures, and on his new perspective on life.

'Sex has been very important in my life, probably more so than for other people. I was an early starter and lived through the era of the Pill, the pre-AIDS generation and so on, when sleeping around was more socially acceptable.

'When my biopsy tested positive for prostate cancer it really took the wind out of my sails. I didn't know what the bloody thing was and I read as much about it as I could and discussed treatment options with a number of doctors.

'I realised that they basically knew stuff-all about it – the causes, rate of progress, how long you could live with it or anything else. The prostate is a pretty mysterious little organ.

'Anyway, the tests showed that the cancer hadn't spread so in the end I decided to have a radical prostatectomy and get the damned thing cut right out. But the statistics concerning the side-effects of the surgery were really terrible: from memory I think they said I had a 15 per cent chance of becoming incontinent and a 60–70 per cent chance of impotence.

'The thought of incontinence was worse than the thought of impotence – wearing adult nappies for the rest of my life . . . ergh!

'I can't really remember the first erection I got after the operation. I had deep anxiety about whether they'd contained the cancer, and I was much more concerned about that and the catheter in my penis.

'That had to stay in place for about three weeks. It was really undignified and painful. I had a few dribbles for a while after that but happily that's completely gone now, although I still have concerns about incontinence when I'm older.

'As for impotence, well, I discovered that the medical definition of that is a joke. That's one of the reasons I agreed to talk to you. They say you're not impotent if you can get an erection capable of penetrating a vagina 50 per cent of the time.

'On that definition, I'm not impotent. But I regard myself as having a much-diminished sexual capacity now. I still wake up in the night with a pretty solid erection but that's about the only time it's like that.

'Orgasmic sensation is seriously diminished as well. I still climax and have an orgasm but there's no ejaculation. The real fireworks just don't happen.

'You still want sex just as much as ever but the spirit and flesh relationship just isn't there any longer. The body doesn't respond in the same anxious fashion that it once did. And it's not as if I have a young demanding wife.

'Prostate cancer is still a subject men don't talk about much, even though it's had a bit higher profile in the media in recent years. Worse still, men tend to joke about it – until it happens to them. Women discuss breast cancer in great detail and know all about it.

'It's obviously a cultural thing. There's a great deal of sensitivity among men about sex. And when they do talk about it they tend to overstate their ability.

'Look at those surveys that show a lot of men who've had prostate surgery later claim they don't have impotence problems, but when you ask their wives they all say the opposite.

'I play cards regularly with a bunch of fellows about my age. I didn't mention it to them. They'd make the odd joke about it but I let it pass. They didn't offend me but I couldn't join in the laughter. Then one day I told them. I said: "Listen, you should grow up. This could happen to you."

'Even now they still don't like to talk about it as a group, but I notice that they've come to me on their own and want to talk about it one-to-one. A relative of one of them is now dying of it and that's brought it home to them.

'You realise that life's a gamble. I'd have hated it to happen to me when I was any younger. I guess it just makes you a little more disinterested – not uninterested – in the world around you.'

On the chemistry side, some prescription drugs, especially those used to treat high blood pressure or depression, are also sometimes responsible. More rarely, ED can result from hormonal imbalances, such as lowered testosterone levels. Stress and anxiety play a key role in only about 20 per cent of ED cases, although they undoubtedly contribute to problems in many more, according to Goldstein. A few failed erections can certainly dampen a man's confidence and start a cycle of performance anxiety that only makes matters worse. Sex therapists say that ED can also be the temporary or intermittent result of psychological or psychiatric problems.

Evidence is accumulating that ED may be an early warning sign of heart disease in particular. Research presented at the American Heart Association Scientific Sessions in late 1999 suggests that doctors should do more to investigate a man's general health in cases where ED may be the result of diseased blood vessels. 'Erectile dysfunction could be called a "penile stress test", and may be another way for detecting diseased blood vessels in much the same way that the exercise stress test, which measures electrical signals from the heart, is used to detect diseased blood vessels of the heart,' Marc R. Pritzker, of the Minneapolis Heart Institute Foundation, told the conference. 'We now understand that atherosclerosis detected in one set of blood vessels markedly increases the chances of having this form of blood vessel disease in other areas of the body including the heart, brain, legs and kidneys. Because the blood vessels that supply the penis are narrower than arteries in other areas of the body, atherosclerosis – the disease process that leads to heart attacks and strokes – may manifest itself as erectile dysfunction before the disease becomes apparent in other arteries. This provides a wonderful opportunity for strong preventive programs that could reduce the risk of heart attacks and strokes.'

Pritzker's comments were based on studies of 50 men with ED who had sought prescriptions for Viagra, and in turn were referred by their doctors for further evaluation. Although none of the men had symptoms of heart disease, 20 were found to have significant heart artery blockages. 'Our population of patients was a very select group,' he cautioned. 'We do not wish to suggest that heart disease is behind every case of erectile dysfunction. However, a man having regular sexual activity who experiences a consistent change in erectile function may be demonstrating signs of atherosclerosis where arteries become clogged and the heart muscle does not receive enough blood.' ED often precedes heart disease by a year or more. Pritzker thinks that between 30 and 50 per cent of ED cases are the result of blood vessel disease. 'The heart disease found in the study participants was treatable, and in many cases the men's erectile dysfunction went away when they quit smoking or got their cholesterol levels under control,' he says. Six of the men in the study had blockages in all three major heart arteries, seven had two arteries that showed narrowing, and one artery was blocked in another seven men.

Although the penis has an outwardly sturdy construction, its support mechanisms and inner workings are delicate and vulnerable to damage, so its capacity to achieve erections can be thwarted in many ways. Serious cyclists who regularly ride for hours at a time, for example, can suffer from the sustained pressure of a narrow, hard bicycle seat on the blood vessels or on the nerves that control the penile vein valves. Much of the connective plumbing and wiring on which the workings of the penis depend passes through the perineum, the delicate area between the scrotum and anus. Two vessels – the pudendal arteries – carry blood to the penis. After emerging from the pelvis, they branch into two smaller arteries – the dorsal and cavernous arteries – and then branch off again into even narrower arteries. Since the smallest of these are just 0.4 millimetres wide they are prone to blockage, especially for men whose lifestyles make them susceptible to diabetes and heart disease.

Injuries to the perineum certainly involve a high risk of ED. And it's no wonder; Goldstein and colleagues have calculated that a 70-kilogram man who slips off his bicycle seat onto the crossbar below while riding at about 30 kilometres an hour will suffer an eye-watering 230 kilograms of force on his perineum. Cyclists who ride on rough roads or tracks can suffer perineal injury as well by repeated, lesser trauma from the narrow nose of the bicycle seat when bumping over rocks and potholes. It may be that keen riders suffer ED problems simply as a result of compression of arteries during the extended time they spend in the saddle. Tests by Goldstein's group showed that arterial blood flow could be cut by as much as two-thirds through nothing more than the pressure of the rider's body weight, a finding confirmed more recently in a study at the Mayo Clinic. A scare rippled through the men's cycling world in 1997 when *Bicycling* magazine published articles on the issue. In one of them, Ed Pavelka, a former executive editor of the magazine, admitted that his penis had become 'as soft as overcooked rigatoni' after he clocked up about 34,000 kilometres riding in a single enthusiastic year. Goldstein believes the ideal design for a bicycle seat would be like that of a toilet seat, supporting the rider's weight without pressure on the perineum. Now that would certainly raise a few chuckles. Perhaps the more practical option is to opt for a seat that is as soft and broad as possible.

For most of last century, there was precious little progress in understanding or treating ED. Before new medical therapies, such as implants, started to come along in the post-war period, most ED men apparently went without treatment. Those who sought professional help were likely to find themselves on a couch being psychoanalysed. One study found, for example, that as recently as 1985 the number of US men being treated for ED was about 525,000, less than 1 in 20 of the actual number of men who had the problem. Another study of US war veterans found that half those who acknowledged having ED refused further evaluation and treatment.

When the only real options were a visit to a urologist with limited expertise and even more limited tools of investigation and treatment, or to a psychologist or psychiatrist – who 'did not even look to see if the patient had a penis, but treated him happily in endless sessions', as one veteran researcher puts it – men's lack of interest was understandable. Early in the twentieth century surgeons did try to help men with ED by implanting stiff pieces of bone or cartilage into their penises, but normal scavenging processes within the body meant that these were quickly broken down and absorbed. The 1940s saw the introduction of the first treatment that really worked – a surgically implantable rigid plastic strut that conferred a permanent erection, but it wasn't until the introduction of medical-grade silicone in the 1960s that a flexible implanted rod became available, according to Professor Arnold Melman, a urologist and co-editor of the *International Journal of Impotence Research*.[1]

More anatomically appropriate implants soon followed, including semi-rigid rods that are straightened by hand for an erection then tucked away into a more practical, everyday position, Melman recalls. Then there are hydraulic devices: when a bulb placed in the scrotum is manually squeezed it pushes saline solution out of a sack implanted in the abdomen and into a cylinder inside the penis. After sexual activity is completed, a release valve in the bulb allows the saline fluid to escape from the penis and return to the sack. 'The average age of a patient choosing a prosthetic is 50,' Melman says. 'Implants seldom wear out, even after decades of use; each implant carries a manufacturer's lifetime guarantee. Implants are safe and almost 100 per cent effective. In addition, the approach offers a particular advantage not present in any other impotence treatment currently on the market: [it] allows coitus without prior planning. That fact greatly increases the overall satisfaction of the men and their partners who choose this option.'

Another standby is a vacuum constriction device, which uses a pump to create a vacuum around the penis to draw blood into the organ. A constricting ring is then placed around the base of the penis to trap the blood inside it. Some men long ago discovered this helpful trick of sexual physics on their own. One 84-year-old man confided to me that he still at times has an active desire for sex but when his penis will not perform, a simple mechanical remedy is readily at hand: 'I just roll up a Kleenex tissue and tie that firmly around the base of my penis when I'm ready; it lets the blood in but doesn't let it out until I'm done.'

Now, with one male Baby Boomer reaching the problem age every few seconds somewhere in the world, erections – or the lack of them – are literally becoming a growth industry. But the accent on mechanical solutions began to change radically in the 1970s as advances in medical science and technology enlisted the services of vascular surgeons, plastic surgeons, radiologists, biochemists, clinical and neurophysiologists and especially pharmacologists. The first anti-impotence drug was discovered – as so often happens in science – as a result of a fortuitous mistake. During diagnostic tests in 1979, French surgeon Ronald Virag intended to inject saline solution into a patient's penis. Instead, he accidentally used the drug papaverine, a smooth muscle relaxant. To their mutual surprise, the man's penis became erect within minutes. 'This discovery highlighted for the first time that smooth muscle relaxation was the key erectile mechanism and set the direction for the next generation of basic research,' Melman wrote. It later became clear that relaxing the penile muscles let blood flow more freely into the organ and so engorge it.

Another extraordinary moment in the birth of this new approach occurred at a 1983 meeting of the American Urological Association in Las Vegas. An inventive and bold British doctor, Giles Brindley, dramatically stepped aside from the speaker's podium to reveal unmistakably how a shot of an experimental drug he had given himself a short time earlier had produced an upstanding erection. It was a graphic start to a new era of openness in the public discussion and treatment of what was once virtually a taboo subject. Some doctors reportedly began prescribing Brindley's treatment within weeks of his startling demonstration, even though official approval of it took some years. By 1996, American men were spending US$25 million a year on such drugs alone, despite the discomfort of having to use a needle to inject them into the penis to achieve the desired result. A variety of other devices and creams accounted for an unknown but certainly much larger market in both helpful and dubious remedies for ED.

But these were mere scene-setters for the blaze of scientific, medical and commercial interest surrounding the official release of a little blue diamond-shaped pill, the anti-ED drug sildenafil citrate, better known as Viagra. Within a fortnight of its approval by the US Food and Drug Administration on 27 March 1998, the manufacturer Pfizer saw this misnamed 'superstud' drug being sold at the rate of 40,000 a week. It is now available in more than 60 countries, and has become the preferred treatment for most erectile dysfunction cases. The total number of prescriptions written for it passed 9 million in the US alone at the time of writing, according to Pfizer; its worldwide sales are expected to reach several billions of dollars a year. Some pundits have predicted it could be the most profitable drug ever sold. Bob Guccione, the publisher of *Penthouse*, claimed that Viagra's social influence could be as great as its commercial success because it would 'free the American male libido in the same way the Pill did'. Dr Harin Padma-Nathan, director of The Male Clinic in Santa Monica, California, made a similar prediction in 1997 when he said that such oral therapies 'may have as dramatic an impact on the field of sexual medicine as the birth-control pill had on the human sexual revolution'.

Whoa! These are hefty claims, so let's briefly backtrack here and see if we can get away from the hype for a reality-check. Scientists at Pfizer's research centre at Sandwich, in the English county of Kent, discovered Viagra's beneficial effect on ED by accident in the 1980s. They had been experimenting with treatments for hypertension and angina, seeking a compound that lowered blood pressure. Sildenafil citrate failed to control abnormally high blood pressure but it soon became stark-staring obvious that the drug either enhanced or prolonged erections in male subjects; it's not the kind of side-effect you'd fail to notice. Ultrasound studies had already revealed that thickening and hardening of the arteries made erections more difficult for men, but Viagra worked by sidestepping that problem and relaxing the penile muscles, thus allowing more blood to flow in. How the process happened, however, was still a puzzle when the Pfizer scientists began developing the drug.

An unrelated line of basic scientific inquiry that began around the same time eventually provided the answer – and a curious link to urban air pollution – almost a decade later. In the early 1980s, Robert Furchgott, of the State University of New York, was puzzled that some drugs acting on blood vessels often had contradictory effects: sometimes they caused the vessels to contract and sometimes to dilate. He later showed that in order to receive a signal that causes blood vessels to dilate, the endothelial cells lining those veins and arteries have to be intact. Furchgott concluded that those cells must produce some unknown substance – which he dubbed endothelium-derived relaxing factor (EDRF) – to relax smooth muscles. In 1986, Furchgott and Louis Ignarro of the University of California, Los Angeles, independently unmasked the identity of EDRF. They told surprised colleagues that it was none other than nitric oxide, a simple gas best known as a hazardous component of smog. It was the first time a gas had been shown to have a biochemical signalling role in the body and it sparked a flurry of research that has since confirmed that nitric oxide plays a broad and potent role in many body processes. We now know, for example, that nitroglycerine is a useful treatment for heart disease because it releases nitric oxide and so relaxes heart muscles. Their discoveries earned Furchgott, Ignarro and Ferid Murad a Nobel Prize in 1998.

In 1991, the Pfizer researchers discovered that nitric oxide is a key to success in erections as well, because its presence is needed to give the go-ahead to smooth muscle cells in the penile blood vessels to relax. Viagra apparently beefs up the signal in the nerves and cells lining the corpora cavernosa (by inhibiting an enzyme that breaks down nitric oxide), letting them open far enough to permit the flow of blood. Incidentally, there's evidence that nitric oxide may play a comparable role in women: a study found that the gas is generated in the clitoris, just as it is in the penis, and so may regulate smooth muscle activity in the erection of that organ as well. Anecdotal reports suggest that at least some women who have experimentally taken Viagra have increased clitoral sensitivity as a result.

Viagra may have confirmed that ED is not all in the mind, but the popular mythology surrounding the drug suggests that many people still misunderstand what it does and what male sexual arousal is all about. It is definitely not an aphrodisiac (a drug or food that arouses sexual desire) because it acts on the chemistry of muscles, not the brain. It does not make a man want to have sex, but merely lets his sexual plumbing work more normally, and then only briefly. In general, Viagra works successfully in about 65–70 per cent of all men with ED. However, the greater the degree of damage to the normal erection mechanism, the lower the overall success rate. Men whose ED has a psychological cause have the best responses. More than half of diabetics and men with spinal cord injuries respond successfully, and more than 40 per cent of men who acquire ED after radical prostate cancer surgery – the most difficult group to treat for ED – report improved erections.

Pfizer's own research suggests that on average, Viagra will enable a man to achieve about 80 per cent of full penile rigidity for about 10 minutes. What's more, the increase in blood flow it provokes is not restricted to the penis, since the drug is circulating throughout the bloodstream and affecting the whole body. That is probably why more than a few men who take Viagra report that it also gives them headaches, swollen nasal passages and flushed skin. A few even report a mild transient change in their ability to distinguish some colours (especially blue, aptly enough considering the colour of Viagra pills) after taking the drug, an odd side-effect related to its impact on the chemistry of vision. Uncertainties remain about whether long-term high-dose use of Viagra may cause this visual effect to be a medical problem rather than just a scientific curiosity.

Despite the Viagra hype, several clinical studies have now hinted that, given a choice, a significant proportion of ED men would prefer the direct injection method, not least because it seems to offer a more rigid erection. A recent Italian study of Viagra's effects also highlights that ED is not simply a male problem but a 'couple's disease': almost a third of the steady sexual partners of the 60 men involved in the study remained dissatisfied about their sex lives despite their man being able to achieve more reliable erections. It's worth remembering that no amount of penile rigidity can kick-start a flat sex drive or be a substitute for a well-synchronised sexual relationship. It's worth noting as well that men taking nitrate compounds for cardiac problems use Viagra at the risk of worsening their heart condition – apparently not for biochemical reasons but because of the physical strain posed by the sudden and unaccustomed exertion of having sex. Even that risk, though, has not deterred some men with serious heart disease from ignoring the warnings and ending up in a morgue. It's hard to imagine a more striking illustration of the power of desire than a man prepared to die for sex.

An inability to achieve an erection is not the only problem that can affect the penis. Sometimes the opposite can happen – an erection that simply will not go away. That rare condition, known as priapism, usually has nothing to do with sexual excitement. Indeed, pleasure is said to be the last thing on the minds of men unfortunate enough to have this problem; it is almost always painful and distressing. Priapism is defined as a period of prolonged erection lasting more than six hours. It is generally the result of a plumbing problem in which blood continues flowing into the penis faster than it can escape, sometimes due to obstructions caused by large blood clots or tumours in the penis. It can also be caused by traumatic accidents that damage a penile artery, letting it bleed into the surrounding erectile tissues. Boys can have brief episodes of priapism due to full bladders, local irritation or over-enthusiastic masturbation. The medical literature records other possible causes as an inflamed urethra, urethral calcium stones, prostate gland infections and rectal parasites. Prolonged cases can arise from congenital syphilis, leukemia, or sickle cell anemia. Cocaine abuse can sometimes have this effect as well.

Ironically, injections of smooth muscle relaxants aimed at treating ED can also sometimes end up causing priapism, while some antidepressants also have the side-effect of episodes of priapism and enhanced nocturnal erections. Very rarely, exceptionally extended and rough sexual activity can cause a clot to form in the vein that vents blood away from the penis, resulting in priapism that may last for days or weeks. Case reports record that the penis is at first stiffly erect and extremely tender to touch and can remain semi-erect and painful for weeks unless early medical treatment is sought. Left untreated, once the penis returns to a flaccid state it will usually never again be able to erect normally because the erectile tissues are too scarred and damaged after their prolonged swelling.

If Viagra allows a man have sexual intercourse when he otherwise could not, that is no mean feat. In its wake the medical treatment of other sexual dysfunctions is bound to become more common and sophisticated. It is likely that in the years ahead we will see an increasing range of ever more subtle drugs and other treatments aimed at specific sexual problems, for both men and women. New delivery systems, such as nasal sprays, may help drugs to work faster. Further experimental drugs are being developed to stimulate the hypothalamus, and thus induce erection from the very start of the erectile chain of command. New therapies aimed at repairing, or even bypassing, damaged nerve pathways between the penis and the brain are likely new candidates, as are gene therapies. 'Gene therapy represents a new area of research, one for which the penis is particularly well-suited,' Melman says. 'Because the penis is external and easily accessible, a tourniquet can be readily applied (for up to 10 minutes) to prevent any injected genes from entering the rest of the body. Moreover, vascular smooth muscle cells, the probable targets for many gene therapies, have a low turnover rate, increasing the chances for the effects of the therapy to last for weeks or months. Gene therapy can be used in different ways, including the insertion of genes into penile cells to produce proteins that are lacking because of missing or defective genes. Injected DNA could also generate proteins that would make the penis more sensitive to compensate for an organic disorder.'

But the key lesson we have learned about ED from advances in medical science in recent years is a time-honoured piece of doctor's advice – an ounce of prevention is better than a pound of cure. For most aging men, staying fit, eating sensibly and going easy on alcohol and cigarettes will help keep them sexually healthy and active well into old age. It may also be obvious to you by now that there's another valuable insight to be had here, by comparing the different effects of the different ED treatments. Ronald Virag's accidental papaverine injection and Giles Brindley's dramatic display both showed unequivocally that erections can be induced without any sexual stimulation at all. As Melman points out, papaverine acts near the base of the chemical cascade needed for erection. Newer drugs act higher up in the chain, and several are now used in combination to enhance the overall effect. Viagra alone won't give you an erection unless you're sexually stimulated as well. So what does all this tell us? Not only that the process of getting an erection is more complex and subtle than was once thought, but that it's only one piece of the jigsaw of understanding men and sex. All those men who have endured surgery and then overcome their squeamishness about injecting needles into their penises to enable them to achieve erections emphasise how motivated men can be in remaining sexually active into advanced age, and how they regard the involvement of their penises as central to the expression of their sexuality. But the treatments also reveal that an erection is little more than a mechanical component of that expression. Most men with ED are still at least technically capable of achieving a sexual climax and of fathering children, and in the vast majority of cases a flaccid penis bears no relation to a man's hormonal or genetic status as a functioning male. As we'll see in the next chapter, a man plainly does not need to get an erection to be able to have either an orgasm or an ejaculation. In that sense, the age of Viagra and our new insights into ED should help us all to better understand what makes men tick.

10

AROUSAL: Why gentlemen prefer blondes

'She was so extraordinarily beautiful that I nearly laughed out loud. She . . . [was] famine, fire, destruction and plague . . . the only true begetter. Her breasts were apocalyptic, they would topple empires before they withered . . . her body was a miracle of construction . . . She was unquestionably gorgeous. She was lavish. She was, in short, too bloody much . . . Those huge violet blue eyes . . . had an odd glint . . . Eons passed, civilisations came and went while these cosmic headlights examined my flawed personality. Every pockmark on my face became a crater of the moon.'

Richard Burton

IN THE BRIGHT living room of her elegant London home, Jung Chang goes to a drawer and takes out a small object wrapped in fine fabric. She places it reverently on the coffee table between us and gently unfolds the cloth to reveal a tiny black silk slipper, beautifully embroidered with traditional Chinese designs in red and blue. 'This is one of my grandmother's shoes,' she says softly. I'd read all about it in Chang's wonderful book *Wild Swans*, yet it set me back in my seat to see it there. It was smaller than my hand and much thinner. The sole was a long thin triangle. It was lovely, fascinating and horrible, three sentiments evoked time and again as you read Chang's family story. It starts with her grandmother's birth in 1909, in the dying days of the 260-year Manchu dynasty. It tells of the turmoil that China and its people endured in ensuing decades.

The shoe is a striking symbol of how great that change was, and of much else besides. To look at it, you cannot imagine how an adult's foot could possibly fit into it. But her grandmother, Yu-fang, was subject to a strong and long-held custom when her feet were bound at the age of two. All her toes but the big one were bent inward and held under the sole of her foot with tight cloth wrapping. Stones were used to crush her arch, causing extreme, relentless, lifelong pain. It was a practice inflicted on Chinese women for a thousand years. The aim was to force their feet into a male aesthetic ideal – feet like 'three-inch golden lilies'. Crippled in this way, such women had no choice but to shuffle in tiny steps 'like a tender young willow shoot in a spring breeze'. The sight was said to induce erotic and protective feelings in men. But there was nothing sexy in the mangled, smelly reality beneath the bindings. Men rarely saw that. Beneath the bindings, a woman's feet 'were usually covered in rotting flesh and stank', Chang told me. She recalled how Yu-fang would sigh with relief as she soaked her aching feet in hot water. 'Then she would set about cutting off pieces of dead skin. The pain came not only from the broken bones, but also from her toenails, which grew into the balls of her feet.' Yu-fang led a remarkable life. Given at 15 by her father as concubine to a feudal warlord, she spent just six days with him before he left without a word for six years, leaving her a prisoner of spying servants. Only on his death could she flee with their infant daughter.

I met Chang in 1993 when I interviewed her in the course of my job as a newspaper reporter, but my encounter with Yu-fang's shoe still provokes in me a sense of wonder about the lengths to which men, and women, will go to satisfy their wants. It was also a graphic reminder that one man's meat can be another's poison. Of course, the tradition of foot-binding speaks volumes about the oppression of Chinese women at the time, but it was the perceived erotic effect on men that puzzled me most. I see nothing sexy or appealing in crippling the object of your desire, yet Chinese men apparently thought the result seductive enough for the practice to persist for a millennium. So the question of what turns a man on is by no means easy to answer and it seems to vary over time and across cultures. In 'Anything Goes', Cole Porter reminds us that a glimpse of stocking was once considered shocking. Sexual arousal and attraction are remarkable – mind and body conspire in anticipation of being rewarded with pleasure, and strange and marvellous outcomes can follow.

Women's magazines have thrived for years on exploiting their readers' curiosity about how to get men 'interested' in them. Their hopes and dreams have been fed a steady diet of advice – how to look, what to wear, what to say, what to cook, how to behave and so on – about supposed sure-fire ways to a man's heart. But the magazines aimed at heterosexual men are far less coy on the question of attraction: their overworked but successful strategy (just think of the endurance of *Playboy*) seems ample evidence that the heart is not the organ at issue, and that many a man's sexual fire can be kindled quickly and simply by the sight of exposed female flesh.

The contrast between the two types of magazine is stark. The first targets romance, appearance, personality, relationship and an intimate and complete meeting of mind and body. The second centres on shallow impersonal fantasy about sex with a total stranger – mere anatomy is the cue. Either type of magazine could give the distinct impression that what turns a man on is not just well known but also well understood. That is far from true. The folklore of male sexual arousal is narrow, skewed and often defective.

'In the old popular belief, the sexual impulse was viewed as a biological drive or instinct,' Erick Janssen and Walter Everaerd, of the Department of Clinical Psychology at the University of Amsterdam explain.[1] 'It was seen as the expression of a "need of evacuation" (of male semen), or as a biologically driven impulse to reproduce.' This pressure-cooker view of male sexual arousal is understandable. People the world over have long observed that puberty can plunge a teenage boy into a stormy sea of pressing sexual thoughts and powerful longings, that men are generally quicker than women to become aroused, that they generally want to have sex more often, that they reach orgasm during intercourse sooner and more reliably than women, that they are more likely than their spouses to seek out affairs and that they are more likely to retain an active interest in sex into old age.

But as one early sex researcher put it in the 1950s, 'no genuine tissue or biological needs are generated by sexual abstinence . . . What is commonly confused with a primary drive associated with sexual deprivation is in actuality sexual appetite, and this has little or no relation to biological or physiological needs.' In other words, a man may want to have sex but it's certainly not going to kill him if he doesn't get it. By contrast, think of the dire consequences that can follow if he fails to satisfy needs that unquestionably have a biological basis, such as eating or sleeping. Consider as well the fact that he may still want sex even when it is physically impossible for him to have it. Men who have been castrated, who are impotent or quadriplegic can and do still have lively sexual appetites. Then there's the flipside, where men who are perfectly capable of having sex physically may have little or no desire for it – men with psychological problems, such as chronic depression, or men who choose a life of celibacy for religious reasons. Sexual appetites vary greatly in intensity between men, and within individuals at different times. There is no universal sexual appetite ticking away inside every man, nor does it always turn over at the same pace. Yet it is true that the overwhelming majority of men desire and actively seek out sex, and very few fail to get it. That more than 90 per cent of men find a mate at some stage of their lives underlines the near-universal nature of their sex drive: various studies have shown that virtually all men (and only slightly fewer women) report that they have experienced sexual arousal.

A man's sexual response system can be thought of as a 'complex triad involving physiological, psychological . . . and behavioural components', say Janssen and Everaerd, adding that some of the folklore of male sexuality does have a basis in fact. Men are born with a strong inbuilt capacity for sexual arousal. With the help of new technologies that allow a growing fetus to be observed we now know, for example, that boys can get their first erections months before they are born. Male babies can also get erections within minutes of birth and their penises often become firmly erect while nursing. These are not examples of precocious sexual desire, since they clearly don't occur in a sexual context.

Other evidence points to the fact that even very young boys can experience sexually pleasurable sensations. Since the 1930s studies have reported that infant boys will readily manipulate their genitals and that they may smile and coo when they do so, and even react with body movements that indicate they are experiencing orgasm. More than a few dismayed parents have witnessed similar events while bathing their infant boys, or have discovered their toddler son lying on his stomach happily rubbing his penis rhythmically against a nappy or his bedding. Older boys who have not reached puberty can masturbate and reach orgasm (indeed, they may be more easily orgasmic than adult men) although they are not yet capable of producing sperm or ejaculating. While that would seem to clinch the popular idea that men are born with a ready-to-go sexual appetite, what happens to that system later in life makes it plain that it is far more complex than that. As Janssen and Everaerd point out, 'it is clear that as age increases, psychological and social factors become progressively more important determinants of the responsivity of the sexual system'.

Most healthy men are aware that their penises become erect several times a night when they are asleep, usually for no apparent reason, but no one is sure why this happens. We do know, however, that these erections coincide with phases of fairly shallow REM (rapid eye movement) sleep, which is also when we dream. Men often wake in the morning after one of these REM phases, still with a so-called 'morning glory' erection. Researchers at the Kinsey

Institute for Research in Sex, Gender and Reproduction are studying this curious trait in the hope that it might provide a window into the way sexual impulses are managed by the brain. The institute's director, Professor John Bancroft, notes that human sexual responses seem to be under 'dual control' by two opposing forces. We usually respond positively, of course, to pleasurable stimuli from the senses, such as the thrill of the touch and sight of a familiar lover. But it's also plain that we can respond in the opposite way to negative stimuli, such as the doubt or fear we might experience from having sex with a new partner or from not using contraceptives.

Bancroft is interested in nocturnal erections because he is trying to learn more about the inhibitory role played by norepinephrin, a chemical messenger involved in the transmission of nerve impulses in the brain. He says there is no doubt that norepinephrin is involved in inhibiting sexual responses and that, in men, it effectively puts the brakes on erections. It seems to do so by dampening the sexual arousal messages that travel from a site in the brain, known as the locus caeruleus, to the penis and other parts of the body. During REM sleep, Bancroft explains, the locus caeruleus virtually switches off, so it seems likely that this takes the brakes off the erection process. That would not fully explain why the erections occur, he says, but it does give some insight into how they happen.

During his teens, erections can seem mysterious indeed to a young man. One of my tennis mates and I were talking in the pub after our usual weekly game, about our early teenage years and the dubious delights of being an adolescent male. 'Oh God, I'll never forget it,' he said, with a hearty roar of laughter. 'I was like an inferno – I couldn't stop. I thought it would fall off at one stage. I was supposed to be studying in my bedroom at night and I could just feel it come up under the desk and I knew I wouldn't be able to concentrate. So I'd duck off to the bathroom and get rid of it. Then I'd have to do it again before I went to bed to make sure it didn't wake me up in the night. It was relentless.' When our sexual urges awoke within us, we felt a bit like Rip Van Winkle – the world had changed, beyond our ken or control. Girls, in particular, seemed to have metamorphosed overnight into the most desirable and bewildering creatures we had ever laid eyes on. We suddenly thought about them, fantasised about them and wanted them in ways we had never before imagined. And since we had motive – truckloads of motive – and very little opportunity to do anything about these aching desires, masturbation was the most common outlet for them.

I recalled how two boys newly arrived from Scotland had come to our school; they were twin brothers who had previously been at boarding school. There they had learned the dark secret of self-abuse and were only too willing to pass on this remarkable knowledge. It was like a virulent contagion passing through my classmates over the next few weeks. They were suddenly spending longer in the toilet or developing a hitherto unknown interest in the clandestine study of nature in the bushland beside the school. Pretty soon some of them were doing it warily in company, even blatantly in groups, and some individuals began boasting about not merely having done it the previous night, but of how many times. Gales of laughter greeted the most enthusiastic convert when he arrived at school one morning holding up six fingers: his hair was tousled, his clothes crumpled, his eyes were bloodshot and he looked a wreck from lack of sleep. That incident seemed to be a turning point for many of us: the fever had peaked, and from then on it was rarely so intense.

More than 30 years on, I can't for the life of me remember what it was that had us all so slavishly worked up (thankfully, my hormonal peaks and troughs now aren't nearly as extreme). It was partly group-think, partly the dawning realisation that we had arrived on the threshold of adulthood, partly the thrill of something secret and rebellious. Mainly, though, sex was a wondrous new source of fun. It seemed that we had discovered an amazing capacity in ourselves for an indefinable physical and mental pleasure we had only heard gossiped about before. So this was what all the fuss was about!

More recently I watched in awe as our family dog went through a similar phase once he discovered the same joys: for a while he caused us no end of embarrassment by his eagerness to mount the legs of visitors to our home and start thrusting. What was striking about our dog's behaviour (and in retrospect the sexual urges of my teenage years) was how readily and easily it seemed to be sparked off. It took only the slightest stimulus to excite him, and it didn't need to be anything to do with female dogs. One day near my home I was astonished to see a male dog happily attempting to copulate with an empty plastic garbage bin that had fallen on its side: he had mounted the bin and was rolling it back and forth, rubbing his exposed penis against it and seeming perfectly content with the arrangement. I also recall a teenage friend being a little frightened by the fact that he had ejaculated for the first time in his sleep – a 'wet dream'. And it is indeed unsettling to discover that this arousal can seem to happen all by itself.

Many male animals require only an approximate stimulus to prompt them to initiate sexual behaviour, regardless of the context: a well-known scientific example was recorded in the 1980s when a male *Bombyx* moth was observed reflexively trying to copulate with a piece of filter paper soaked in a female sex pheromone. The cane toad, *Bufo marinus*, is infamous in Australia for attempting to copulate with dead female toads flattened by cars, and for invading garden ponds and mounting goldfish so enthusiastically that they have drowned the poor fish. More recently Benjamin Sachs, a psychologist at the University of Connecticut, has shown experimentally that at least one mammal, the rat, can get erections simply from being exposed to the smell of a female in estrus. The rats got erections from her scent alone, whether or not they could see or hear her and whether or not they were sexually naive or experienced.[2]

That may help to explain why many male mammals seem to be on a shorter sexual fuse than females. This certainly seems to be the case in humans. Smell, in the form of chemical compounds known as pheromones, is known to play an important signalling role in mammal behaviour. Many males and females mark their territories or signal their presence and/or reproductive state through non-volatile scents in urine and secretions from glands. Sniffing and licking these secretions is known to promote sexual arousal and mating behaviour. Sachs's finding is the first to link volatile airborne odours to sexual arousal in mammals and so, in one sense, these are the first scientifically confirmed aphrodisiacs. This is doubly intriguing because, as Sachs points out, there's ample evidence that male rats and men have similar sexual mechanisms: 'Suffice to say that across the large evolutionary gap between rodents and humans there has been a striking conservation of relevant elements, including the basic anatomy of the penis, the mechanics of erection, and the neural structures regulating erection.'

Animal breeders know from experience that pheromones are involved in some way in mammal reproduction. Pig breeders, for example, can bring sows to puberty earlier than normal by placing them in the same pen as a boar for about 30 minutes daily, even if the boar has been vasectomised. Boar pheromones will induce a sow in estrus to freeze stock-still, enabling the boar to mount her and induce her to mate with him. Recent research supports the widespread suspicion that pheromones may also play a role in human reproduction. It has been suggested recently as well that girls with doting dads reach puberty later than those whose fathers are very distant or often absent, possibly through less exposure to pheromones or through stress reactions from contact with unrelated males, although the research did not consider possible maternal influences.

Some women are sensitive to what they say is a characteristic and strong 'male' odour, especially notable in adolescents. Whether this reflects poorer hygiene, less use of artificial perfumes or a rampant sex pheromone is unclear. Some researchers claim, with varying degrees of experimental evidence, to have found such substances and some are already on sale as sexual attractants. It is assumed that the evolutionary retention of pubic and armpit hair in humans relates in some way to their capacity to trap odours. Given the commercial potential of human sex pheromones, it seems a certainty that if and when they are isolated in the future they will find a large and ready market.

Men also seem to crave a variety of sexual partners, more so than females. David M. Buss, a psychologist at the University of Michigan with a special interest in the evolution of sex, suggests that this craving may be an ancient psychological solution to the differing reproductive interests of males and females. A study of American college students, for example, found that at every stage of their lives men would ideally like to have more sex partners than women would. Asked to nominate, for instance, how many sex partners they would like to have in the next year, male students on average wanted 6 while female students wanted just 1. Over a lifetime, the men said they ideally would like an average of 18 partners, while women wanted only 4 or 5. Likewise, men seem to need a much briefer getting-to-know-you period than women before they are ready to have sex. The same study found that men and women were equally likely to say they would have sex with a desirable partner they had known for five years, but the shorter the length of acquaintance, the less likely women were to feel that way. 'Five years or six months – it's all the same to men,' Buss says. 'They express equal eagerness for sex with women they have known for either length of time. In contrast, women drop from probably consenting to sex after five years' acquaintance to neutral feelings about sex after knowing a person for six months.'[3]

Of course, evolutionary forces might have little or nothing to do with this result. It could be argued, for example, that it reveals men as self-indulgent and irresponsible when it comes to satisfying their sexual desires or committing themselves to relationships, or that they are simply making the most of their grip on social power to do more as they please: that's for gender politicians to debate. Even so, science can offer plenty of fodder for discussion. As mentioned earlier, for example, females of many mammal species are now known to initiate sexual activity far more than previously thought. In one sense, that shouldn't be surprising because a male mammal needs to be highly motivated to engage in sex. He often must expend energy searching out females, competing with other males for access to them, then be aroused enough to achieve and maintain an erection, be enthused enough to insert his penis into a female's vagina and to thrust long enough to achieve an ejaculation of sperm. It's a big ask, when you look at it like that. A clear invitation from a similarly motivated female certainly can't hurt in making the effort seem worthwhile.

Sexual arousal in men is nothing if not rich in its complexity and variety of individual tastes. Yet it does follow some common trends; underlying patterns of behaviour can be found, and it is from them that we gain scientific insights into the process. For starters, there's the technical side, the details of which are pretty consistent from man to man. When a normal healthy man becomes sexually aroused, his brain, spinal cord, blood vessels, nerves, hormones and penis go through some well-recognised and consistent stages. Regardless of what starts the process – a lover's naked body and delicate touch, a vivid memory or sheer fantasy – the ensuing response follows a well-defined and familiar pattern. His breath quickens and his heart beats faster, his blood pressure rises, his body surface warms up due to the extra blood in his skin capillaries and his nerves carry go-ahead messages from the brain to his penis, which engorges with blood. His sensitivity to touch increases, his sensitivity to pain decreases, his nipples harden and so on. The rhythmic thrusting of intercourse stimulates nerve endings and amplifies the intensity of these and other events. Soon the muscles in the scrotum contract and raise the scrotum closer to his torso, the muscles in his epididymis and vas deferens also contract and move his sperm through the vas, secretions from the seminal vesicle and prostate gland mix with the oncoming sperm and he reaches a climax. The muscular contractions of his ejaculation give rise to a flood of pleasurable feelings and a release of tension, followed by a release of blood from the penis and an overall sense of warmth and tiredness. Within a few minutes the rest of his anatomy returns to normal, though he is unable to achieve a new erection and ejaculate again for at least 10 minutes but usually up to an hour – the so-called refractory period. His testosterone levels drop after orgasm.

That's the bare-bones description of male sexual arousal and its successful resolution. But if you've ever tried explaining those events to one of your kids you'll know how difficult it is to describe, not least because it is such a subjective and highly personal experience. Many parents resort to comparing it all to a sneeze. After all, they both involve an initial ticklish feeling, followed by a build-up of anticipation and muscular tension, then a climactic release. But parents aren't the only ones struggling to come to terms with the idea of orgasm, or to see parallels with sneezing. Indeed, the whole concept of orgasm is being questioned and redefined scientifically as a result of studies involving men and women who have suffered spinal injuries, and of research into unwanted side-effects of some surgical and drug treatments. Beverley Whipple – best-known for popularising the discovery of the G-spot in the 1980s – has spent many years investigating human sexual responses at Rutgers University in the US. The surprising results of her recent research involving women with spinal injuries have made her one of the chief protagonists of an emerging new view of orgasm. With Dr Barry Komisaruk, she has reported that women with complete spinal-cord injuries experience orgasm. Stimulation to sensitive parts of the body above the point of the injury – the breasts, neck and face, for example – can trigger the tell-tale build-up of muscular tension and release that is experienced as a pleasurable orgasm.

Rather than a term associated only with sexual climax, Whipple argues that orgasm should be used more generically to describe any bodily process involving the characteristic build-up and sudden release of muscular tension. A sneeze, she says, should be seen as a 'respiratory orgasm'. A yawn might fit the bill as well.

Despite popular conceptions to the contrary, male orgasm can and does occur independently of both erection and ejaculation: it is a mostly cerebral event. As Richard Millard, a urologist at the University of New South Wales, lightheartedly puts it, most people don't appreciate that 'orgasm is what occurs between your ears and ejaculation is what makes the wet patch in the bed that nobody wants to sleep in'.

A recent review by William Dunsmuir and Mark Emberton of research into the male sexual climax raises as many questions as it answers.[4] 'Although probably essential for the survival of the species, very little is known about male orgasm,' the authors say. Drug side-effects reinforce the idea that erection, ejaculation and orgasm can be distinct from each other. As many as 1 in 5 men taking antidepressants, such as the much-publicised Prozac, find that the drug can prevent orgasm but not ejaculation. Some men who lose penile sensation as a result of surgery report that they can experience normal orgasmic sensation with or without simultaneous ejaculation, as do some men with Parkinson's disease and multiple sclerosis. After prostate surgery, many men lose their ability to experience orgasm: a total prostatectomy leaves about 80 per cent of men without the ability to reach orgasm.

Operations on the spinal cord can sometimes cause a loss of orgasmic sensation as well but – as with the women studied by Whipple and Komisaruk – the site of the surgery seems to determine whether this happens or not. Dunsmuir and Emberton speculate that 'certain areas of the brain have intense electrical activity during orgasm. Indeed, orgasm can be induced by direct stereotactic stimulation of the septal nucleus, the area of greatest activity during orgasm.'[5] Complex neural interactions seem to occur during male orgasm, they suggest, along with subtle chemical changes in specific parts of the brain: upset that system in some way and it may not be possible for it to reach its usual conclusion.

Naturally, our old friend testosterone comes into play with sexual arousal, helping to maintain and regulate the sex drive. Testosterone can have marked effects on both male and female libido. But when alcohol enters the arousal equation, the effect is markedly different. The male tactic of plying a woman with drink to encourage her to have sex has a solid basis in sexual chemistry. In a study of women aged 18–35, Peter Eriksson of the National Public Health Institute in Helsinki found that their testosterone levels rose quickly after even just a little alcohol, especially in women who are taking the Pill or ovulating.[6] But despite its power to loosen inhibitions in both sexes, alcohol is no friend of a man intent on having sex. As Shakespeare once wrote, it 'provokes the desire, but it takes away the performance . . . it makes him and it mars him; it sets him on and it takes him off; it persuades him and disheartens him; makes him stand to and not stand to . . .'

A big boozy night or regular long-term drinking can both significantly cut a man's testosterone levels, because alcohol directly suppresses the Leydig cells that make the hormone in the testes. It causes 'brewer's droop' by hindering the transmission of nerve impulses from the brain to the smooth muscles in the penis, interfering with the relaxation that allows blood to flow in. 'Alcohol acts directly on the nervous system,' says David Schwartz, an adviser for the Impotence World Association.[7] Michael Wilks, of the British Medical Council for Alcoholism, says that long-term alcohol damage to nerves can leave a man permanently impaired with erectile dysfunction. Chronic boozing can also shrink the testes by suppressing sperm production (since the vast bulk of their size is taken up by sperm and its associated structures), and there's growing evidence that it can also reduce a man's fertility by damaging sperm. Worse still, for male drinkers concerned about their body image, those who regularly consume large amounts of grog can lose muscle mass and strength and become more feminine: alcohol seems to speed up the conversion of testosterone into estrogen and so can cause such men to lose body hair, put on fat and develop larger breasts.

If they haven't overdone it with alcohol the night before, many men experience greater sexual arousal first thing in the morning. It's not simply that they often wake with their final nocturnal erection still very evident. Again, fluctuating testosterone levels seem to be the key to this, because they are usually at their highest between 4 a.m. and 6 a.m. in men. According to Theresa Crenshaw: 'Since testosterone levels are routinely higher in the morning, it may be one reason many men feel more vigorous and virile at dawn than at dusk, especially as they age. When well rested, with a morning erection in the vicinity and a naked woman at arm's length, nature obliges.'[8]

That seems straightforward enough, but what gets a man so interested in the first place? Why, for example, does the sight and touch of one women stir his loins while another leaves him cold? What if our randy man awoke to find at arm's length a naked, spotty, warty, hirsute, obese, bad-smelling woman with rotten teeth giving him the come-hither look? Would nature be so readily obliging? And why do men seem so stereotyped in what turns them on when both they and women come in all shapes, sizes, colours and personalities? Look at one of the most famous loin-stirrers for heterosexual men of Anglo-Celtic descent, Marilyn Monroe. At the height of her popularity Monroe seemed to have the complete package: curvaceous; young; blonde; clear, pale skin; full, firm breasts; well-rounded bottom and thighs; full red lips; pearly white, regular teeth; large eyes set in a symmetrical face with a diminutive and graceful jawline. Why would I, and countless millions of other modern men, be equipped with a brain that is so effortlessly attracted to that combination of physical attributes? And why is having sex with such a woman – or rather the thought of it – more pleasurable to so many men than with a woman who is a little older, darker-haired or even larger-breasted?

Donald Symons, an anthropologist at the University of California, has thought about these issues more than most people. And, at least for the purposes of this book, he argues persuasively that satisfactory answers can only be found through Darwin's theory of evolution by natural selection. As he puts it, that theory is the only scientific explanation for how all manner of living things look and behave – there simply is not a known or even a suspected scientific alternative to it. We cannot, of course, directly interrogate our ancestors to discover whether the theory is right, but we can use it and other evidence to make some educated guesses.

In a nutshell, Monroe had all the sexually attractive attributes our male ancestors had been evolved to respond to in a woman. Those responses are hard-wired into the brains and bodies of today's men, regardless of whether they are all still relevant or not, Symons believes. 'We take for granted that small differences in things like skin texture and facial hair can have large effects on a woman's sexual attractiveness, but why this should be so is not obvious,' says Symons.[9] When we choose an apple to eat, for example, we know from experience that apples can vary greatly in how sweet, juicy or flavoursome they are. We also use our senses to help us decide – we know we can judge by how the apple looks, feels and smells because we have learned that these traits reliably predict what an apple will be like. Presto! As we grow, we discover that our brains carry an inbuilt solution to the apple-picking problem. Likewise, our early ancestors were clearly faced with many other kinds of information-processing problems: not just finding food, but choosing mates, selecting places to live and so on. Eligible women vary in how much or how little they will promote the reproductive success of the men who mate with them, and vice-versa. Thus, for men each woman had a potential mate value – just as different foods or habitats varied in value. Because each problem needed its own solution, our brains must include many complex mechanisms specially designed to solve diverse problems in different domains, Symons reasons. The psychological mechanisms for food choice, for example, are exceedingly unlikely to be identical to those for mate choice, if only because the criteria that decide 'food value' are utterly different to those that determine 'mate value'. 'In short, there is no such thing as a general problem solver because there is no such thing as a general problem.'

How to pick the best mate must have been a perennial problem for men throughout time. Sexual attraction might not have been the only basis on which our ancestors made their choices, but it was certainly a key one. Men might have found women skilled at food gathering to be attractive (and therefore to have a high mate value), since they would be likely to be healthy and to provide well for their children. But skills and status are abstract concepts and a woman's physical attributes are more easily observed, described and quantified, Symons contends, and so easier to be scientific about. Indeed, ancestral men must have learnt that they could reliably predict important things about a woman's mate value by careful observation: 'Selection thus produced psychological mechanisms of sexual attraction specialised to extract and process this information: male sexual attraction was designed to vary in intensity directly with perceived cues of female mate value,' Symons asserts.

Two important categories of information probably determined a woman's mate value among our male ancestors, he argues. The first category was her age, hormonal status, whether she had had a healthy baby already, and her fecundity. The second was her health and what Symons calls 'design quality'. Good health involves relative freedom from disease, parasites and severe injuries; good design overlaps with good health but embraces such observable cues as body symmetry. Combined, those features effectively point to good genes and a robust immune system.

Clearly, some of these qualities are impossible to observe: you can't see a woman's estrogen levels, whether she is about to ovulate, whether her womb contains an embryo. Neither is her childbearing past or future easy to discern. So a nubile woman – one who is just beginning her ovulation cycles and who has not yet become pregnant – would be the most solid bet and thus rate as most attractive. We all know that the sexual attractiveness of women declines as they age. Surprisingly, there's very little science to give us a deeper understanding of why that should be. It is 'a theme that runs through the ethnographic and historical records, folk tales, great literature, less-than-great literature, movies, plays, soap operas, jokes and everyday experience,' Symons points out. 'It accounts for a large portion of the billions of dollars spent annually throughout the world on make-up, cosmetic surgery, diets and exercise.' Yet few studies have even tried to work out at what age a women begins to lose her sex appeal and what visual cues men use to determine that change.

Symons points to extensive studies of preliterate people, such as the Yanomamo of southern Venezuela and northern Brazil, which show a clear trend. On average, Yanomamo girls first begin menstruating soon after they turn 12, then they pair off with a man within two years, have their first baby by the time they're 17, are at their most fertile between 20 and 24 and have had their last baby by the time they're 40. In ancestral times, women were probably at their most nubile between 15 and 18 years of age. Symons concludes: 'The data on living natural-fertility preliterate peoples strongly implies that for tens of thousands of years, at least, women almost always were married by the time they were nubile, the biological father of a woman's child was very likely to be her husband, and women typically began their reproductive careers at nubility, could rear no more than one child every three or four years, and nursed each child intensively for a period of years.' So ancestral men who married a nubile woman had the best opportunity to sire the most children by her during her most fecund years. But even men who had no interest in long-term marriage would have been likely to find nubile women most attractive as well, if siring children was their main aim. Because breastfeeding has contraceptive effects by suppressing ovulation, Yanomamo women, for example, typically are either pregnant or lactating for the equivalent of all but two years of their reproductive lives – assuming they are fertile on just three days of each menstrual cycle in that time, they can potentially conceive on just 1 per cent of all the days within those two years. Whatever a man's reproductive strategy – long-term commitment or wham-bam, thank-you ma'am – a nubile woman was far and away his best chance for siring children, says Symons. Evolution is thus very likely to have equipped men psychologically to find her most attractive.

So how do men judge nubility? Because women conceal their ovulation, their potential to be impregnated is not immediately obvious. Pregnancy itself, breasts swollen with milk, a clinging toddler, stretch marks on the belly or greying hair are unmistakable signs that a woman is not nubile. One reasonably reliable cue that she may be so, however, is her waist-to-hip ratio (WHR). In childhood, boys and girls have virtually identical WHRs, but hormonal surges in puberty markedly change all that: testosterone fills out a boy's waist and estrogen broadens a girl's hips and thighs, creating an obvious difference between the sexes and between nubile and pre-pubescent females. Several studies have shown that before menopause, healthy women typically have a waist that is 70–80 per cent as wide as their hips (for healthy men, the corresponding figure is 80–95 per cent), or a WHR of 0.7–0.8. Women tend to deposit fat very quickly and early around their pelvic girdle region in early pregnancy, making WHR a reasonable guide to that condition; rapid fetal growth soon makes the diagnosis obvious. Some of that increase in WHR remains after the first child is born, but a 22-year-old woman has much the same WHR as she did when she was 17. During menopause, women's WHR takes on basically the same configuration as men's. So the WHR is one obvious cue for men seeking nubile mates.

What's more, modern research studies have found, as ancient peoples no doubt knew by experience, that WHR is indeed a reliable guide to fecundity: an average WHR of about 0.7 genuinely does indicate a woman who will conceive more easily than one who is very fat or very thin (one famous study found that women appearing in *Playboy* centrefolds over a period of 30 years typically had a WHR of 0.7). What's more, a bloated belly – and so a high WHR – can also be an accurate sign of poor health. It has been shown to be a more reliable indicator than total body fat or other physical signs of parasitic infections, menstrual irregularities, diabetes, heart problems, gallbladder disease and breast and ovarian cancer. If so, no wonder men are attracted by an hourglass figure, or that women go to so much trouble and expense to achieve one.

Other subtle signs may yield further information about a woman's nubility, Symons adds. It seems likely that ancestral men also used skin colour, for example, as a bridal guide. Humans tend to be born with paler skin than that of their parents. They become darker through childhood but at puberty skin colour lightens again for boys and even more so for girls. Female skin is lightest during the period of nubility (it even lightens a little more around the time of ovulation). Pregnancy tends to darken a woman's skin again, especially in places that are usually darker in relation to the rest of the body: in freckles; around the nipples, genitals and anus; in the armpits; and in a characteristic line that runs vertically up the centre of the belly from the pubic region. Many of those skin areas – such as around the nipples – then remain permanently darker. Many children are also born with light-coloured hair that darkens with age and there is anecdotal evidence that hair colour also darkens during pregnancy, so light-coloured hair may be a subtle sign of youth and virginity: perhaps that explains the cliché that gentlemen prefer blondes. Anthropological studies and historical records suggest a broad cross-cultural preference among men for women with relatively light skin (even in historic times among Japanese men, who had not encountered Caucasoid women).

Healthy, clear skin may also be a useful cue to a woman's reproductive status: one study of 139 women who sought medical treatment for acne, for example, found that 90 per cent of them had relatively high testosterone levels and almost 60 per cent had some kind of ovarian dysfunction. Clear skin after puberty is thus more likely to indicate a woman with relatively low testosterone. Full lips also suggest nubility: lip fullness in women peaks at the age of 14 in Western populations, according to one study. Full lips with a healthy blood supply contrast strongly with pale skin in adolescent girls. High cheekbones may also be another indicator of a relatively low level of testosterone in a woman, Symons proposes, since men's larger body size, greater aerobic capacity and larger nasal airways make them more robustly built in that area of the face.

Pregnancy can induce many small visible changes in a woman's body: varicose veins in the legs; vascular 'spiders' on the face, neck and arms; extra body-hair growth; swollen eyelids; small skin growths; and darkening and swelling of the gums. None of those features is likely to feature high on men's most-wanted list of attractive features in a woman. Pregnancy may also cause a woman's hands and feet to grow longer (does that partly explain the perceived erotic appeal of small feet?). Symons notes that pregnancy also promotes a woman's bone-formation rate and that her exposure to the growth hormones released by her growing baby may cause her face to lengthen and 'coarsen'. Having a male baby additionally exposes a women to testosterone from her fetal son's testes, which may remodel her face even more.

A string of research studies into what people perceive as beautiful in a woman's face suggests that what rates most highly are very symmetrical features, a relatively short lower face and a slender, 'gracile' jaw. Adulthood tends to lengthen human faces vertically while testosterone tends to promote bone growth in the lower jaw (which may be why, conversely, the classic square-jawed male face is perceived as handsome).

Randy Thornhill, a biologist at the University of New Mexico who is prominent in this field of research, has looked at the relationship between developmental symmetry and human sexual behaviour. 'Body symmetry is a measure of how well an individual has coped with insults during development,' Thornhill told a media briefing at the 1997 annual conference of the American Association for the Advancement of Science. 'Perfect symmetry is the goal of development and insults such as diseases, adverse physical conditions, toxins, inbreeding and mutations throw development off track and lead to facial and body asymmetry.' Both men and women rate symmetrical faces as more attractive. (Oddly enough, though, the consequences of having a symmetrical face seem to differ for men and women. Thornhill's research team found that symmetrical men, but not women, invest less in their romantic relationships, have more sex partners, begin sex earlier in life and earlier in their relationships, cheat more on their partners and are more likely than non-symmetrical men to stimulate orgasm in their female partners.) There's some evidence that a healthy symmetrical body is also an honest advertisement for a healthy well-developed mind: the more symmetrical a person's features, the better they tend to perform on cognitive skills tests, the team has found.

As a sidelight, male fetuses may effectively sabotage the attractiveness of any subsequent brothers they may have. Recent Canadian research suggests that the more older brothers a man has, the more likely his body is to be lopsided in some key features.[10] A team led by Martin Lalumière, of the Centre for Addiction and Mental Health in Toronto, studied 40 psychiatric patients and 31 hospital employees. They checked the men for random symmetry differences between the two sides of their bodies, ruling out any that might be related to left- or right-handedness. Hand- and ear-width and the lengths of the ear, third and fifth finger stood out: those subjects who had an older brother were more likely to be asymmetrical in those features; and the more older brothers they had, the greater the asymmetry (as the youngest of four brothers, you can just call me Wonky). Having older sisters, however, made no difference. The team guesses that male fetuses may provoke an immune reaction in their mothers, possibly because her body detects the presence of 'male-only' genes on the Y chromosome. If so, having more sons in future would be likely to increase the intensity of her immune response. The researchers noted that other studies had shown that the placenta – which, among other tasks, shields a fetus from the maternal immune system – becomes larger the more sons a woman has.

Meanwhile, all of these physical signs of health and virginity in a woman still do not answer one crucial question for a man: does she look nubile simply because she's infertile? There is no obvious physical sign of that and choosing such a mate would be disastrous for a man intent on passing on his genes. But, as Symons points out, a woman who reaches the age of about 25 without having had a child in Yanomamo society is extremely rare. Very few infertile Yanomamo women have been recorded, and 95 per cent of them have had at least one baby by the time they are 20. If that were generally so in ancestral times (most studies suggest that 95 per cent of women in preliterate societies marry), an infertile woman would have been fairly obvious, especially in a small community where sexual and menstrual activity was carefully monitored (some cultures have even ritualised that monitoring process, requiring women to go into seclusion or spend time in special huts when they are menstruating – such comings and goings are watched and noted by men and women alike).

In short, Symons argues that men's sexual preferences tie in closely with observable signs in women's bodies that reliably indicate their nubility, and that this preference 'is the product of a specific selective history, not of a mysterious physical or biological law that applies to animal species in general'. Male rhesus monkeys, for example, show sexual preferences that relate specifically to their life situations: for them, experience and maturity rate highly in a female. When a dominant male has a choice of receptive females (as often happens), he will tend to prefer an older female over one who is displaying the fact that she is ovulating for the first time. As rhesus monkeys pair for only short periods, he does not have to help feed or protect his mate's existing offspring, and an older female is not only far more likely to conceive but also to bear a healthy baby and raise it successfully through its first year of life. Likewise, Austrian researchers have found in recent studies of facial preferences that men are not attracted to women with babyish facial features – they prefer at least some signs of maturity.

One recent British study has suggested that men are somehow able to assess a woman's 'medically correct' weight for her height, and that is what attracts them most. Study subjects were asked to rate the attractiveness of women of all shapes and weights. Sexy curves counted for very little, while the weights they preferred turned out to match exactly what is healthy and best for producing children. Martin Tovee, of Newcastle University, and his colleagues believe women's body shape has been over-rated as an attractive feature to men. Even anorexic women can have an 'ideal' WHR of 0.7 and they are often infertile.

Tovee's team showed 40 male students colour photographs of 50 women (with faces hidden) who were underweight, normal, overweight or obese and asked the men to rate how attractive they found them. Each weight category included a range of body shapes, from hourglass to less curvaceous. Without fail, the men opted for women whose height-to-weight ratio was in the optimum range for good health, regardless of shape. Women in the underweight range scored worst, while those in the overweight range scored less badly. The results tally well with the likely fertility of such women: being underweight is more likely to be linked to poor fertility than being a little overweight. In all, women's weight accounted for 75 per cent of men's preferences, while WHR accounted for just 2 per cent. Tovee says that the ideal weight for attractiveness in a woman seems to be exactly that preferred by men's magazines for centrefold models.

Of course, what men find attractive and how they actually fare in mating are two vastly different things. It's hard to overstate the influence of human culture here: many cultures opt for arranged marriages in which wealth, status, religion and politics play major roles and biological forces only minor ones. Even when there's free individual choice, the inbuilt cues to attractiveness are only part of the story. Countless men may be attracted to an exceptionally beautiful or sexy woman, for example, but few will be likely even to speak with her, let alone have intercourse or babies with her. Women come in all shapes and sizes, and most find a man who sees them as attractive. Yet men do seem to carry an 'ideal' woman template in their heads, against which they measure attractiveness. As one scientist has pointed out, few 50-year-old American or British men will ever have sex with a 20-year-old woman, but *Playboy* and *Penthouse* don't need to publish special editions for them featuring older women. What men generally find attractive and arousing, they seem to keep finding arousing, from their youth until well into advanced age – making allowances for those inevitable times when they are stressed, sick or feeling down. And, by intentionally focusing here only on what men find appealing in women, I've given a very one-sided view of what is really mutual attraction between individuals, whatever the gender or orientation. If I have inadvertently suggested to any readers that it is men who make all the running in mate selection, or that all men are exclusively straight and perennially sexually active, forget it.

Just because evolution equips living things with special problem-solving adaptations to better suit them to their environments does not mean that the resulting design changes stay relevant when conditions change, Symons argues. Men are not larger than women by chance, for example. There must have been a pressure in the past for that size difference to emerge – it somehow promoted survival and reproductive success – but, like Yu-fang's tiny shoe, there's no obvious reason why it should persist. It's a remnant of an earlier age when its value may well have been obvious to our ancestors, but seems to serve less purpose today. Likewise, male attraction to an 'ideal' woman and to such cues as pale, smooth skin and perky breasts is no longer such a reliable guide to child-bearing ability. For one thing, plastic surgery and cosmetics allow men and women alike to sidestep nature and cheat. Modern cities are also ethnically diverse. My own local government area in inner Sydney contains 85,000 people of more than 120 nationalities, and the faces I see on the street are every shade of black, white, brown and yellow.

Last but not least, glance back to the start of this chapter and read again Richard Burton's rich praise of the magic of sexual passion: there are things other than science. And remember, his divine Elizabeth Taylor is a brunette. She has no trouble continuing to attract men even though she is no longer young nor her 'medically correct' weight. *Vive l'amour!*

11

CHEMISTRY: The hormone from hell

'A dozen millennia or so ago, an adventurous soul managed to lop off a surly bull's testicles and thus invented behavioural endocrinology. This experiment . . . certainly generated an influential finding – something or other comes out of the testes that helps to make males such aggressive pains in the ass.'

Robert Sapolsky

I AM WATCHING intently from the sideline of the playing field at the Waterloo Rugby Union Football Club, in a quiet middle-class suburb beside the yawning mouth of the muddy Mersey River in Liverpool, England. It is a sunny autumn Saturday afternoon and a match is in full swing, but it's a one-sided affair. The visiting side – from the delightfully named Vale of Lune – certainly has met its Waterloo. They are taking a pasting from the home side. The Waterloo players are generally bigger, stronger, faster and better trained. They cut through the Vale defence time and again, working the ball out to a well-built winger who towers over everyone else and has the long lean-muscled legs of a sprinter. Next thing you know the ball is touched down over the Vale line again. Their opponents try to rally themselves amid stirring cries of 'Come on Vale!' but you can see that they're goners, hands on hips and with no more energy reserves to call on. Mostly they've played in good spirit but there's a bit of spite creeping into their play – a harsh word here, a stray elbow there – yet even in that department they're coming off second best. Waterloo's crunching tackles and aggressive rucking have sidelined several Vale players with injury and an ambulance has had to be called for one of them. Even the biggest member of Vale's solid forward pack – thick thighs and barrel-shaped body – is red-faced and bushed, drained of strength from being outshoved in the scrums and brought down hard onto the ground in tackles.

By game's end, the score is an embarrassment for the visitors and they leave the field with heads down, sore and sorry. Their coach consoles them. It's him I've been watching as much as the players. He's a big man: broad-shouldered, narrow-hipped, square-jawed and muscular. His T-shirt and shorts reveal that there's hardly a scrap of fat on him. He's obviously very fit and strong and he's been pounding up and down the sideline for the whole game, urging his players on, cajoling them, despairing of them at times, barking instructions, getting flushed with anger and doing lots of finger-jabbing into the air. It's been stressful for him. I have especially noticed his intense bouts of machismo because in this match all the players have been women.

Despite its growing acceptance, a women's rugby match is still not a common sight. It was virtually unheard of when I was a boy.

Rugby was a man's game. Invented by males, for males. It was 'the game they play in heaven', but a heaven almost exclusively organised, supported and populated by men. The game itself is clearly designed to suit male attributes, with its elements of bull-necked muscle, group competition, high pain tolerance and conflict. But so is its social side – lots of back-slapping and bonding, heavy boozing and swapping laughs with the lads. Women's rugby? You gotta be joking, mate!

But these women were playing hard, robust rugby and they were certainly being trained and encouraged to behave that way by their coach. This aggressive aspect of rugby training was plainly on show the next morning, when squads of young boys on that same playing field were being drilled by their coaches. Deep-voiced adult men bellowed at the boys almost constantly, inciting them to tackle, push and shove each other, and goading them into competing ever harder. By passing on the benefits of teamwork, their coaches were showing them how to make alliances and so be even more effective in their pursuit of competitive victory over other boys just like them.

Competitive team sports, especially those like the various codes of football that involve physical contact between players, are not merely for having fun, getting exercise and sharpening your wits. They are also forms of ritualised combat. You can put a positive spin on that and see them as being cleverly designed to channel youthful human energy in a constructive way that teaches the individual to control his aggression. But you could just as easily assert the contrary view: that they are designed to foster aggression, to train young minds to take an offensive – as opposed to defensive – attitude and follow through with the relevant physical approach, albeit under tightly limited rules of engagement.

Science can shed some light on all this. And where it can do so is in the realm of the old nature–nurture debate: are men born aggressive or do they learn it? Or is it a bit of both? And even if nature and nurture are mutually dependent, are some men – and women – born more aggressive than others? More to the point as far as this book is concerned, is there a biological reason why men are more likely than women to attack other people with words, fists and weapons? Do their genes and body chemistry incline them that way? Or have we all inherited something quite different from our ancestors – a culture that encourages male aggression and suppresses it in women? Certainly some women are capable of great aggression and violence. But, as Robert Sapolsky points out, men generate a vastly disproportionate amount of social violence: 'Whether it is something as primal as having an axe fight in an Amazonian clearing or as detached as using computer-guided aircraft to strafe a village, something as condemned as assaulting a cripple or as glorified as killing someone wearing the wrong uniform, if it is violent, we males excel at it.'

Two targets stand out as the recipients of male aggression: other males, and females with whom the aggressor has an intimate relationship. Why is this? The tendency for boys to be more aggressive – as seen in their rough-and-tumble play and acts of bravado – than girls is apparent from early childhood. In adulthood, men are responsible for far more crimes of violence and killing (in the US, for example, they presently account for more than 85 per cent of all recorded simple assaults, aggravated assaults and murders). Those trends are seen across most communities and nations the world over and thus it has become a truism that 'male' violence is innate, and specifically that 'male' hormones are largely to blame. One hormone in particular, testosterone, has come to be seen as the villain of the piece – the hormone from hell.

We should really be using the terms androgens and estrogens to distinguish between the hormones that usually predominate in the bodies of men and women respectively. But the androgens are all cast from the same mould, either being made directly by the testes or being modified forms of testosterone. Because it is by far the best-known androgen, I use testosterone in this book as shorthand for all of them.

It's also wrong to think of testosterone or estrogen as exclusively male or female hormones. Men and women produce both: women make some testosterone, for example, in their adrenal glands and men make some estrogen in their testes. The levels of testosterone and estrogen in the blood fluctuate markedly from time to time, and the relative proportions of the blend change. It is true, however, that on average men have far higher levels of testosterone swimming around in their bodies than do women.

The adrenal glands, which sit on top of the kidneys, play a vital sex-related role in male and female bodies. They produce the body's most abundant hormone, dehydroepiandosterone (known simply as DHEA). It's been a bit of a celebrity in its own right in recent times, with claims that DHEA fights off the effects of aging, heart disease, diabetes and so on. Many people have bought DHEA supplements off the shelf for that reason, but older men in particular should be wary of doing so: DHEA is converted to testosterone in the testes (and into estrogen in women's ovaries). Kids have very little of it, but levels rise after puberty and peak in the late twenties before starting a long, steep decline into old age. Testosterone fuels tumour growth in the prostate gland, so older men may be living dangerously if they take DHEA for supposed health reasons. Adrenal hormones also kick off the testosterone surge that marks the start of puberty about 6 to 12 months later: they spark the first growth of pubic hair and seem to prime a boy's body for when his testes later switch on full testosterone production. But it is unknown what keeps the testes in check from shortly after a boy's birth until puberty.

Hormones can and do have strong and obvious effects on bodies and minds. The way birds respond so dramatically to the advent of the breeding season and then to the arrival of their young, for example, is triggered by hormones. But such examples may create a false impression of their power. Usually the effects of hormones are far more subtle than causing bright plumage to sprout or involving a sudden desire to spend all day gathering caterpillars for a squawking baby. That said, it was long ago realised that castrating a male – whether it be a mouse, a dog, a ram, a boy soprano or a harem guard – had significant consequences. Glaringly obvious among those changes is that he becomes less aggressive. So you might reasonably conclude that testosterone causes aggression (and a lot else) in men, but you'd be wrong. As Sapolsky points out: 'Times of life when males are swimming in testosterone (for example, after reaching puberty) correspond to when aggression peaks. Among numerous species, testes are mothballed most of the year, kicking into action and pouring out testosterone only during a very circumscribed mating season – precisely the time when male–male aggression soars. Impressive, but these are only correlative data, testosterone repeatedly being on the scene with no alibi when aggression occurs. The proof comes with the knife, the performance of what is euphemistically known as a "subtraction" experiment. Remove the source of testosterone in species after species and levels of aggression typically plummet. Reinstate normal testosterone levels afterward with injections of synthetic testosterone, and aggression returns.'

So it would seem that males suffer from a sort of hormonal attitude problem, a collective case of testosterone poisoning. There's more damning evidence against the suspect as well. Sample the testosterone levels of a wide range of men and you'll find a pretty clear correlation: those with the highest levels of the hormone also tend to be the most aggressive. That would seem to clinch the case. But there's a wrinkle: you can't predict at all reliably how aggressive a man will be from his testosterone level, as many studies have confirmed. When you put a group of men together, the ones with the most testosterone initially aren't necessarily going to be the most aggressive. In fact, the ones who behave most aggressively are those whose testosterone levels *rise* most – in other words, the hormone level is a response to aggression, not a cause of it. And if you sample one man's testosterone as its level varies (highest in the morning but it can soar and dive by as much as 50 per cent in the course of a single day), the high points on the chart plainly don't tally with when he's most aggressive.

It's now clear from a wide range of studies that the link between aggression and testosterone is far from simple. In short: 'You need some testosterone around for normal aggressive behaviour – zero levels after castration, and down [aggression] usually goes; quadruple it (the sort of range generated in weightlifters abusing anabolic steroids) and aggression typically increases,' Sapolsky says. 'But anywhere from roughly 20 per cent of normal to twice normal and it's all the same; the brain can't distinguish among this wide range of basically normal values.' It seems that within that spread, tes-tosterone isn't causing aggression but may enhance it when it happens. When you watch electrical signals from a region thought to be involved in aggression being received by the part of the brain where emotional activity is focused, the traffic between them doesn't begin to flow in response to the presence of the hormone. Only if that pathway is already switched on does testosterone boost the rate at which the sparks fly. 'It's not causing aggression, it's exaggerating the pre-existing pattern of it, exaggerating the response to environmental triggers of aggression,' Sapolsky says.

Another researcher with a keen interest in aggression, psychologist John Archer, of the University of Central Lancashire, notes that 30 years of research aimed at determining a link between testosterone and aggression have failed to reach a clear conclusion. His research has shown that comparisons of groups of men, often jail inmates, who have a history of violence or non-violence, 'generally show higher testosterone levels among the more violent men than the less violent ones'. But specific comparisons between individuals have yielded conflicting results. Giving men a little extra testosterone doesn't make them all a little more aggressive. Yet it may do so to some men if they are already aggressive – some animal studies have found that testosterone does elevate aggression in aggressive individuals but not in non-aggressive ones. So it seems that testosterone can be produced by aggression or as a result of it, and that its impact varies according to the individual.

Animal and human studies have found that testosterone

levels do rise and fall in line with victory or defeat in combative encounters or sporting contests. One found that men taking part in a judo competition had higher testosterone levels than when they did an equally energetic session of exercise. Other research suggests that it is the intensity of competition that dictates how much the levels rise or fall. And men apparently don't even need to be directly involved in competition to make their hormone levels change. In a group of Brazilian and Italian fans at the 1994 World Cup soccer final, testosterone levels rose in 11 of the 12 'winning' Brazilian fans by an average of 27.6 per cent and decreased by an average of 26.7 per cent in the 9 'losing' Italian fans. That finding and others suggest that success and failure (even experienced second-hand) does alter men's testosterone levels and, in turn, their alertness, sense of well-being and anxiety are affected. One theory put forward to explain these linkages is that men who succeed in competitions – or those who experience a gain in 'eminence', to use the jargon – whether through sport, business or job, are rewarded with a hormone boost that enhances their mood, fends off fatigue and calms them.

If so, it's no wonder that men tend to be attracted by combat and competition: you feel great when you win. King of the hill. Nawaz Sharif, then Prime Minister of Pakistan, expressed that sense of triumph with shocking rawness in 1998 after his nation detonated five nuclear devices in response to nuclear tests carried out earlier by India: 'Today, we have paid them back.' His crowing words could just as well have come after a street brawl between rival gangs.

But testosterone is only part of the aggression story. Despite what we may suppose, men are not especially prone to violence when compared with other animals. Decades of field research have revealed that injury and death resulting from combat between animals of the same species is not as rare as we once believed. As one researcher has pointed out, among most mammal species the 'murder' rate is actually higher than it is for people in large American cities. Modern evolutionary game theory suggests why violence isn't more common – the self-interest of the individual combatant takes precedence. Escalating from low-intensity 'ritualised' combat to higher-intensity injurious combat occurs only when the first fails to resolve the issue, or when the stakes for one or both combatants are so high that the risks of fiercer combat are worth the gamble.

What sort of rewards would make men resort to physical means to solve conflicts and so risk death or serious injury? Here our ancient animal ancestry seems to play a part. The sexual success that comes with high status is an obvious candidate because, for men at least, it greatly increases their chances of reproductive success. Males that do not father children in effect experience reproductive death – their genes peter out. A pattern is evident among mammals in which males are typically more aggressive than females, and it seems likely that this pattern is the product of sexual selection: most male mammals and many male birds have to compete with each other for access to females, and females are typically choosy about which partners are acceptable to them. 'The greater willingness to commit acts of physical aggression to other males, and towards mates to stop them mating with other males, can be viewed as part of a wider reproductive strategy of males,' Archer says. 'Male sexuality contributes directly to the pursuit of genetic posterity, whereas male aggressiveness does so indirectly.'

Mind you, just because the effect is indirect does not mean it can't be highly effective. Anthropologist Napoleon Chagnon's famous studies of the Yanomamo, the indigenous Indians who live on the Venezuela/Brazil border, illustrate the latter point well. Yanomamo men are often said to be the most aggressive and violent of any society. In the past at least, murder rates were extremely high and the men who killed most often attracted several wives, while weaker men opted for a bachelor life. Chagnon studied a group of 113 men and found that just 16 of them accounted for more than half of all the grandchildren that could be traced from the group; 4 headmen alone had a total of 191 grandchildren.

Where men do seem to stand out from other male mammals, though, is in their propensity for organised warfare. Carolyn Nordstrom, an anthropologist at the University of Notre Dame, has spent many years studying war at first hand. She argues that there's not much evidence that men are especially inclined towards war by biology; rather, she believes it's a cultural invention. By way of example, she cites two studies which found that in World War II, 80–85 per cent of soldiers did not fire their weapons in the heat of battle. 'Apparently, a large percentage of soldiers were willing to go to war for their country, they were willing to work on the front lines, but they were not willing to kill,' Nordstrom says.[1] In the Vietnam War, the situation was reversed: 90–95 per cent of American soldiers fired their weapons in battle, as a result of military training specifically aimed at overcoming the reluctance discovered in World War II. That training 'success', however, came at the cost of a great increase in traumatised soldiers and in community censure of government and military institutions over the number of civilian casualties. 'Clearly, the vast majority of people do not want to kill and may not be able to unless careful training is given,' she says. And while most of us carry images of war that revolve around fighting men in battle zones – images reinforced by books, films, war museums and art – the reality of modern war is somewhat different: most of those killed are non-combatants. They are usually children, women, the aged and the frail. In World War I, only 10–20 per cent of all casualties were civilians; in World War II, 50 per cent were civilians; in Vietnam, 80–90 per cent were civilians. Human rights violations and sexual assaults are all more likely to occur during war, and military servicemen are disproportionately responsible for domestic and sexual violence.

'Without dismissing people for the ethical responsibility of their actions, the soldiers I have seen who violated human rights had themselves generally been brutalised. Harsh and degrading training has often been successful in producing harsh and degrading strategies.' Indeed, war propaganda often aims to dehumanise an enemy as well, to help create a sense of moral distance from normal civility and law and so legitimise state-endorsed aggression and violence. Whatever else it is, that's not biology. As Nordstrom puts it: 'Whether in war or in peace, violence is not a biological eruption of genes encountering environment, but a culture-bound system of learned rules, ethics, and actions. Like all cultures, these rules are made, enforced, reinforced, and changed through human interaction.'

There's other evidence that male aggression is not wholly dependent on testosterone to fuel it, and that it can respond to cultural forces: it's likely that once you've experienced being aggressive, for example, you don't need testosterone for that behaviour to persist. In animal studies, it's been shown that the more social experience an individual had of being aggressive before castration, the more likely that individual is to stay aggressive afterward. Says Sapolsky: 'Social conditioning can more than make up for the hormone. "Testosterone equals aggression" is inadequate for those who would offer a simple solution to the violent male – just decrease levels of the pesky steroids. And "testosterone equals aggression" is certainly inadequate for those who would offer a simple excuse: boys will be boys and certain things in nature are inevitable. Violence is more complex than a single hormone.'

Yet testosterone is central to understanding men. It seeps through the male body, mostly in trickles and surges but at times in great waves, from the moment the testes are able to make it. And it seems to play a pivotal role in just about every aspect of mind and body that makes men stand out from women – muscles, beards, deep voices, competitive urges, risk-taking behaviour and sexual drive. As Sapolsky puts it: 'This hormone binds to specialised receptors in muscles and causes those cells to enlarge. It binds to similar receptors in laryngeal cells and gives rise to operatic basses. It causes other secondary sexual characteristics, makes for relatively unhealthy blood vessels, alters biochemical events in the liver too dizzying to even contemplate, has a profound impact, no doubt, on the workings of cells in big toes. And it seeps into the brain, where it binds to those same "androgen" receptors and influences behaviour in a way highly relevant to understanding aggression.'

People have long suspected that a certain magic something must be contained in the testes. Ancient Egyptians believed the organs must have medicinal power, and men in other ancient cultures are said to have sometimes consumed animal testes before going into battle (more recent claims have suggested that, for similar reasons, some German troops ate androgenic substances during World War II). As long ago as 1000 BC, medical texts recommended eating testicular tissue as a treatment for impotence, while a German compendium of remedies published in 1754 mentions the use of horse testes.

Castration is still used medically today in the treatment of some male breast cancers and prostate cancers when a rapid response is needed (since testosterone fuels the tumours' growth). But the modern pioneer of testes-as-therapy was a French doctor, Charles Édouard Brown-Séquard. In 1889, he announced that he had rejuvenated his 72-year-old body with injections of a liquid extract from the testes of dogs and guinea pigs. He claimed to have grown stronger in body and sharper in mind, as well as being cured of constipation and even able to pee in a longer arc. Most scientists now agree that Brown-Séquard was kidding himself – responding to the power of positive suggestion, not some positive ingestion. Even so, he was the first scientist in modern times to propose that a bodily secretion could regulate body functions – as hormones do – and that those same secretions could be used to restore lost or diminished functions.

The colourful story of experimentation with male hormones was traced in an article in *Scientific American* by John Hoberman and Charles Yesalis.[2] They recorded how Brown-Séquard's novel suggestions about his '*liquide testiculaire*' sparked a rush of experimentation around the world, with the extract being tried as a cure for tuberculosis, cancer, diabetes, paralysis, gangrene, anemia, heart disease, influenza, Addison's disease, and even hysteria and migraine. Some years later, two Austrian scientists who were inspired to join the throng injected themselves with liquid extracts from bull's balls, with questionable results. But the idea behind their experiment was to see if these extracts could improve muscle power. The concluding sentence of their scientific paper pointed out: 'The training of athletes offers an opportunity for further research in this area and for a practical assessment of our experimental results.' It was the first proposal to inject athletes with a hormone. The scientists could hardly have imagined how ardently their suggestion would be taken up.

Another key finding in the discovery of sex hormones was reported in the 1920s by two German scientists, Bernhard Zondek and Selmar Aschheim. They were intrigued to find that when they injected extracts from the urine of pregnant women into female rats and mice, the rodents went into estrus – that is, they became sexually aroused and receptive to mating. The special ingredient that achieved this striking response was quickly isolated and purified by other researchers, Adolf Butenandt in Germany and Edward Doisy in the US, and was named estrone. That hormone influences the development of the female reproductive tract and turned out to be just one of a number of sex hormones associated with femaleness. Butenandt went on to isolate progesterone, which regulates the condition of the inner lining of the womb. His work on male hormones included creating a synthetic form of testosterone. Indeed, his was one of three research groups, all sponsored by pharmaceutical companies, to publish scientific papers within a few months of each other in 1935 describing the hormone and how to make it synthetically. For his pioneering work in finding and explaining the roles these compounds play in the body (which also paved the way for the development of birth control pills), he was a co-winner, with Leopold Ruzicka, of the 1939 Nobel Prize for Chemistry.

'Since then, testosterone and its derivatives, the anabolic-androgenic steroids, have led a curious double life,' the *Scientific American* article notes. 'Since the 1940s countless elite athletes and bodybuilders have taken these drugs to increase muscle mass and to intensify training regimens. For the past 25 years, this practice has been officially proscribed yet maintained by a $1 billion international black market. That testosterone products have served many therapeutic roles in legitimate clinical medicine for an even longer period is less well known.' Mind you, even the hormone's legitimate medical reputation has been sullied, with one sexologist dubbing it one of the most abused, misused and over-prescribed medications for male sexual dysfunction in medical history.

The first testosterone trials were aimed at treating male infertility and impotence, and it was later used to treat people with wasted muscles, such as survivors of Nazi concentration camps. It has also been used in the treatment of depression and – because it stimulates the production of red blood cells – anemia, as well as to stimulate puberty in boys with developmental delays and to stimulate growth (in conjunction with human growth hormone). Testosterone was also used from early on to treat a variety of female conditions, including breast cancer and irregular periods. It has been used in treating advanced breast cancer in older women, as doctors long ago observed that even if the hormone did not stop the cancer from growing, it relieved pain, increased appetite and weight and resulted in a greater sense of well-being. Equally, from the earliest trials, it was apparent that testosterone could reawaken or intensify women's sexual appetites, and it has often been used specifically for that purpose. When a woman's testosterone levels are below normal, replacement therapy can help to restore her libido, but testosterone supplements for women can also have many unwanted side-effects. They can make a woman become more masculine, causing her body fat and muscle ratios to change, her hips to narrow, her breasts to shrink, her voice to become lower, her moustache and other body hair to grow and her clitoris to enlarge (as long ago as 1939 one researcher reported that daily applications of testosterone ointment enlarged the clitoris of one of his female subjects, who then became able to achieve orgasm).

Jack's story

Jack is a 29-year-old writer who lives in New York. Born female, he is undergoing a transsexual change to become male. He has been taking testosterone for 4 years, as well as having both breasts removed and chest tissue reconstructed. He has found the social world tougher as a man, with people making fewer concessions to him and being far less courteous. Male hormones have transformed his inner world as well.

'I didn't want to believe that testosterone really made a qualitative difference in how men and women see the world, how they act in the world. I really wanted to believe that gender was a cultural creation. A lot of it is, but a lot of it's not. It's hard for me to convince some people of that; you kind of have to go through it to believe it.

'Since I started the transition I have done a lot of studying about testosterone and I know now that it has actually changed my brain.

'I'm a writer and my verbal ability, since I've been on testosterone, has decreased. Words don't come to me like before. I have to look up a lot of words I used to know. It's a little spooky.

'Under the influence of testosterone, you become more visual. Your whole visual/spatial reality shifts. Men like pornography because they're more visually stimulated, while women, generally, prefer to read romance novels – I used to think that was bullshit, but I don't think that anymore.

'All our lives, we hear the same thing about men, that they think about sex every five seconds. As a feminist I wanted to believe that this was just male propaganda. But the fact of the matter is testosterone makes you crazy sexually.

'Before testosterone I'd be sitting on the subway and I'd see an attractive women and I'd think, "She's attractive. I'd like to talk to her. If I talk to her, we might talk about this or that. I'd learn her name, I'd ask her on a date, we'd go out, we'd get dressed up, we'd get to know each other, I would lean in for the kiss, I'd take her home, we'd have sex."

'After testosterone, I'd see a woman on the train . . . no, let me amend that, I'd see a woman's knee on the train and instantly aggressive, violent, sexual images of just [expletive deleted] this woman would flood my mind. There was not even a split second between seeing the knee and having the flood of images.

'It's just instantaneous, and it's unstoppable. You can't get it

> out of your brain. I felt out of control. I felt like a monster. I felt horribly distracted. I mean, I have a job. I'm expected to be able to concentrate on the task at hand, and there was no way I could do my work because all I could think about was tearing the clothes off all the women around me. They didn't even have to be attractive. They could be very unattractive. It didn't matter at all.
>
> '[Now] it's mellowed out and levelled out and I'm also used to it. Now my fantasy life is sort of a combination of before and after testosterone. There's a little bit of narrative, but the stories in my head are a little more aggressive than they used to be. Sexual desire is much more manageable now. It's not overwhelming.'

Testosterone in women causes extra hair growth because the hormone is intimately involved in boosting the hairiness of the parts of the body that help a male to advertise his masculinity and maturity. No doubt these sex differences evolved long ago in our ancestors as useful social signals, despite the presumed loss of most of the rest of our body hair as compared with our ape ancestors. A beard certainly makes a major difference to a man's appearance and to how other people react to him, as I found one Christmas holiday period. Being from hairy stock, I fight a daily battle with my face fungus. The heck with it, I thought. Why spend good money on razors, shaving soap and brushes? Why start each day by dragging a sharp metal blade over soft cheeks, puckered lips and tender throat in a blood-letting, rash-making ritual? It seemed as irksome and repetitive as washing the dishes, only far more pointless. Electric razors suit me no better. And what a waste of time:

someone has calculated that a man of 60 who has spent 10 minutes shaving each day since he was 18 has used up a total of 2555 hours – 106 days – of his life.

It was only when I stopped shaving, though, that I really began to get an inkling of why men do it. Most of us don't denude our scalps, root out our eyebrows, scrape our armpits naked or mow our chests on a daily basis. We may get haircuts and pluck the odd wayward strand but we don't harvest the entire crop every day. After enduring the usual itchy-scratchy 'don't-kiss-me-Dad' phases, my new thatch grew soft and neat. The plan was to keep it short and tidy, avoid the Charles Darwin look, routinely remove all breadcrumbs and not offend others by twiddling it or using the moustache as a drink-strainer.

But it's hard to persuade some people that in itself a new beard does not make a man become subversive, rebellious, layabout, artistic, excessively hetero or homo, demonic, unclean, older, younger, quieter, more aggressive, wiser, dumber, fatter or slimmer. He is not wearing an Identikit face: he just looks the way that genes and testosterone, left to their own devices, are primed to make him look. Being keenly attuned to visual signals – like our closest relatives, the chimpanzees – thick facial hair is a most conspicuous sign of gender and sexual maturity. Women and boys don't have it. Left untrimmed, an average man's beard – except those from races where hairiness has retreated even further – will grow 30 centimetres every two years, and its curliness accentuates its bulk. Shrubbery like that is quite enough to leave even distant observers in no doubt that they have encountered an adult male: that's a useful thing, given our aggressive tendencies. For most of history, it seems that letting beards grow has been the norm, especially for men of high status. Ancient Persian kings cultivated large beards (often dyed, perfumed and adorned with jewels) and the Egyptian pharaohs wore long false beards on ceremonial occasions to highlight their rank. At one time Elizabethan society even had a beard levy, enabling the upper classes to flaunt their wealth by displaying their ability to pay what was in a sense a testosterone tax. Conversely, hair removal has often been an act of submission: prisoners of war were shaved to humiliate them; men who join religious groups shave to show humility and devotion. Shaven men have been the mark of militaristic cultures as well: Alexander the Great ordered his foot soldiers to shave to deny enemies a grasping point in combat.

Desmond Morris suggests that shaving has become a sign of submission in a new way, a strong signal of conformity that flags to other men and women a man's willingness to socialise, suppress his ancient pugnacity and be cooperative. It certainly makes men look more 'juvenile' and 'well-groomed' in an era when youth is promoted over age, and good hygiene and self-consciousness are highly valued. Significantly, shaving also effectively makes a man's face more womanly, enabling clear expression of a full range of emotions. In short, it would seem that lopping off his beard helps a man give the impression that he is friendlier, cleaner, neater, younger and more feminine – altogether less liable to have his mind ruled by the hormone from hell. Come to think of it, perhaps it's their beards that put Hell's Angels into the renegade camp, every bit as much as their motorcycles.

The thicker face, chest and limb hairs that signify manhood need testosterone to stimulate their growth. Those hairs begin to develop at puberty, about two years after pubic hairs start to emerge. Although the enlargement and maturing of the testes and a subsequent flood of testosterone from them is the main hormonal event of puberty, that change is preceded by up to a year of higher testosterone output from the adrenal glands. It's thought that another hormone released by the pituitary gland in the brain triggers that change, but its identity remains unknown. Likewise, it's still unclear how puberty itself is triggered. It begins in boys from 9 to 14 years and takes 3 to 5 years to complete. Once they get started, beards grow vigorously until a man passes the age of 30. But testosterone doesn't make more hair grow: rather, it is thought to make hair grow longer and faster by giving the hair follicles more time to be active. Hair follicles turn on and off in fits and starts and the hormone extends their so-called anagen period – the hair-growing phase – in men to an average of more than 50 days a year, compared with just over 20 days for women. The growth of pubic and armpit hair also depends on testosterone, although apparently less of the hormone is needed to make that happen, since women and men differ little in this respect (in women, the adrenal gland produces enough testosterone for the task). Increasing baldness in old age ties in with gradual declines in men's testosterone levels, but genetics clearly come into play here.

The market for products to treat hair loss is huge: creams, pills, personal care products, surgical procedures, hair replacement and wigs collectively persuade American consumers alone – mainly men – to part with an estimated $7 billion a year. So it's no surprise that scientists have long sought cures for baldness, but a stumbling block has been the lack of a way to coax the adult scalp to produce new hair follicles. Those follicles start to form in human embryos in the first single layer of skin, where they can be seen as tiny depressions as the skin grows in the fetus. The fetal forehead and scalp form a structure of tissues containing the follicles, but after about five months' gestation the follicles on the scalp keep growing while those on the forehead don't – this leads to the hairline being formed. Soon after birth, the follicles over most of the body shrink back and produce only tiny, fine hairs. The scalp follicles, however, mature at the same time and develop two distinct layers of cells that surround the hair shaft. In adults, hair follicles produce a protein called keratin – the stuff that also makes toenails and fingernails, animal hooves, horns and feathers. Keratin gets blended in with dead cells from the budding occurring within the follicle: as this mixture forms it gets pushed up and out from the skin surface and a hair is formed (sorry but, yes, your hair is dead) at the rate of about a centimetre a month. The average person has about 100,000 scalp hair follicles, of which only about 85,000 are growing at any one time. The remainder are either resting or in regression – that is, they drop their hairs and don't make a new one until they start to actively grow again. That's why finding loose hairs in your comb or brush each day is perfectly normal. But balding men (and some women) soon start to notice more and more hairs dropping out – the result of increasing numbers of follicles going into regression and not re-entering the growth phase. Those follicles may have been shrinking for some time beforehand, producing fewer and shorter hairs before they stop completely.

Most men go increasingly bald as they pass through middle age, but as many as 40 per cent of them experience substantial hair loss much earlier in life, in what is known as male-pattern baldness. It's a trait they share with our orang-utan cousins and at least one species of macaque monkey. Usually starting in their twenties, but as early as their teens, they progressively go bald from the forehead and temples and then the crown, their formerly long and sturdy scalp hairs often being replaced initially by short, downy, baby-like hair. They are eventually left with a wreath of hair at the sides and back, surrounding a hairless, shiny pate – like Friar Tuck. Oddly, even though testosterone boosts hair growth in most of the rest of the body, in the case of male-pattern baldness it has the opposite effect – indeed, such men often have generous body hair elsewhere. This tendency seems to be inherited and so is strongly suspected to have a genetic origin, and the balding seems to coincide initially with rising testosterone levels. Drugs used to treat baldness usually aim to counter the hormone excess.

Much of what limited amount we know about hair growth comes from animal studies. Sheep, for example, have about 100 genes that regulate keratin production, although the roles they play are largely a mystery. US researchers recently announced the discovery of the first gene that seems to activate hair follicles in humans.[3] The find emerged from studies of a Pakistani family in which 11 members lost all their hair. They were born without eyebrows or eyelashes and never grew pubic hair. Although they were born with a normal head of baby hair, no new hair grew to replace it. Researchers from the biotechnology company FibroGen and a team led by dermatologist Angela Christiano at Columbia University traced several common genetic markers in the bald members of the family. Christiano had also isolated the human version of a mouse gene known as 'hairless' – found in a special type of bald laboratory mouse used for decades in skin research – and learned that it lay in the same chromosome region as the markers she identified in her bald subjects, each of whom was found to have a single mutation in the hairless gene. That gene is though to be a kind of master gene that controls others in the hair-making sequence; if it doesn't give a signal the rest won't come into play. Because this gene is as active in women as men, it is unlikely to be involved in male-pattern baldness, the team believes. But it should pave the way to better understanding the process and so boost the chances of finding a remedy for what many men find to be a distressing problem (isn't it odd that we mourn the loss of scalp hair and yet so assiduously remove face hair?). 'The discovery of this new gene gives us endless possibilities that may allow us to effectively treat hair loss and possibly baldness within the next five years,' Christiano said. 'It is now within our reach to design ways to grow hair, remove hair, even dye hair genetically and, best yet, this can all be accomplished topically, reducing possible side effects.'

Other facets of the balding process are beginning to yield their secrets. Several proteins that act as receptors for testosterone have been isolated and they seem to play a part in regulating the process. One seems to actively suppress testosterone in hair follicles. More hope on that front has emerged recently from a research team led by Elaine Fuchs, a Howard Hughes Medical Institute investigator at the University of Chicago. For the first time the scientists were able to induce new hair follicles to form in mature mammals. Getting new follicles to form was a surprise because it was thought the number in adulthood was limited to those formed in the womb. 'During development, you're given a set number of hair follicles for the rest of your life,' Fuchs explains.

In mice genetically engineered by Fuchs and her colleagues, however, new follicles start to emerge within a month of birth and keep doing so throughout life. The new hairs arise from skin cells between, or even from within, existing follicles. Hair did not form, however, on the footpads or on other naturally hairless areas. It seems that a previously unrecognised signalling pathway exists that can command adult skin cells to make new hair follicles, says Fuchs. A key component of this pathway appears to be a protein called beta-catenin, which usually breaks down quickly in adult cells. The team created mice whose skin cells had a gene encoding a sturdy form of beta-catenin that resists degradation. In some skin cells, but not all, this added beta-catenin sparked new follicle growth. The scientists suspect that some still mysterious signal, perhaps released by existing follicles or other nearby cells, determines why only certain cells react to the extra beta-catenin. But the new hair growth in the mice was not fully normal. Often the new follicles were set at the wrong angle, so the hairs they made did not emerge from the skin but grew within it, making it thicker. Another significant downside was that the growth-boost sometimes produced tumours – the beta-catenin is thought to have stimulated so much activity in the follicles that it caused tumours to grow. So the discovery does not offer an imminent cure for baldness, but it may be possible to stimulate skin cells by this new pathway for long enough to form new follicles but not so long as to induce tumours.

Getting to the bottom of testosterone's effects on mind and body is far from simple. The timing of a male's exposure to it in his formative months and years may play a vital role in influencing how it affects him in later life. In chickens, for example, it seems there are crucial 'windows' of time when its influence can have a marked impact. A chicken's sex can be manipulated experimentally with hormones until about four hours after hatching. If a newly hatched female chick is injected with testosterone, it will develop into a fully functional cockerel. When injected into male or female chicks at later stages of growth, it causes both sexes to experience extra-early growth of the comb, crowing and aggressive behaviour. In the 1960s, girls exposed to abnormally high levels of testosterone in the womb – after their pregnant mothers took synthetic steroids – not only had masculinised genitals but also seemed to have their brains irreversibly influenced as well. They later preferred typically male toys (cars over dolls), and showed more interest in male-typical play and activities.

Sex therapist Theresa Crenshaw, in her book *Why We Love and Lust*, records how a woman in her late thirties was referred by her general practitioner for a second opinion on the testosterone treatments she had been taking for about two years for low sex drive.[4] Before she began the treatments, 'she was a different person – withdrawn, shy, without confidence, depressed and sexless. With the shots, she developed a voracious sexual appetite, felt happy and assertive and got along much better with her husband.' From his point of view, her husband felt that he could now 'communicate with her like a man. She was "logical and made good sense". Off it, she was hopeless.' Despite evidence of physical side-effects (a changing figure, deeper voice and extra body hair), and despite the long-term consequences to her health, she decided to continue with the treatment: 'She said she just didn't like the person she was without it.'

It was once believed that testosterone might be used as a 'treatment' for male homosexuality – in the 1940s it was thought that gay men simply had an excess of estrogen. Clinical trials were conducted, in some cases by legal orders forcibly imposed by courts and parental injunctions. Naturally, the 'therapy' failed. Hoberman and Yesalis describe how one trial on 11 subjects wrecked the theory: 'Indeed, given that five subjects complained of increases in their sexual drive, the researchers conceded the likelihood that "the administration of androgen to the active (or aggressive) homosexual would rather regularly intensify his sex drive" instead of reducing it.'

In that same era, the hormone's anabolic power to build up muscle tissue was also discovered. Muscle cells are weird, and we'll need to get a little bit technical to explain what they are like and how testosterone helps them grow. Rather than having just one central nucleus, containing the chromosomes, muscle cells can have several nuclei and may grow several centimetres long. Surrounding these nuclei are countless tiny tube-like strands known as myofibrils, which contract and expand like a collapsing telescope when you flex and relax. But muscle cells can't divide to form whole new cells, so it's a puzzle how they manage to grow – as they obviously do when you exercise them regularly. It is known that the myofibrils thicken in response to exercise, but how they do it is not known. The large amounts of proteins they need to do so are made under instructions from the genes in the nuclei. It's thought that exercise prompts the muscle cells to 'borrow' more nuclei from nearby satellite cells to boost their protein-making capacity. Those satellite cells are not there by chance: they are apparently attracted to the surface of muscle cells as part of the body's repair team. Their routine role is to patch up tiny rips and tears that occur in muscle fibres in normal use. So increased exercise probably damages muscle cells more than usual and attracts a larger repair team to patch them up. Some members of that team are then enlisted into the cell itself to help build more myofibrils.

Testosterone plays a vital brokerage role in all of this. Circulating in the blood, it can penetrate the outer wall of muscle cells and enter them, where it is detected by special free-floating receptors. They link up and together enter the inner sanctum of the nucleus. There they activate a gene that directs the making of the proteins from which the myofibrils are made. Synthetic versions of the hormone exploit this same natural process, which is why weightlifters and bodybuilders use them. In the US alone, it is estimated that about 1.5 million people, mainly men, are in effect testosterone abusers. The Canadian Centre for Drug Free Sport reported in 1993 that an estimated 83,000 young people between the ages of 11 and 18 had used anabolic steroids in the prior 12 months. In Britain, the Drugs and Sport Information Service conducted a survey of 43 gyms across the north-west of England in 1996 and found that 30 per cent of those attending 'hardcore' gyms were using anabolic steroids at the time. Almost half the doctors in Liverpool during that year reported being aware of having treated at least one anabolic steroid user.

Anabolic steroids can and do help to increase lean body mass, shed fat and increase power, size and strength. They also help to facilitate heavier training regimes and to cut the recovery time between training sessions. But other users take them because they seek the hormone's influence on their state of mind – people lacking confidence in their jobs, for example, believe testosterone will provide the sense of well-being and aggression they feel is necessary to succeed. In fact, a number of studies have now shown a link between depression and low testosterone levels. 'This suggests that testosterone is not only a natural aphrodisiac but an antidepressant as well,' Crenshaw comments.

Taking testosterone doesn't prevent other psychological problems from emerging. There's one paradoxical group of men (and some women) who believe that they're such scrawny weaklings they must shun social invitations, avoid the beach and pool, and wear heavy clothes even in summer to hide their bodies. But it's all in their minds: remarkably, these people are actually dedicated bodybuilders who have spent hours each day in the gym and even taken steroids to make themselves muscular hunks. Their condition is known as muscle dysmorphia. Although the vast majority of people should become healthier and fitter from bodybuilding and sport, muscle dysmorphics can never be satisfied, no matter how big their muscles become. Like its puzzling predecessors in the 1980s – the eating disorders anorexia nervosa and bulimia – muscle dysmorphia emerged in the '90s among people with grossly distorted images of their own bodies. 'I know of one young man whose sole aim in life is to reach a weight of 100 kilograms,' one researcher into eating disorders told me. 'What's more, he doesn't think he has a problem.'

When it comes to testosterone, more is not always better. Giving a lot of extra testosterone to normal men can cause the usual controls over hormone production to go haywire – the pituitary gland, for example, may detect the increase and interpret it as a sign to shut down hormone production in the testes. Testosterone supplements can also cause salt and fluid retention, not to mention the chance that a man may become more aggressive or surly. As Crenshaw points out, testosterone is a funny drug – a 'libido booster that makes you obnoxious' and 'an antidepressant that makes you irritable and warlike'. Testosterone abuse in both sexes has been linked with liver and kidney disorders, coronary heart disease, stunted growth, sleeplessness, nosebleeds, depressed immune systems and acne. For men, it can cut sperm production and render them infertile, shrink the testes and cause hair loss and the growth of breast tissue. Women abusers can experience menstrual problems, a deeper voice, more body hair, smaller breasts and an enlarged clitoris. Naturally, many of these effects are irreversible.

Many studies over the past 20 years have suggested that there are benefits in hormone replacement therapy (HRT) for men with too little testosterone; it not only helps to restore and heighten their sex drive but also increases their sense of well-being. And there's other emerging evidence that testosterone does have positive benefits for men. Men with higher than average testosterone levels are less vulnerable to high blood pressure, heart attacks, frequent colds and obesity, says Alan Booth, professor of sociology and human development at Pennsylvania State University. As well, such men are more likely to rate their own health as excellent, a rating supported by physical examinations. 'The benefits of higher testosterone levels have a downside, however,' Booth comments. 'Some, but not all, men with higher levels of testosterone are more likely to engage in behaviour that cancels out the beneficial effects of testosterone.' Those men are more likely to smoke, drink too much alcohol and behave in other risky ways.

Booth's research team recently studied testosterone and health in a sample of 4393 men between the ages of 32 and 44 who had done military service. The men were interviewed and medically examined. Testosterone was measured in blood samples taken each morning; these tests revealed that they had an average of

680 nanograms per decilitre (the range of testosterone levels considered normal is very broad, anywhere between 250 and 1250 nanograms per decilitre). Compared with subjects who were slightly below average, those whose levels were slightly above average were 45 per cent less likely to have high blood pressure, 72 per cent less likely to have experienced a heart attack and 45 per cent less likely to rate their health as fair or poor. Yet the hormone seems to be a two-edged sword – men at the higher level were 25 per cent more likely to report one or more injuries, 32 per cent more likely to imbibe five or more drinks a day and 151 per cent more likely to smoke. 'We don't yet fully understand how testosterone benefits health or leads to behaviours detrimental to health,' Booth says. 'More studies are needed to discover the missing pieces to this puzzle. What is clear is that men with higher testosterone levels are at higher risk for negative health outcomes. But there are many men with higher testosterone who don't engage in high risk behaviour and who do realise testosterone-related health benefits.'

The negative side of testosterone for most men's health, though, is that it is probably in part responsible for shortening their lives. Researchers at the Heart Research Institute in Sydney have found that testosterone has an adverse effect on blood vessels and increases men's risk of developing vascular disease. It makes the walls of blood vessels more 'sticky' and so lets cholesterol build up there more easily, and makes the cells in the walls more likely to 'load up with fats', says David Celermajer, who headed the research team. 'This means that maleness is a risk factor for heart disease, like diabetes, and high cholesterol and high blood pressure and obesity.'[5] A typical Australian man in his forties has a 1-in-2 chance of developing coronary disease, while his female counterpart has only a 1-in-3 risk. The risk rises for women after they go through menopause, pointing to the protective effects of estrogen. But Celermajer explains that even two decades after menopause the risk of heart disease is still higher for men. Men who have been castrated or have been given anti-androgenic drugs as part of their treatment for prostate cancer were found to have healthier blood vessels six months later. The team also tested women who had been treated with testosterone during female-to-male gender reassignment and found that their blood vessels were less healthy than those of untreated women the same age. The results suggest that men should be especially careful about having a healthy diet, not smoking and regularly exercising.

David Handelsman, an andrologist at the University of Sydney, has a long-standing interest and expertise in testosterone. He is sceptical that differences in testosterone levels between individuals are especially relevant to differences in body growth or aggression (which he describes as 'an undefinable term used usually by those who have never stopped to think what it means – it is about as valid as defining an alcoholic as someone who drinks more than me'). 'The most useful metaphor I know to illustrate the effects of testosterone is that testosterone is like petrol in a car – so long as there is more than a threshold amount, the car will run. It runs just the same whether the tank is ¼, ½ or full.'

Handelsman is also wary of claims that older men should routinely have testosterone HRT. The existence of a so-called 'manopause' or 'andropause' – the male equivalent of the female menopause – is controversial in itself. Many studies are underway internationally at the time of writing, aimed at providing a more considered answer. But that fundamental doubt hasn't stopped drug manufacturers and some health professionals from actively promoting HRT for men. There's no real medical need to make up for the normal declines in testosterone levels known to occur in older men, Handelsman argues, and he is worried that profit-driven entrepreneurs may overstate the significance of its effects: 'There's no doubt that there is a small, gradual fall in testosterone, as men age. It is very modest. It is nothing like what occurs in menopause, and it is sufficient that it raises the question whether replacing this relatively small fall is worthwhile. It's not immediately obvious that it would be beneficial, but it could well be, and that's the subject of very carefully controlled studies which are under way at the moment.' The decline can be accelerated by the presence of some diseases, such as diabetes and high blood pressure. For such men, the early indications are that there may well be some benefits to HRT, such as the ability to maintain bone structure and muscle mass.

'There is tremendous over-reaction in the use of testosterone based on age alone, or based on not feeling 100 per cent, or not feeling as well "as I felt ten years ago",' Handelsman argued in a recent interview.[6] 'This kind of use for subjective symptoms without careful evaluation of a need for testosterone is at the very least wasteful, and is perhaps very misguided. It could be harmful, I think that remains to be seen whether it really is harmful or not. My own guess is that it's not very harmful, but it's bad medicine and it's wasteful. In fact, whatever you hear about things like male menopause, or andropause, whatever glamorous, conjured-up names there are, most of these really have little basis in medical knowledge or in science, they are really a front for some form of commercial scam.'

Men with genuine testosterone deficiency need to be carefully evaluated by a doctor, Handelsman points out. They may show a wide variety of symptoms, often not very specific. Tiredness and weakness are common, but they alone don't indicate a problem without reliable confirmation of biochemical tests. Such tests actually need to be done on two separate occasions to get consistent findings: 'One of the things that endocrinologists have discovered over time is that if you take people who aren't really androgen deficient and put them on testosterone, you definitely get a placebo effect to start with. People feel great for a little while and then it wears off, and that is very frustrating for the patient, it is very frustrating for the doctor and it's just not good medicine. Basically in that situation, it's also then very difficult to establish whether there really was androgen deficiency in the first place or not. So it's very important that the evaluation is done by people with experience and carefully done before testosterone treatment [is] started.'

It is even possible that declining testosterone levels with age have something of a protective effect against prostate cancer. Most of the testosterone that enters the prostate is converted there to a far more active and potent form, known as dihydrotestosterone. In effect, the prostate gives the hormone a turbo-charge. To develop, prostate cancer seems to require exposure to testosterone early in life followed by sustained exposure over decades. Studies into the origins of the disease show that for at least the 10 years before the disease is detected, there is no apparent relationship between blood levels of testosterone and prostate cancer. Handelsman said: 'There is certainly a relationship: you don't get prostate disease without male levels of testosterone, but it could be, and it seems likely, that it's very early life exposure that's very important here, and also sustained exposure to normal levels throughout life. This is again very similar to the way in which ovarian cancer or breast cancer depend on a lifetime of exposure, the net exposure, to ovulatory cycles and oestrogens. So it's not a very simple relationship one to one; again, the experience we've had with oral contraception in women is that there are also non-contraceptive benefits of oral contraception, and it's very important to keep that in mind. For example, benign breast disease is less common in women who use oral contraceptives, and it's quite likely that benign prostate disease is just as likely to be benefited as to be harmed by the long-term use of testosterone, so long as it's maintained in a physiological range and not in excessive amounts.'

Yet the public perception that a manopause exists, and that its negative effects can be slowed or reversed, already seems to have been established. And that perception – along with the positive expectations it produces – may prove to be more important than mere science in deciding whether mass testosterone therapies become accepted. As one prominent specialist in aging put it in 1995: 'I don't believe in the male midlife crisis. But even though in my perspective there is no epidemiological, physiological or clinical evidence for such a syndrome, I think by the year 2000 the syndrome will exist. There is a very strong interest in treating aging men for profit, just as there is for menopausal women.' Judging by the mushrooming number of clinics aimed at 'treating' normal male aging, he was right.

So much for the waning of a man's desire. But there's a lot else going on inside men's heads. Compared with women, they seem to have a very different attitude to sex – and as we'll see next, there's a growing body of evidence that they may very well think differently because their brains differ in some small but significant ways.

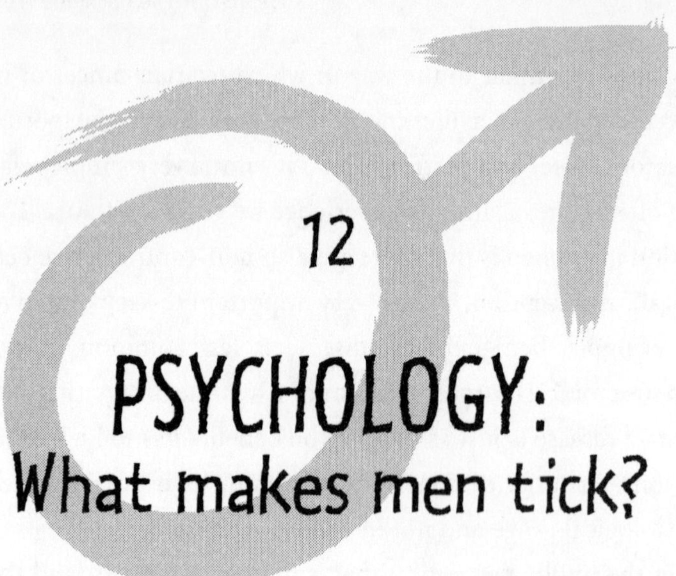

12

PSYCHOLOGY: What makes men tick?

'Heterosexual men would be as likely as homosexual men to have sex most often with strangers, to participate in anonymous orgies in public baths, and to stop off in public restrooms for five minutes of fellatio on the way home from work if women were interested in these activities.'

Don Symons[1]

A CHILL WIND is keening at my ears as I walk along this dim inner-city back lane. I'm not surprised when the locked door I'm looking for turns out to be so unremarkable: apart from a sign, it is barely distinguishable from the adjoining rear entrances to a repair workshop and an office for an import/export business. I ring a buzzer and after a brief exchange through an intercom a woman's voice instructs me to enter and go up a staircase. At the top is an elaborate wooden reception counter and beyond this is a featureless hallway. It's warm in here and I am welcomed just as warmly from behind the counter by an attractive and well-groomed woman in her late twenties: despite the fact that it is the middle of the day, she is wearing a tight dark-blue evening gown and her face is fully made-up with cosmetics. I cannot fail to notice that the front of her dress is cut so low that it barely contains her very large breasts. On the wall behind her are some framed paintings of nude women and I can hear lively music and a woman laughing from another room behind her.

I am inside one of Sydney's busiest massage parlours. Men come here, 7 days a week, 24 hours a day. I am trying informally to learn a little more about who they are and why they are willing to pay strangers to engage in such a personal and intimate act. This is just one of countless thousands of sex establishments for men in cities everywhere around the world. Most of them show a discreet face to the society in which they operate. The receptionist's smile fades slightly when I explain that I want to pull back that veil a little, that I am writing a book about men and hope to gather some insights from women working in the sex industry. 'Oh God, we could tell you some stories about what men want . . .' she laughs cynically, 'but you'll have to speak to the boss.' A few minutes later I have been shown into a small room off the hallway – nondescript except for another painting of a nude on the wall, two lounge chairs and a coffee table with a copy of *Penthouse*. The manager soon enters – a businesslike woman in her late thirties, wearing glasses, a long-sleeved and buttoned dark jacket and skirt. Again I explain my purpose and request her permission to talk to the staff. 'I'm sorry,' she says bluntly. 'We can't help you. This is a massage centre. We don't do sex.' I was taken aback. The place oozed sex, as did its advertising, including an internet site featuring nude photographs of the women who worked there and promises of 'sexy massage' and bare-breasted dancers. But the interview progressed no further. No sex took place here, and that was that.

So I went back one night ostensibly in the role of prospective client. My first name was recorded, prices and facilities were explained and I was ushered into a well-appointed lounge area, with pool tables, a refreshment bar, music and a bare-breasted dancer. It was a quiet night. Half a dozen men of various ages – from their twenties to early fifties, and all white – were sitting somewhat nervously and well-spaced from each other, chatting to the 'ladies'. Several of these women soon approached me, greeted me by my name and introduced themselves. I was suddenly the centre of interest for three attractive and attentive women. As soon as it was clear that I had a rapport with one of them, she suggested that she show me around. The other two women left with a smile and wandered over to join other men. It emerged that for the price of about a day's pay for an average working man, I could have a private room and drink a glass of champagne while I shared a hot spa bath with my masseuse, both of us naked. Then I would receive my massage. The whole thing would take about an hour and I was assured that this was no simple rubdown. I could not have sex with her, she said, nor touch her 'below the waist' nor kiss her lips. But she told me that she would remain naked while she worked, that I could touch and kiss her breasts and I was left in no doubt that my penis would soon be in her expert hands (and, no, it wasn't). I seriously doubt that many wives would agree with the parlour manager that this was not sex of some sort; Bill Clinton would be proud of her.

I'd guess, however, that more than a few men would probably find it convenient to take the same view as Clinton – that this sort of thing is not 'really' sex. Of course, many sex establishments make no bones about it. They offer much more than intimate touching, oral sex or masturbation. As one man who frequents massage parlours and brothels told me: 'You can always get more – whatever you want really – if you're willing to pay.' One prostitute had recently offered to let him have a 'special extra' of unprotected anal sex with her for a mere A$100 more than the A$75 price she asked for half an hour of her time, including protected vaginal intercourse. Her need for money must have been great to risk infection with HIV or another sexually transmitted disease for such a small sum, but what would motivate a man to take up such an offer? His risk of disease – and, if he was married, his risk of discovery as well – would be at least as high as hers, in exchange for a few minutes of sexual release. The fact that some men turn to prostitutes for sex of any kind is puzzling enough to many women; that they would risk acquiring a potentially fatal disease and passing it on to their partner seems inexplicable.

Yet when you look more deeply into the hows and whys of the way men think, the pieces begin to fall into place a little better (this is not to condone or excuse what they do, merely to try to comprehend it). Risk-taking is part and parcel of life as a male and, indeed, for at least some men it may be an end in itself. Men tend to see less risk than women in just about everything, from riding motorcycles to nuclear power plants, according to several large-scale surveys and studies. There's even a substantial proportion of men in the US who see virtually no risk in anything, according to Paul Slovic, a psychologist at the University of Oregon. With colleagues, Slovic has recently found that it is mainly white males who fall into that category: 'It appears that white men are causing the gender effect and that a subset of 30 per cent [of them] are really driving the effect,' says Slovic. When the research team analysed what made these men different, the distinction was in the way they thought about politics and society in general: they tended to be highly authoritarian, anti-egalitarian and they trusted experts. But people who identified with the phrase 'I often feel discriminated against' – notably women and non-whites – perceived life to be much less safe. 'People in a more vulnerable position, socially and economically, see the world as more risky,' Slovic explains.

There's no dodging it: most men think in very different ways from women. It's plain in the way they behave, the way they speak and the opinions they hold. Ask yourself, for example, why poor people are poor: is it their own fault, has society failed them, are they exploited or were they simply born unlucky? If you are a woman, you'll tend to believe poverty can be explained by bad luck or by events beyond individual control. If you're a man, though, you're more likely to view the poor as lazy, spendthrifts or having loose morals. At least, that was the outcome of one 1980s Australian study by Patrick Heaven, a psychologist at Charles Sturt University. Men were more likely to agree with statements such as 'the seriousness of poverty is overstated' and 'in the Western world, there is really no such thing as poverty'. Women tended to blame poverty on low wages, poor schools, prejudice, lack of jobs or exploitation by the rich.

Obviously, poverty exists for many reasons, but why should men be so personally critical of the poor and women so empathic? Slovic's study suggests that your own status in society is what matters most here – not your race, gender or intelligence, but how much you feel in control of your own life. And in the modern world, that's a reflection of prevailing cultural norms that favour males, not some pre-ordained natural law or irresistible genetic command. But some important aspects of male psychology do indeed seem to have a biological basis. If you're a woman, for example, your man may seem a bit slow to pick up when you're peeved or cranky with him. And, if this is the case, it may be because you're not as dangerous to him as a man. Lisa Goos, a psychology graduate student of York University in Toronto, Canada, showed 58 women and 56 men college students photographs of the faces of men and women displaying four negative emotions: anger, fear, disgust, or sadness.[2] The test subjects saw each photo for a mere 30 milliseconds (a millisecond is one-thousandth of a second). Males who were exposed to angry female facial expressions recognised them only about 30 per cent of the time. That was surprising, because 'reams of research have shown that most expressions are perceived better when the expresser is a woman,' says Goos. 'The reversal of the pattern is predictable by evolutionary theory, which says that information important for survival will be taken in, and used, in very special ways.' A next step, she says, might be to try to identify special brain regions involved in anger recognition. Psychologist Ruben Gur, of the University of Pennsylvania Medical Center, says the findings are 'consistent with evolutionary theory: because men are physically stronger, it's less important for them to know whether a woman is upset.'

Men also tend to be more inclined to be impulsive – and yes, selfish – in gratifying their wants and needs. As one married man who occasionally goes to brothels for sex told me: 'The thing is that I can have sex there when I want it: not tomorrow night or next week or when she [his wife] is in the mood, but when I am.' Evolutionary psychologists Martin Daly and Margo Wilson see ancient roots in men's greater propensity for risk-taking and impulsiveness. Men, especially young ones, are more reckless drivers, greater drug and alcohol abusers than women, and less likely to worry about the effects of pollution or sexually transmitted diseases. 'They are also more inclined to choose immediate rewards over larger but later ones and more often experience a close brush with danger as a rewarding thrill,' Daly and Wilson say. 'The ubiquity of these tendencies across cultures implies that they cannot be simply a consequence of modern society.' They have also found that a man is 20 times more likely to kill another man than a woman is to kill another woman. Men are also more likely to kill women than vice-versa.

'These facts, together with the observation that males are the more aggressive sex in nearly all mammals, have led many people to suppose that men are unavoidably aggressive and that homicide is a natural consequence of male biology,' say Richard Nisbett, co-director of the Culture and Cognition Program at the University of Michigan, and Dov Cohen, assistant professor of psychology at the University of Illinois, who have studied how culture and nature intersect in male aggression.[3] 'Yet the striking variation in homicide rates among different societies makes it clear that, whatever men's predispositions may be, cultures have a great influence on the likelihood that a man will kill.' The homicide rate is 10 times higher in the US than in Norway, and in Colombia it is 15 times higher than in peaceful Costa Rica.

Even within nations, regional differences appear that demand an explanation. Nisbett and others have shown that in small cities in the South and South-west of the US, for example, the homicide rate for white males is twice that of the rest of the country. A white man living in a small Southern county is four times more likely to commit a murder than his peer living in the Midwest. Researchers have found that one special set of conditions reliably provokes a high homicide rate: 'It occurs when men face danger from the actions of other males and the state does not provide protection. Men respond by resorting to self-protection and demonstrating that they are strong enough to deter aggression. This type of social system is known as a culture of honour. A man establishes his honour by tolerating no challenge or disrespect, responding to insults and threats to his property with threatened or actual violence.'[4] It's a cultural theme that dominates the Mediterranean region, the former colonial outposts of Spanish culture, the Masai tribesmen of Africa, the horsemen of the central Asian steppes and inland parts of my own country, Australia, in cattle and sheep-grazing regions.

In each of these cultures, animal husbandry is a common feature: for instance, the US South was largely settled by Scottish and Irish pig- and cattle-herders under fairly lawless conditions, while the North was colonised mainly by English, Dutch and German crop-growers. Those in the North were at far less risk of having their assets stolen – it's not as easy to rustle wheat as cattle – and it better served their interests to get along with their neighbours and to be more conciliatory. The historic male bluster and bravado of the South seems to have continued to the present day: the high homicide rate there is, according to FBI statistics, overwhelmingly due to incidents arising from insults, bar brawls, lovers' triangles or neighbours' quarrels. Nisbett and Cohen's team has found that Southerners are more likely than Northerners to think it justifiable to use force to protect home and property, more likely to respond to an insult and more likely to advise their sons to fight bullies rather than reason with them. That code of honour is even enshrined in law, with many statutes in the South endorsing a 'true man' rule, which permits a man to stand his ground and kill an aggressor rather than be expected to retreat. Looked at like this, all those gunslinging cowboys having showdowns in the American movies of my youth seem more comprehensible.

The team has also conducted experiments in which unwitting volunteers are confronted in a narrow passageway by a man who bumps into them and swears at them. Subjects from the North tended to shrug off the incident, but their testosterone and cortisol levels surged, suggesting responses of stress and aggression. The experiment was immediately followed with another, in which subjects found themselves facing a tall and heavily built man walking towards them down the middle of a corridor and showing no signs of deviating from his path. Southerners who had been insulted in the previous experiment tended to wait until the big man was a mere metre away before stepping aside, while those who had not been insulted stepped aside when he was still three metres away. Such results show that the culture of honour remains strong in the South, although it is gradually diminishing. 'It has already come a long way since the era when a man would ask a prospective son-in-law if he had ever done any "sparkin" – putting his life on the line in combat,' Nisbett and Cohen comment. 'Economic and social changes, together with immigration from other regions, will eventually erode what remains of the tradition. In the meantime, the contrast between North and South shows that violence by men is a matter of nurture as much as one of nature. Male aggression is not inevitable. Whether a man reaches for his gun or his civility when insulted is a matter of culture.'

So we're still a long way from understanding why men think as they do, and what aspects of their behaviour are malleable to cultural change. As many studies like those of Nisbett and Cohen reveal, what seems an inbuilt biological trait can easily turn out not to be so at all. Our thinking about sex and gender is subject to many subtle cultural influences and attitudes can be hard to shift. One recent study, for example, found that in the 1970s male cartoon characters outnumbered female characters by almost four to one on American TV. Despite apparently fundamental social change in the intervening 20 years, male cartoon characters still outnumbered female cartoon characters almost four to one and were still stereotypical. Cynthia Spicher and psychologist Mary Hudak, of Allegheny College, found that male cartoon characters were not only still more prominent than female characters, but they were also portrayed as powerful, aggressive and smart. 'Occasionally there's a token female cartoon character but she's like lime jello – she's bland,' Hudak said.

When it comes to sex, research tends to confirm what many people believe. Men generally want to have sex more often than women, so there's a disparity between demand and supply. Men are also able to have sex more often: they don't menstruate, have babies or nurse infants. In many cultures, men are also more 'permitted' to have sex: young men can 'sow their wild oats', for example, before settling into marriage, and double standards often apply to acts of infidelity among those in relationships. And men often have more means and opportunity to have sex: like it or not, child-rearing does tend to tie women more to the home, while men's jobs mainly take them out of the home and sometimes out of town.

Brad's story

Brad's job included free air travel and a party lifestyle, both of which he actively pursued for many years – between and during several marriages. At one stage he commuted between dual lovers in his hometown, Auckland, and a South-East Asian city. He is now 53 and faithful to Jodie, his present wife, but financial burdens resulting from divorce settlements and alimony payments strain their marriage. His experiences have left him angry with women . . .

'My first marriage left me feeling devastated. After three years, my wife just told me she didn't love me. She came from an ethnic culture where all the sons were given cars and property when they reached adulthood, but because she was female she got nothing. Well, she got them from me. I think she saw me as a way to get her share and that she never loved me in the first place.

'It took a long while to get over that. But then I had an absolute ball for about five or six years. I slept with a lot of women. In the house I was sharing it was party, party, party. I had regular sex with a married woman, Sharon. It was convenient for her because I didn't want commitment and I didn't care because I'd lost respect for marriage. She knew I was sleeping with other women; I was quite open about it.

'Eventually Sharon's marriage ended – her husband was having affairs as well – and our relationship just kind of evolved, until she got pregnant. I married her because I was taught to "do the right thing" and take responsibility when that happened.

'But it was never going to work. My heart wasn't in it and I'd just met Jodie and I really liked her. I used to pretend to go out jogging at night with coins taped to my backside so I could call Jodie from a pay-phone. We'd talk for ages and then I'd sprint home to make myself look red-faced and sweaty.

'Later on, when Jodie and I fell in love and started having an affair, I would drive to her place then change afterwards into sweaty jogging clothes that I kept specially in my bag. That way Sharon wouldn't smell anything, but as it turned out I probably didn't need to bother because she was having an affair as well.

'But I haven't once been unfaithful to Jodie since we married. I love her and find life very fulfilling with her. There have been times when, if a woman with a reasonable body came along and offered some loving care and attention, I might have gone for it.

'But those sorts of offers don't come anymore. I don't have the looks, the disposable income or the time and now I really don't have the inclination, quite frankly. It sounds corny but these days I'd be quite happy to have a platonic relationship with a woman and just be good friends.

'I couldn't have imagined myself saying that 15 years ago. I guess my attitude at that time was summed up by what one of my mates said when a woman told him that she just wanted to be friends. He said to her, "I've got all the friends I need, I just want a f...".

'It's difficult for men of my generation. We had all the wild times from the 1960s and so on, but there's still that lingering thing of the man being the head of the household.

> 'I'm angry with women now because they expect men to be the same as them and blame men if they're not.
>
> 'I was reading the advice column in a women's magazine recently. This woman had written in about her boyfriend watching porn videos. The responses from other women were typical – they saw it as dirty and filthy, degrading to women and so on.
>
> 'There was no effort at all to see it from a man's perspective. Women and men are different. Men are titillated by the visual thing and I don't think women are to the same extent.
>
> 'I'm angry about their double standards as well: they want equality – equal pay, equal jobs, equal housework and looking after the kids – but deep down, when the s... hits the fan in the household finances, they turn to the man and say, "Where's the money?" The buck still stops with the man. Women want to be the chief executive officer but not the chairman of the board.'

Men are far more likely than women to find anonymous casual sex appealing. Among adults who are not in steady relationships, men are six times more likely to answer 'certainly would' when asked if they would have sex with an attractive member of the opposite sex if they could do so without fear of discovery, disease, pregnancy or of having to commit to a relationship, according to one American study. Even among people in committed relationships, men were four times more likely than women to be 'sure' that they would do so, the study found. The massage parlour I visited fits that bill for many men – their money buys not just the pleasure of sex but freedom from the effort of courting a woman's interest, freedom from any other involvement with her, and her complicity in keeping his infidelity secret. That approach makes sense in terms of the psychology bequeathed to men through their animal ancestry, evolutionary biologists argue. Women, on the other hand, have far more to lose from sex without commitment: an unwanted pregnancy, for example, or more severe social sanctions.

Even textbooks that deal in great depth with all scientific aspects of *Homo sapiens* struggle when it comes to sex differences. *The Cambridge Encyclopedia of Human Evolution*, for example, addresses the issue only briefly and raises as many questions as it does answers. The key entry, written by Georgina Mace, of the Zoological Society of London, reads: 'Humans are sexually dimorphic in size and strength (males are larger and more muscular), in physiology (males have higher metabolic rates), in hair distribution and in life history (males have higher juvenile mortality, attain sexual maturity later and die younger). Darwin postulated that differences in size and strength between men and women are, as in other primates, a product of sexual selection. Many discussions of human sexual dimorphism are preoccupied with separating genetical from environmental influences in dimorphic traits. However, the two are always closely intertwined. For example, genetically based hormonal differences must have implications for patterns of growth and development, which will generate disparities and mortality, susceptibility to certain diseases, strength and other physical distinctions, and some behavioural disparities. However, cultural influences are so strong in human societies that they will nearly always disguise any broad patterns of human sexual dimorphism.' That's not to say there's not a wealth of useful material to delve into, it's just that Mace's summary reflects the fact that it's easy enough to observe that 'men are from Mars and women from Venus', as pop psychologist John Gray puts it, but much harder to say scientifically how, and harder still to say why.

These are not trivial questions, though. Far from it. Men in Australia, for example, are about four times more likely than women to successfully commit suicide. While the overall suicide rate has been pretty constant for more than a century, the stable total masks an important underlying trend – the suicide rate for women seems to be falling, while for men it is rising. That trend has been evident since the 1960s and is most obvious among young men aged 15–24, and more so in rural communities than in cities.[5] Suicide risk is known to be linked with mental illness (especially depression), and alcohol and drug abuse. While substance abuse is increasing in both sexes, it seems to be a more important factor in suicide for men than for women. The impulsiveness of young men forms a lethal combination when it is mixed with drug abuse, violence, depression and access to the means to commit suicide.

Homosexuality is another risk factor. A recent Canadian study showed that young gay men are far more likely than heterosexual men to have suicidal thoughts and actions: of 750 subjects, only 13 per cent were gay males, yet they accounted for 62.5 per cent of suicide attempts in the sample. A 1969 Kinsey Institute study of 575 predominantly gay males in San Francisco made a similar finding – being gay rather than straight meant the suicide risk was about 14 times higher. Men also tend to choose more violent and lethal ways to kill themselves than women – the no-second-chance gunshot, hanging, high-speed crash or gassing with car-exhaust fumes.

And there's other persuasive evidence from therapists, counsellors and doctors that all is not well with the male psyche in many Western nations. Many men seem depressed, confused and 'absent', in the sense of being missing in action. 'They are absent from themselves, not in touch with their own feelings and they don't know what they want or what is good for them,' says Don Edgar. 'They are absent from their partners, can't communicate or engage in mutual self-disclosure and barely have enough time for a "quickie" every now and then. They are absent from their children, leaving home before they are out of bed and getting home too late to play or read a story or to ask how their day has been. And then they are absent from work because their neglect of family life rebounds on them in marital and parenting problems, or neglect of themselves has resulted in stress, depression and ill health.'

So let's look at what we do know about what makes men tick differently from women. Some of those differences seem to be in the way their brains function. For starters, it's long been known that men are better than women at performing certain tasks (just as women perform better in others). Men have repeatedly been shown to do better in tests that involve mathematical reasoning or finding two items that match in a jumble of similar items. It's also well-established that men tend to be better able to mentally rotate a three-dimensional object, or figure out where the holes punched in a folded piece of paper will be when the paper's unfolded. They're also better at tasks in which motor skills are needed to guide or intercept a projectile accurately. As a boy, it seemed obvious to me that most girls weren't as good as boys at throwing stones, balls, sticks or whatever at targets – girls were 'cack-handed' by our standards. Women are better able to work out whether an object has been displaced in a group of objects they recently saw, better at mathematical calculations and precision manual tasks and better able to recall a list of unrelated words.

In some small but apparently important ways men seem to think differently from women because their thinking equipment – the brain – is different. It's not so much a question of size. Even though men's brains are larger (about 15 per cent on average), the size difference probably relates mostly to their larger body size. And it's not that men are any smarter than women, despite what many scientists and philosophers once asserted. But men and women do differ significantly in certain talents. 'For the past few decades, it has been ideologically fashionable to insist that these behavioural differences are minimal and are the consequences of variations in experience during development before and after adolescence,' notes Doreen Kimura, a Canadian psychologist.[6] 'Evidence accumulated more recently, however, suggests that the effects of sex hormones on brain organisation occur so early in life that from the start the environment is acting on differently wired brains in boys and girls.'

Neither of the wiring alternatives seems to have a clear-cut advantage over the other. 'Major sex differences in intellectual function seem to lie in patterns of ability rather than in the overall level of intelligence,' Kimura says. 'Men, on average, perform better than women on certain spatial tasks . . . They outperform women in mathematical reasoning tests and in navigating their way through a route.' Women, on the other hand, recall landmarks from a route better.

The sex difference in navigation is intriguing. Why should a woman be better at remembering to take the left fork in the road when you come to that large tree just past the church, while a man successfully travels the same route by following his directional nose? The old complaint about men being reluctant to stop and ask for directions seems to have an element of biological truth. If our ancestors were mildly polygynous, there may be a sound reason for the difference. Males of most such species roam more than females, covering large home territories to boost their chances of encountering females or providing resources to support more females. A male orang-utan, for example, may have a large rainforest territory that overlaps with those of several females and will patrol his boundaries to deter other males. As they reach sexual maturity young males are also more likely to be driven away by older males, so having good spatial skills to help them negotiate long distances and unfamiliar terrain is a definite plus. But females, constrained to smaller territories by motherhood, may benefit more from having brains wired for remembering specific visual cues – such as a fruit-bearing tree to feed her children. Various anthropological studies have shown that boys range further from home than girls – whether they live in the Kalahari Desert, rural England or American cities – and that this difference between them becomes even greater as they approach puberty.

Dean Falk, an anthropologist at the University of Alabama, and her colleagues have suggested a plausible evolutionary explanation for men having larger brains than women. The team studied 414 male and 390 female human brains, comparing males and females of the same body weight. Falk was surprised to find that 'at any body weight, men have bigger brains than women'. For those with a body weight of 60 kilograms, for example, women's brains weigh about 1256 grams and men's about 1373 grams, a difference of about 9 per cent. The same trend was found in comparable data for 39 male and 44 female rhesus monkeys, a species in which males leave their birth groups at puberty in search of mates: the pattern was 'remarkably consistent' with that of humans. Falk suspects that the extra 'luggage space' in the male brain is used to process visual information and to construct mental maps of environments. There's no such sex difference among gibbons, where males are monogamous and stay home. Some male voles – from polygynous species – also travel far afield during the mating season in search of an appropriate mate, whereas in monogamous species the males are stay-at-homes. 'In polygynous but not monogamous species, males have better navigational skills than females – useful for getting to and fro during mating season,' Falk says. 'Men have better mapping skills than women, and your computer needs extra memory to process complicated graphics.'

But how and when do these kinds of differences first arise between men and women? Psychologists at the University of Massachusetts have recently suggested a surprising primary influence on the formation of men's brains – their mothers. The team leader, Christine Wagner, explains that scientists have known for almost two decades that there are structural and neurobiological differences between the brains of men and women. It was thought that sex hormones produced by fetuses and infants themselves were solely responsible for bringing about those distinctions. Remember that if you castrate a male rat pup immediately after birth it will grow up behaving more like a female – as an adult it won't mount other rats so much and it will arch its back when it is receptive to sex. Give a newborn female rat androgens and she'll grow up behaving more like a male. 'These lifelong effects of early exposure to sex hormones are characterised as "organisational" because they appear to alter brain function permanently during a critical period in prenatal or postnatal development,' Kimura says. 'Administering the same sex hormones at later stages or in the adult has no such effect.'

Scientists at Johns Hopkins University in Baltimore, Maryland, recently uncovered 'striking' differences between men and women in a part of the brain linked with ability to estimate time, judge speed, visualise things three-dimensionally and solve mathematical problems.[7] These differences may help explain why more men than women are architects, mathematicians and racing-car drivers. The team showed that a brain region called the inferior parietal lobule (IPL) – part of the cerebral cortex found on both sides of the brain, just above ear-level – is significantly larger overall in men. Men in the study, which involved detailed brain scans of 15 people, had roughly 6 per cent more IPL tissue than women. The difference is asymmetric, with men having a larger left IPL and women having a larger right, although the asymmetry is less obvious in women. 'This is the same part of Albert Einstein's brain that was particularly large compared with controls,' says psychiatrist Godfrey Pearlson, who headed the project. 'Scientists have noticed this region is also larger in the post-mortem brains of other physicists and mathematicians. The inferior parietal lobule is far more developed in people than in animals and has evolved relatively recently.' It is involved in processing information from senses such as vision and touch, and in types of thinking involved in selective attention and perception.

Other studies have linked the right IPL with working memory of spatial relationships, the ability to sense relationships between body parts and awareness of a person's mood or feelings. The left

IPL is more involved in perception, such as judging how fast something is moving, estimating time and having the ability to rotate three-dimensional figures mentally. But the sex differences in the IPL don't automatically mean men are better at some tasks than women. As Pearlson says: 'It's easy to find women who are fantastic at math and physics and men who excel in language skills. Only when we look at very large populations and look for slight but significant trends do we see the generalisations. There are plenty of exceptions, but there's also a grain of truth, revealed through the brain structure, that we think underlies some of the ways people characterise the sexes.' Pearlson has also shown that two crucial language areas in the frontal and temporal lobes of the brain are significantly larger in women.

The bundle of nerve fibres connecting the two sides of the brain – the corpus callosum – also seems to be larger in women. In addition, there's recent evidence that men have more 'grey matter' in their brains, while women have more 'white matter'. Grey brain tissue is involved in transferring information between distant regions of the brain, which is vital for the highest levels of spatial performance. White brain tissue is used for computation. The difference may explain why men do not score higher than women in intelligence tests despite having greater brain volumes, which are known to be linked to higher intelligence. Male intelligence, it seems, is not better or worse than female intelligence, but simply different.

Such organisational changes can be seen in the brains of some animals as well. In songbirds, for example, the part of the brain that deals with singing is six times larger in males than in the non-singing females. In male rats, part of the hypothalamus – which plays a central role in how the brain directs sexual behaviour – is visibly larger (between five and eight times) than it is in females. Likewise, a parallel nerve clump in the human hypothalamus is larger in men than in women. Intriguingly, it seems that our gender identity and sexual orientation may be related to such differences in anatomy: neuroscientist Simon LeVay has reported, amid some controversy, that this nerve clump is smaller in homosexual men than in heterosexual men.

A team led by Dutch neuroscientist Dick Swaab has found a further brain difference between gay and straight men. Another region of the hypothalamus linked to our circadian rhythm – or biological clock – is thought to help time daily variations in the production of sex hormones. That region is thinner in men and fatter in women, and it is twice as large in gay men as in straight men; researchers led by Jiang-Ning Zhou have found evidence of similar differences between heterosexual men and male-to-female transsexuals.

Meanwhile, very recent studies of rats by Wagner's team suggest that, during pregnancy, the maternal hormone progesterone may play an important role in shaping the brain for gender-specific behaviour. 'The sex differences in the brains of rats seem to parallel those found in humans,' Wagner says. 'Therefore, this finding may offer us a window into the fetal development of human brains.' Progesterone is the most abundant hormone in the mother's body during pregnancy and is essential for maintaining the pregnancy. 'Our research demonstrated that progesterone from the mother's blood can enter the blood and brain of the fetus.' There the hormone fits into certain receptors, like a lock and key, and once joined they actually modify the way brain cells work. Fetal males seem to be more sensitive to the hormone, having many more progesterone receptors than do female fetuses. This is because the growing baby boy is producing testosterone and when it enters part of the brain called the medial preoptic nucleus, it undergoes a chemical conversion. This, in turn, switches on a gene that activates the production of progesterone receptors.

It has been suggested that sexual orientation may be influenced through that process, or a similar one. Some researchers have wondered whether gay men, for example, can trace the roots of their attraction to other men back to hormonal disruptions in the process of brain-building in the womb or soon after.

I should point out here that the terms homosexual and lesbian weren't coined until the 1850s (replacing 'inverts', the earlier Victorian term), when same-sex lovers came to be seen as having potential for study, treatment or even cure. That began a period of interaction with science and medicine that was a very loaded and negative one for homosexual people, since much of the intent of that scrutiny was to control, inhibit or eradicate people such as themselves. Just as the concept was redefined then, some social historians argue that the flowering of the modern 'gay' male identity is yet another reinvention, albeit one self-adopted and more positive.

For the purposes of this book, there seems little point in trying to pin down homosexuality with a definition when the depth and breadth of same-sex activity in the human race is so extensive and makes such a shifting target. So I'll be unscientific here: like biological sex, anatomy and gender identity, sexual orientation embraces the full spectrum – from exclusively heterosexual, through asexual, to exclusively homosexual. At each point along the spectrum, sexuality can be expressed in the usual inventive range of human ways. At Sydney's famous annual Gay and Lesbian

Mardi Gras parade, for example, men of every shape, size and persuasion take part: tubby men, hairy men, muscle men and queens; construction workers, flight attendants, businessmen, police, farmers and doctors; men into leather, men into lace, men into pleasure and men into pain. Some are promiscuous, some live in stable long-term monogamous relationships. I even know of one gay man (a former priest) who is happily married to a lesbian (a former nun) and they have a clutch of children.

Such a marriage would have been frowned upon by Magnus Hirschfield, an early sexologist who believed that same-sex orientation was nature's way of ridding the gene pool of defective stock. Beliefs like this found fertile ground in the eugenics movement and Nazism, and were applied with equal vigour to a wide range of people on the basis of their race, mental capacities, criminal history and so on. What we can say simply as a matter of fact (not opinion or moral stance) is that a sizeable proportion of human males can and do seek sexual pleasure with other human males – either briefly in their youth, occasionally or regularly in adulthood, or exclusively for life. There are few, if any, reliable statistics to quantify that proportion, and it is unlikely that there will be any in the near future. Establishing the facts of this (and many other facets of human sexual behaviour), would entail research that would run foul of most ethics committee these days. Let's face it, some of the observations made so obsessively by Alfred Kinsey and his colleagues in the 1950s were tacky and invasive, regardless of the question marks hanging over the scientific validity of some of their work. Yet Kinsey's team was the first to systematically study sexual orientation in the US, collecting the personal sexual histories of some 20,000 individuals. These revealed no real discernible pattern – homosexuality occurred in all families, locations, ethnic groups and socio-economic divisions.

Likewise, social scientists have now documented a wide diversity of attitudes towards homosexuality. Barring a few societies, such as those from Melanesia in which sex between men and adolescents is socially institutionalised in male initiations, homosexual activity (as distinct from an exclusively homosexual lifestyle) is widely seen as 'immature' conduct to be forsaken once marriage and heterosexual intercourse become possible, says anthropologist Alice Schlegel. In short, it's generally viewed as a surrogate sexual outlet for young men whose access to women is prohibited or restricted (you'll note, of course, that jails, seminaries, the military and remote outposts impose these circumstances on men of all ages). In parts of the Philippines, it is quite acceptable for boys to sit intimately close, limbs entwined, whereas adult male friends sit close together but are careful to avoid such touching. Among Nyakyusa people in Africa, boys move into special villages of their own when they reach puberty and parents turn a blind eye to their sons' sexual experimentation, which includes interfemoral intercourse – that is, thrusting their penises between a partner's thighs – with both males and females. And no doubt many adolescent boys in modern industrialised societies have their first experiences of sexual activity with other adolescent boys.

Grigor's story

Grigor started experimenting with sex when he was about 11 years old. Now in his forties, he has been in a happy, stable and monogamous relationship for 20 years. He

has always been attracted to women as friends and companions, but never in a sexual way. Here he tells how he came to realise that he was homosexual.

'As a kid, my closest friends were three girls. We played all the usual games so long as they involved taking your clothes off – doctors and nurses, strip poker or whatever. There was a sexual element to it, of course, but never any sexual activity.

'My best male friend was gay as well, but we didn't know that at the time. We used to play pop stars, putting pegs in our hair to make it look long. One of us would perform and the other would be the fan and, of course, pop stars had sex with fans. That was how it started, just a bit of mutual masturbation. It was fun and it felt good.

'We both liked girls because they were into fashion and we thought it was cool. One day our teacher sent home a letter to both of our parents saying that we were spending too much time with the girls.

'His parents reacted with total denial and tried to have the teacher sacked. Mine were calmer about it and their reaction was that I had to play sport, join a football team. I told them I didn't want to and managed to talk them out of it.

'I had my first sex encounter at the end of that year when we were on holiday. I was vaguely aware that something was going on at the public toilets at the end of the road by the beach. I went up there to have a look one evening and pretty soon a car was following me. I wouldn't get in the car, even though I was excited, so the guy had to open the door and had oral sex with me while I stood there beside it. It was all over very quickly, but I liked it.

'When I was 12 I wrote away for a men's underwear catalogue and haunted the mailbox for days afterwards to avoid detection by my parents. After it arrived I spent a lot of time in the toilet with an "upset stomach"!

'It all became more obvious at high school. I had long hair and the other boys called me a nancy and I got beaten up. I avoided trouble as much as I could but it got pretty heavy. I didn't think of myself as gay, though.

'I had girlfriends, because that's what everyone did. The funny thing was that I could get all the good girls because I was very fashionable and I could talk to them.

'In fact, I got a date with the hottest babe in school. I took her on a picnic and took food and – can you believe it? – a game of Scrabble! She just wanted to go walking in the bushes and I couldn't figure it out. I had no sexual desire for her at all.

'It was a relief in some ways when I left school at 16 and went into the fashion industry. I was still getting a bit of action at the beach during the day, but I just saw it as an outlet – it was exciting but I thought I would eventually find a girl.

'My cousin took me to my first gay club but they were bitchy queens and I wasn't like that; I was scared.

'When I was about 17 I started suffering bad headaches. My doctor recommended that I go to a psychiatrist and I was really lucky – he was great. I suppose I was beginning to have doubts myself. When we talked about sex, I was saying how I fancied pop stars, and that my boss and the guys I worked with were gay.

'His advice was to go out and find a girl – an easy girl, if you know what I mean – and give it a go. If nothing was happening for me, I was gay. I walked out of there so relieved. I think I'd been given approval to be myself. I didn't have to go out and find the girl. That was it. The load lifted off me. I was gay – it was okay.

'Mum had a nervous breakdown – literally – when she found out. Dad couldn't understand why. I said: "Dad, Mum knows that I'm a homosexual." He looked blank, so I added: "I'm a pansy, a queer," trying to think of terms he'd understand. He kind of groaned and put his head down in his hands and that was it. He never mentioned it again until years later when he and Mum were watching a TV program about homosexuality and he turned to Mum and said: "Grigor's grown out of that now, hasn't he?"'

It is plain that human males have long been motivated and/or permitted to pursue their sexual desires in many ways. More than a century before Christ, the great Roman comedy playwright Plautus set out guidelines that persisted into late antiquity: he advised his male audience that it was okay for them to seek sex outside of marriage and 'go the public way' – that is, visit prostitutes – and that 'as long as you do not make a path through posted land, as long as you hold off from brides, single women, maidens, the youth and free boys, love whatever you want'. These guidelines, flexibly interpreted, ranked sex with other men as a simple question of individual preference. So a free-born Roman man could have sex with slaves (male, female, young or adult) and prostitutes (male or female) pretty much without fear of social censure. Yet there was a double standard in operation: if he was the recipient of anal sex or gave fellatio to another man he would be the target of malicious gossip and ridicule, according to anthropologist and historian Will Roscoe. Like the Greeks, the Romans admired youthful males with long, flowing hair but publicly detested effeminate men – a scorn often used by politicians to attack their opponents by accusing them of being *mollis* (soft and feminine). And allowing sexual penetration was a surefire way for a man to be seen as having lost his masculinity. What a contrast to the Sambia of New Guinea who, you may recall, deemed that adolescent males could acquire masculinity only by ingesting semen after fellating older males.

All this cultural and historical diversity, of course, suggests that nature, not nurture, is at work. This, in turn, has prompted more questions about a biological basis for sexual orientation. Studies conducted in the 1950s suggested that homosexuality runs in family lines, with a male identical twin being highly likely to be homosexual if his brother was. Further twin studies confirmed those findings, pointing to inheritance being a factor for lesbians as well. More recently, factors as diverse as maternal stress during pregnancy, birth order, number of siblings, age of parents, age at puberty, left- and right-handedness, finger length and the architecture of the inner ear have been scrutinised for more clues. Hormonal influences, especially fetal exposure to high levels of testosterone, remain a focus of research. A recent Canadian study, for example, re-examined the genital sizes of more than 5000 men whose intimate details had been recorded over 25 years by the Kinsey Institute. On average, gay men had penises that were longer and broader than those of straight men – a result suggesting a joint hormonal influence on brain and body. Recent twin studies have cast doubt on those of the post-war era: a study on the sexual orientation of some 5000 Australian twins, for example, suggests that genetic influences are weak – an important finding because the study included twins of all kinds, most of whom weren't gay.

While some homosexual people find the whole idea of such research offensive, worrying or simply irrelevant, others support it as a way to satisfy their curiosity about themselves or to provide facts as ammunition in the fight against homophobia. There's no evidence that people choose their orientation, since it usually emerges early in life before sexual experience is acquired, nor that it can be changed by choice or by psychotherapy. 'Over 35 years of objective, well-designed scientific research has shown that homosexuality, in and of itself, is not associated with mental disorders or emotional or social problems,' says a recent statement from the world's largest professional psychology organisation, the American Psychological Association. As Roger Short and Malcolm Potts point out in their recent book, *Ever Since Adam and Eve*, a genetic basis for homosexuality seems unlikely. 'Failure to reproduce is death to the line, and if homosexual behaviour were encoded in our genes than it is a trait that would have become extinct long ago,' they argue. It is also possible that brain differences between gay and straight men are a consequence, rather than a cause, of their differing behaviour, they note.

Another puzzle is the fact that men are at much lower risk than women of experiencing major depression. It may be that male depression is different and not so well diagnosed. But it may be that men and women are equally liable to become depressed for biological reasons and that women then suffer an additional risk. It's possible, for example, that men's greater grasp on power in public life and relatively high social status have a general protective effect by giving them that feeling of 'eminence' known to boost a sense of well-being. That may also apply in individual relationships where the balance of power favours one spouse over another. The disparity may be related to their coping styles, experts say. Men tend to use strategies that distract them from what is worrying them. Their fix-it tendency prompts them to respond by thinking and acting in ways that make them feel in control of their problem. But women tend to 'brood' and ruminate more, often with other women: men may find that process of 'talking about' a problem (with women or other men) somewhat pointless and frustrating; their inclination is that 'doing something' is more likely to resolve it. It is notable here that women are often advised to exercise more – for the sense of self-discipline, control and mastery it imparts – as a way of tackling depression and, of course, male culture and biology both tend to promote physical activity and sport.

Men's lesser tendency to depression may also be partly attributable to the way they learn to socialise differently as children. Early socialisation may make women more emotionally reliant, according to Heather A. Turner, of the University of New Hampshire, and her colleagues. In a survey of 1393 Canadian subjects they found a strong link between emotional reliance and depression. Men were significantly less likely to be emotionally reliant, independent of other factors like job and marital status, education and income. 'For men, emotional reliance may be perceived as a sign of sensitivity – perhaps a desirable trait for someone in a more powerful position, but one that does not necessarily create losses in ability or authority,' says Turner. 'In other words, males and females may develop different self-conceptions or personal attributes relatively early in life that influence the likelihood of experiencing depressive symptoms.' The tendency to be emotionally reliant (that is, to rely heavily on the positive feedback of others to maintain self-esteem) is developed in women long before adulthood. 'Identity formation for females is inextricably tied to and dependent upon the development of intimate relationships. As a result, women's self-conceptions are most strongly defined through interpersonal associations.' Adolescent boys and girls differ greatly in their sensitivity to the way other people assess them: girls tend to focus on being liked by others, while boys are more likely to give weight to academic and sporting goals, according to Turner.

Emotional reliance also seems to have less impact on men; even those men in the study who were emotionally reliant were less likely than the women to be depressed. Predictably, married subjects were more likely to be emotionally reliant than those who were unmarried. But, consistent with other studies, the research suggests that the benefits of marriage seem greater for men than for women. Men not only depend more on their partners for emotional support but they also get more benefit from marriage than women do. Research carried out by Laura M. Glynn (now at the University of California at Irvine), and her colleagues suggests that a woman's emotional support is more beneficial to health than a man's. Glynn's team took 109 university undergraduates with normal resting blood pressure, then subjected them to stress by getting them to make an impromptu five-minute speech to a male or female listener. The listeners were trained to behave supportively or non-supportively on command: either through sympathetic nods, smiling and laughing and murmuring 'good point' now and then; or by slouching, withholding praise and not responding when the speaker smiled or laughed. Both men and women speakers had lower blood-pressure increases when female listeners were more supportive than when male ones were. Negative feedback – or none at all – is more stressful and results in much higher blood-pressure increases. 'If you accept the idea that reducing the magnitude of blood-pressure responses to stress can have a protective effect on the cardiovascular system, then people with friends – especially female friends – should suffer less heart disease,' says Glynn. She says the findings are consistent with the notion that married men are healthier than single men, and that women do not profit as much from marriage (or suffer as much from a breakup) in terms of health because the support they gain or lose from their partners is less valuable.

Thus, there's little doubt that there are sex differences in the human brain, but as science journalist Deborah Blum writes: 'they are few, they are slight; we don't know what causes them, and in many cases we don't know what they do. On the other hand, they are real.' Blum points to another option – that men and women may have very similar brains but use them differently. Male stroke victims, for example, can suffer much more than women do from damage to one side of their brains; it may be that women are better able to compensate by using the undamaged side. And by monitoring brain activity, it's been shown that during word-selection tasks most men use only the left sides of their brain, where language is mainly localised, while women's brains are active in both hemispheres. Intriguingly, boys are four times more likely than girls to stammer, and tend to be over-represented in remedial reading classes.

Few credible scientists, however, have been willing or able to try to draw together nature and nurture to provide an overarching view of how and why men and women come to think differently. So I'm going to rely heavily here on Eleanor Maccoby, a respected and refreshing exception to that trend, whose seminal book, *The Two Sexes: Growing up apart, coming together*, elegantly distils the results of hundreds of research studies.[8] Dubbed the 'mother of contemporary gender theory in developmental psychology', Maccoby suggests that nature is a lot more important than we give it credit for. She argues that gender is indeed largely a product of cultural forces, but those forces come into play so early in childhood and are so universal that they must be deeply grounded in our biology. For supporting evidence of the power of biology, you have only to look back at the sorry story of David/Brenda, or at the feminist mothers who have had to admit weary defeat in trying to deter their sons from rough play, toy guns and competitive behaviour.

We do know, because we see it happening every day, that the sexes differ markedly in their behaviour from very early in life. Maccoby has a slightly different take on this: she argues that gender is not so much an individual trait as a property of social groups, for when individual boys and girls are alone their behaviour does not observably differ all that much but when they gather in same-sex groups the difference is pronounced. Boys in groups strongly focus on competition and pecking orders, whereas girls in groups tend to collaborate as equals. Boys and girls also seem driven to segregate themselves in childhood and hence learn very different ways of interacting. This is a fundamental reason why 'men are from Mars', and why their approach to sex, romance, intimacy and parenthood puzzles women (and often themselves) so much.

Here's how the differences seem to develop. Most children can distinguish males and females by the time they start learning to walk and talk, within a year of birth. Young children, like all young primates, have a strong mutual attraction (young orang-utans, baboons, rhesus macaques and langurs will even leave the safety of their family groups to find a same-age playmate). By the age of three, most toddlers can use the right gender labels for themselves and others – and this is the age at which they start to segregate themselves when they are in mixed-sex groups (although they may still form strong friendships with members of the opposite sex). 'But the tendency to prefer same-sex playmates – or avoid children of the other sex – becomes progressively stronger through the pre-school years, until by grade-school age it is powerful indeed,' says Maccoby. By six, most kids seem to be drawn into peer groups and friendships with children of the same sex. Tellingly, this happens in societies across the world, virtually regardless of each individual's social experience, family background or the degree of gender segregation that prevails in the adult world around them. Children raised by single parents or lesbians, and children consciously raised in a gender-neutral way from birth, all exhibit this behaviour. This suggests that children may have a special culture all of their own. They may learn some of their gender-segregation tendencies from older children, and it is possible that adults have very little influence on that culture. Children's games certainly get passed down from generation to generation and can be long-lived; one study in the 1960s found that British children still played games dating back to the time of the Roman occupation. Nyansongo children in Africa have their own language for describing intimate parts of the body that they only learn from older children and do not use within earshot of adults.

All-male or all-female peer groups differ from each other in size, how much they roam during play, how they play and how their members interact. 'Boys in their groups, more commonly than girls in theirs, engage in "grandstanding", risk-taking, rough play, direct mutual confrontation, and striving for dominance; boys are also more reluctant to reveal weaknesses to each other,' Maccoby says. They take less trouble to avoid open conflict or maintain positive social relations within the group and they spend less time communicating with each other and with adults. 'It is a fairly consistent feature of childhood that boys' groups, more than girls' groups, separate themselves strongly from adults, actively test the limits and power of adult rules, exert pressure on their members not to tattle to adults, exclude and ignore children of the other sex, and vigilantly monitor the boundaries between the sexes. In short, boys in their groups achieve more autonomy than girls do in theirs, and probably achieve more group cohesion as well, despite the higher levels of conflict within boys' groups.'

Why do boys seek out other boys? The evidence suggests that they are drawn to each other because the ways in which they play are more compatible. 'Boys' rough, vigorous playstyle is attractive to many or most other boys, while many girls are wary of male rough play and tend to withdraw from it,' Maccoby says. 'Avoidance of girls by young boys is hard to understand in terms of female playstyles, and perhaps is better understood as a male response to girls' lack of interest in the kind of play boys seek.' That gender difference in play really does seem to have a biological basis. Indeed, the similarities with our cousins in the primate world are striking. Some evolutionary theorists have suggested that the pecking orders (known as dominance hierarchies) which feature so consistently across species in male playgroups serve to regulate aggression within groups and to socialise boys for co-operative projects and tasks with other males. It's possible that such segregation may help to minimise inbreeding as well.

Whatever the explanation, it does seem likely that we are genetically predisposed to behave in very different ways according to our biological sex. Girls exposed to excess testosterone before birth, for example, tend to play in tomboyish ways. And at this stage all the signs point to our old friend testosterone as the key: 'So far, no evidence has been found for an effect of female hormones on playstyles,' Maccoby notes. 'We can say, then, that it is primarily the presence of large amounts of androgens during specific periods of gestation that predispose children – usually genetically male children – to male-style play.' Exposure to testosterone before or soon after birth is also thought to help explain why males are more likely to separate themselves from adults. If you expose newborn male monkeys to drugs that block the effects of testosterone, their move away from adults into male peer groups is delayed, one study has found. It's also possible that estrogen (or a lack of testosterone) may help girls to acquire language skills and self-control sooner than boys: that could also explain why they tend to seek each other out, but the evidence is thin as yet.

Support for such ideas has recently come from an unusual source, the African spotted hyena. That species is famous in sex-research circles because the female has such bizarre genitals: she has an empty scrotum and her clitoris is so large that it is indistinguishable from a penis – so large, in fact, that her birth canal runs through its centre (a male must somehow insert his penis into the clitoris to inseminate her). Both male and female fetuses are bathed in testosterone in the womb, which almost certainly accounts for the female's masculinised genitals. As you might expect, spotted hyena society is extremely violent and females dominate socially. The young are born with fully developed canine teeth and start to fight, to the death at times, within minutes of birth.

A team led by Nancy Forger, of the University of Massachusetts, recently studied the brains of six female and four male spotted hyenas (culled from a Kenyan wildlife park for population control) and, not surprisingly, found fewer sex-related differences than in other animals. Yet male and female behaviour is still quite different: play-mounting during sex games among the pups is almost always done by males, and females rarely mount each other. Forger's team looked at two brain areas known to differ markedly in size between the sexes in many species, including humans, and thought to be involved in governing male sexual behaviour. In each species studied to date, exposure to testosterone in early life creates the size difference. In hyenas, one of these brain regions has twice the volume in males as in females (the difference is much larger in many other mammals); it seems that exposing a female fetus to testosterone not only masculinises her genitals but her brain as well, making her behave more aggressively. Male hyenas almost certainly get a second hit of testosterone, probably soon after birth, to complete the process of predisposing them to full male behaviour.

It usually takes an environmental cue to activate a predisposition. Maccoby suspects that the main cue for boys in expressing their distinctive playstyle is simply the presence of other boys. Likewise, a bias towards nurturing qualities in girls is activated by contact with vulnerable young animals or their surrogates, such as dolls. The knowledge and experience children acquire can make a difference, too. Simply being aware of gender stereotypes doesn't seem to matter much to them at first, but the pervasive pink-or-blue labelling of the sexes imposed by adults – not just by parents, teachers, and sports coaches but also through the influence of books, film and television – does have a strong impact over time, making boys and girls behave in different ways. They form a sense of their own gender identity and learn to adapt it to the gender roles created by their community.

It may surprise parents to discover that they seem to have little effect on the process of young children segregating themselves. That seems to be because family homes tend not to be segregated. Parents are generally mixed-sex couples and kids tend to play most with the brother or sister nearest them in age, regardless of gender. Early schooling or childcare doesn't seem to have much effect either: 'In societies where parents send their children to mixed-sex schools or daycare centres, the children separate nonetheless,' Maccoby points out. 'The separation occurs in preschools even when the teachers are making conscious efforts to treat children of the two sexes equally.'

Where parents may have a significant impact is in the way they treat boys and girls differently. Parents of both sexes, but fathers in particular, play with their sons more roughly – and the aggregate effect of all that rough-and-tumble on the way all-male groups play could be large indeed. In many societies boys are more likely to find themselves on the receiving end of physical punishment (in my school years, boys were hit or caned by teachers but girls were not). And various studies have suggested that boys' requests are more often refused and that they are more likely to be told what to do, rather than shown or encouraged. Across cultures and age groups, boys also quickly learn to be less compliant toward their mothers than do girls, which often prompts parents to take a firmer disciplinary approach with sons.

Parents also talk to boys and girls differently. They talk much less to boys than girls about feelings – about how the child feels at given times, and about how things a child says and does may make other people feel. We don't know why this happens. Girls may acquire the relevant language skills sooner; they may be more willing to listen and speak about emotions. Parents may simply think girls 'should' be encouraged this way and that boys should not. I have many early memories of being told (by my parents, brothers, a teacher, a football coach) not to cry, to 'be a brave soldier', to stoically endure pain and fear and so on. Girls were 'crybabies', and boys were ever alert and ready to tease other boys who showed any emotional vulnerability. 'Whatever the reason, the fact is that talk about feelings does occur more frequently between parents and daughters,' Maccoby says. 'And such talk facilitates children's ability to adopt the perspective of other people at a later time.'

Kids may be equally, if not more, influenced about gender roles by observing cultural life around them. So, it seems that biology plays a key role in the way kids self-segregate, while home and society have an important effect on the way children interact when they reach those groups. 'Once the male group process is set in motion, its very existence increases the likelihood that boys will preferentially choose (or be chosen) to participate in it, and that girls will avoid it,' Maccoby argues. In societies where men have the most prestige, boys distance themselves from girls, their mothers in particular and adults in general as soon as possible.

By now you will have twigged that these childhood differences clearly have echoes in later life. Despite the fact that puberty tends to suddenly make the Venusians and Martians mutually attractive, teenage boys and girls keep up same-sex social networks. They refine their peer-group membership rules, though, based on sporting, hobby or academic interests, ethnic background, socio-economic status, drug use or whatever. As they start dating and forming couples, young men and women mix together much more, but the workplace and the arrival of children often promotes gender segregation again. In many societies, different types of work are allotted to men and women. Even in a modern office where both sexes may do identical work, men and women tend to separate into same-sex groups when they go to lunch or have a drink after work. The inescapable biology of childbirth then usually promotes further segregation within marriage: when raising young children, women tend to rely on female social networks while men may work longer hours and spend more time with other men.

Men, in particular, have to learn new ways of dealing with the opposite sex as they mature. Boy–boy taboos about contact with girls are relaxed at puberty. But although teenage girls may be impressed by the heroic feats of a young man showing off his skills, they also want the emotional intimacy that boys are often poorly equipped to provide at first. Later, mixed-sex workplaces can be minefields for young men who do not go further and learn an even more gender-neutral style of interaction that goes beyond teenage flirting, as sexual harassment suits will confirm.

Likewise, in marriage many men must learn new ways of interacting with their wives. Men and women differ significantly in the way they deal with marital conflict. In short, men are more likely to try to avoid it, and do so by withdrawing ('Sorry, I've got to fix the car'), stonewalling ('Honest, nothing's wrong, darling') or backing off ('Have it your own way, then'). 'Stonewalling is something that husbands do frequently, and that infuriates wives, who experience it as disapproval, and feel cut off from any means of reaching a resolution of conflict,' Maccoby writes. Such male tactics may have their origins in childhood, when boys learn to resist the influence of girls (such as by ignoring their suggestions) and mothers, and to stoutly assert and re-assert their position and display anger when in serious conflict with other boys. It has also been proposed – from laboratory studies showing that men disengage verbally and emotionally once their stress responses become elevated – that men simply cannot tolerate states of high emotional arousal (or perhaps only negative ones) as easily as women. But that's plainly not true of male–male conflicts.

Maccoby's alternative hypothesis is that men get so internally worked up by marital conflict because they can't use the tactics that seem 'natural' to them. Males learn early that direct confrontation with other males – as boys or men – can easily turn physical when there's a stalemate. They're also taught that it is wrong to hit girls, and that doing so results in a loss of status and punishment. Most male aggression, she notes, is against other males and it is a long-standing tradition that men are expected not to retaliate if a woman slaps him. So, many men soon discover that guy-style conflict resolution in marriage carries far too many risks – dishonour, legal action and divorce may follow if they fail to inhibit their physical aggression, as many regrettably do. In that sense, withdrawing, stonewalling and backing off may also be seen in a positive light, as purposeful male ways of setting aside or inhibiting their potential aggression. Domestic violence perpetrated by men may in part be an indicator of what can happen when a man fails to successfully withdraw or negotiate, reaches the limits of his anger and allows his inner turmoil to erupt.

Men and women use language differently as well, and there's ample evidence of communication problems on both sides. As linguist Deborah Tannen's best-selling books *You Don't Understand* and *Talking from 9 to 5* have detailed, women have been socialised since childhood not to promote themselves or be pushy, while men have been socialised to grab the limelight, brag and challenge others to better them. Men are more likely to play devil's advocate in conversation, whereas women lean towards consultation and compromise. Men also say 'I'm sorry' a lot less than women do, Tannen notes. Typical girl-talk and guy-talk differ not just in their topics – clothes/hair/kids/health versus sport/cars/technology/politics – but in their style as well. As Maccoby says, boys and men joke, pun, tease and mock-challenge each other, and then: 'When women don't respond to this kind of banter, men often think women have no sense of humour. Among girls and women, a more common form of humour is self-mockery. Women can mistake men's humour for genuine hostility, while men can mistake women's for true self-abnegation, which seems to them out of place.' Women and men tend to get on better in the workplace when women can take part in men's banter, some studies suggest. Others have found that women deliberately downplay their assertiveness when talking to men (women are not less assertive, however, since they don't do this when talking to other women).

Laboratory experiments tend to confirm what magazines advise women to do when talking to a man – especially concerning not firmly voicing their opinions or confronting men too openly. When university students were paired up to discuss a subject on which they initially disagreed, a woman used much more tentative speech when talking to a man. This involves much use of disclaimers, such as 'I may be wrong, but . . .', and plenty of 'maybe's and 'sort of's. When a woman did this, men were more likely to be persuaded by her opinions and to like her more as a person, even though they rated her as less knowledgeable and competent than when she used assertive speech (ironically, women were less likely to be persuaded by a woman using tentative speech).

But within marriage, success is more likely to be found in men bending their wives' way, according to marriage-therapy guru John Gottman, a psychologist at the University of Washington. He suggests that successful marriages seem to have far more to do with husbands being able to yield to the influences of their wives than with spouses trying to practise 'active listening'. Many counsellors have advocated active listening to improve communication, using tactics such as paraphrasing or summarising their partner's statements or feelings – a favourite standby is starting your sentence with 'So, what I hear you saying is . . .'. Gottman's team followed 130 newlyweds for 6 years, observing the ways in which couples interact (data from another 13-year study were analysed as well), and relating them to whether a marriage succeeds, ails or fails. The outcome was a surprise: 'This was the biggest revelation we've had about how conflicts are best resolved in successful marriages,' Gottman says. 'Our analysis suggested that active listening occurred very infrequently in marital conflict resolution and its use didn't predict marital success. We expected that active listening would predict positive outcomes in marriages – we have even recommended this type of conflict intervention with couples in the past.' In keeping with men's tendency to be reluctant to talk about their feelings, it is the wife who usually brings up marital issues for discussion, and she usually also presents an analysis of the problem and suggests solutions, Gottman says. When a husband is willing to accept influence from his spouse, that fact alone is a significant predictor of marital success. 'We found that only those newlywed men who are accepting of influence from their wives are winding up in happy, stable marriages,' says Gottman. 'Getting husbands to share power with their wives, by accepting some of the demands she makes, is critical in helping to resolve conflict.' Successfully married couples rarely used active listening techniques. They also almost never validated their spouse's feelings. 'Active listening is unnatural for couples to do,' Gottman argues. 'People may do it at times, but as a means to resolve issues, active listening requires too much of people in the midst of conflict. Asking that of couples is like requiring emotional gymnastics.'

The study also found that gentleness, compassion and soothing of partners are key ingredients to marital success, and neither men nor women have a monopoly on those traits. Male psychology *is* different to female psychology, but it seems to me that men and women are equally capable of great tenderness and empathy. And there, surely, is the best place for them to find and build on common ground.

13

THE FUTURE: Beyond the Clone Age

'We could have had a male contraceptive at the same time as the female contraceptive was developed 40 years ago. In fact, it probably would have been simpler to develop, but priorities were different.'

David Handelsman, andrologist

COME WITH ME behind the scenes of a modern fertility clinic. We are in a contemporary office building in the heart of the central business district of my home city, in the bright, busy and spotless laboratories of Sydney IVF. We're in the section for guys – through the door labelled 'Andrology Services'. As two young women technicians in hospital gowns prepare semen samples for analysis nearby, lab manager Jacek Kossakowski is waiting patiently by a large blue incubator. We've been chatting about his earlier experiences working with stud bulls, but at the sound of a buzzer, he stops and opens the incubator door. He takes out a tray of small test tubes with yellow caps, marked only with identity numbers. Each contains a carefully prepared semen sample, containing the fatherhood hopes and dreams of one of the clinic's clients. They've been in there an hour, held at exactly 37°C.

'Now these ones are ready to go,' Kossakowski tells me, looking the samples over approvingly. He takes a syringe, withdraws a few drops of liquid from a tube, gently squeezes them out onto a glass slide and slips them into the loading tray of a semen analyser, a featureless grey box topped by a computer screen. The screen comes alive with images of moving sperm, wriggling every which way. His expert eye scans them, buttons are clicked, keys pressed and the sperm are quickly displaced on the screen by a series of scrolling numbers as the machine runs through its programmed sequence of checks. In a few minutes, the verdict is delivered in the form of a list of numbers in various categories. Testing over, the slide is removed, tossed into a disposal container and the next sample is prepared and loaded.

It all happens so smoothly and routinely that it's easy to forget how sophisticated is the process we've just witnessed. It is one repeated for some 60 men a week in this lab alone, which in turn is just one of hundreds around the world. Since each sample entered the lab, it has been measured for volume, washed, mixed with a clear liquid culture medium to nurture it, warmed to body temperature, counted for sperm concentrations and checked for sperm shape and vigour, spiked with progesterone (the female hormone that sends the sperm into their turbo-charged phase in the fallopian tube) and kept warm for another hour. Under Kossakowski's highly skilled eye, the semen-analysing machine has then put the hyperactivated sperm through a battery of sampling tests. He shows me an image on the computer screen from semen sample number 1741, a set of zig-zag green lines overlaid with red lines joining a series of dots: 'You can see how the machine has tracked one sperm's movement here. It samples from 30 reference points in half a second.' It was a good sperm, this one, moving vigorously and symmetrically and with a good tail action, like most of the others in the sample. He reads off the rest of the report and nods his head: 'That's good; this guy shouldn't have any problem fertilising an egg,' Kossakowski concludes with a smile.

In most cases a man with fertility problems can now be told with great precision what his problem is and exactly where it lies. Indeed, he can find out much more about it than he could about a dose of the common cold. He can learn exactly how much semen he has produced and its alkalinity or acidity; how much sperm he has produced and what proportion of them move well and are shaped well; the identity of any harmful bacteria infecting his urinary tract; whether his semen is taking a wrong turn that results in 'retrograde' ejaculation into his urinary tract; how smoking, drinking, drugs or other chemical exposures have affected his fertility; whether his sperm have failed to mature properly; whether there is a blockage between testes and penis that stops sperm being delivered; whether he has varicose veins in his testes; whether he or his partner have antibodies that attack his sperm; whether he carries a genetic defect that lowers or stops sperm production; and whether his sperm fail to carry out some of the more subtle biochemical processes in fertilisation. Armed with all this intricate detail, fertility clinics can then offer remedies ranging from simple surgery to the precise extraction of a single sperm from his testes that will be microscopically injected directly into the body of an egg cell.

It's not so much that these men's infertility can be cured. Indeed, not much progress has been made on that score. No, most of this new knowledge and technology is bypassing the problem altogether. Professor Marc Goldstein, director of the Center for Male Reproductive Medicine and Microsurgery at the New York Hospital–Cornell Medical Center, wrote in a recent *Scientific American* article that most of this information and treatment has emerged only in the past 50 years or so: 'Now the vast majority of infertile men have the potential to conceive a genetically related child. All that is required is time, effort, money – and, of course, a woman.'

Cut and change scene to another room in a two-storey redbrick building just a few kilometres away, on the campus of the University of Sydney. Here Professor David Handelsman is deliberately trying to make normal, healthy men sterile. The subjects are volunteers taking part in the first human trial of a male hormonal contraceptive. Each is aged between 18 and 45 and is in a stable sexual relationship with a woman. Every three months, the men are given an injection of progesterone, which suppresses the pituitary gland from signalling the testes to make sperm. Every six months, the subjects are also injected with a pellet of testosterone, the male hormone that keeps up their sex-drive and maintains other essential male characteristics.

While other research groups are trying to devise a male equivalent of the Pill, Handelsman thinks an injection regime will be more suitable because men are, well, 'less likely' than women to be conscientious daily tablet takers. Certainly their poor track record in looking after their own health lends support to that idea. Of course, that inevitably begs the question of whether women can trust men with the responsibility for contraception, but Handelsman counters that half of all contraception used today involves men, and that this new method is aimed at couples already in committed, long-term relationships: 'Men's involvement is already there,' he says. 'We just have lousy methods. We could have had a male contraceptive at the same time as the female contraceptive was developed 40 years ago. In fact, it probably would have been simpler to develop, but priorities were different.'

Welcome to the paradoxical new world of men and sex. On the one hand we are employing our ever-expanding knowledge of reproduction to try to help even the most infertile of men become fathers – at least, those lucky enough to be able to afford it. On the other, we are using it to render even the most potent of men infertile. But it may be no exaggeration to say that for the sake of our own survival, we surely need such know-how of the subtleties of our own fertility. Never before has it been so vital to understand and manage the issue of human reproduction. Human beings have been so astonishingly successful at multiplying that their sheer weight of numbers now threatens the ecological stability of the planet. The fossil record suggests that not since the extinction of the dinosaurs – perhaps never before – have so many species of plants and animals been wiped out at such a rapid rate as in recent times. The best estimates suggest that over the past 200 million years, vertebrate animals have died out at an average rate of about 90 species a century. Yet it is thought that up to 5000 species are at significant risk of extinction within the next 50 years. The 'higher' plants have probably died out at about 1 species every 30 years over the past 400 million years. Yet about 4000 plant species – 1 out of every 8 known – are now endangered. For all our intellect and invention, we still seem unable to live the way we want without putting countless other life forms at risk.

It's worth recalling here that when the first farmers were still taming animals and domesticating crops from the wild, the total number of human beings alive on the planet was probably less than the number who live today in just one of the world's larger cities. Estimates based on the hunter-gatherer lifestyle suggest that at the dawn of agriculture the world's human population was between 5 and 10 million. Even the highest estimate, which assumes a world 'saturated' with hunter-gatherers, is a mere 15 million people. The global rate of population growth was tiny at the time, perhaps 0.02 per cent a year, according to *The Cambridge Encyclopedia of Human Evolution*.[1] But agriculture changed all that and human numbers began to grow more quickly, at about 0.05 per cent a year. By the birth of Christ the total number of people had soared tenfold, to about 150 million. World population doubled again, to 300 million, by 1350, and had reached 500 million in 1600, by which time the rate of increase had climbed to 0.3 per cent a year. Then it got a real kick along with the Industrial Revolution, and another series of boosts from better living standards, clean drinking water, efficient sewerage and modern medicine. The world's human population did not pass the 1 billion mark until 1804, more than a century after Johan Ham's discovery of sperm, but it was on an explosive growth curve. By 1927, it had doubled again to 2 billion, and then took only 33 years to reach 3 billion, in 1960. It took just 14 years to reach 4 billion, in 1974; only 13 years to reach 5 billion, in 1987; and then 12 years to reach 6 billion, in 1999. When that latest global population landmark was passed, ecologist Paul Ehrlich commented 'this is the single most stunning biological event in the last 65 million years, since something hit the earth and destroyed the dinosaurs'.

More people have been added to the human population in the past 50 years than in the preceding million years. Those living in developed nations in particular are staying alive much longer. The oldest generation of people alive today was born at a time when 1 child in 5 didn't survive to see his or her fifth birthday. The prominent demographer John Bongaarts, of the International Population Council, pointed out recently that human numbers are still climbing sharply and that 'we are just past [the] mid-point' of the growth curve: 'After a record-breaking increase of 2 billion people over the past 25 years, the same increase is projected over the next 25 years, and a further expansion to 10.4 billion is expected by 2100.'[2]

While all this growth has been happening, there has been a counter-revolution in human reproductive behaviour since 1950, with the development and widespread use of effective contraceptives, and consequently lower birth rates. But there are marked regional differences within these two trends. Bongaarts notes that large population increases are still expected in Africa, Asia and Latin America, where fertility is still about 50 per cent above the two-children-per-couple level needed to bring about population stability. At the same time, death rates are declining and better living standards, nutrition and public health services have increased life expectancy by 50 per cent since 1950 (although it will decline in most of the sub-Saharan African countries with severe AIDS epidemics).

The counter-trend is happening in unexpected places, even in very poor countries. A typical Bangladeshi woman in 1975 would have had seven children in her lifetime; today she would probably have three. But it is most evident in Europe, North America and Japan, along with some of the rapidly developing South-East Asian countries, where steep falls in population growth rates have occurred since 1960. Immigration, rising life expectancy and population momentum, however, are expected to keep their population levels roughly steady for several decades at least.

We've all heard fears aired about the potentially adverse effects of aging populations and long-term population declines in these wealthier regions – a population 'implosion' – but Bongaarts argues: 'This concern should not be overblown . . . since reported fertility measures do not reflect the fact that couples are still having about two children, they're just having them at an older age. Fertility rates are not as low as they appear to be.' He seems to be on solid ground in suggesting that worries about underpopulation in developed countries have been exaggerated. In France, for example, the annual total fertility rate has been well below the replacement level since the mid-1970s, but by the time French women have reached the end of their childbearing years they have averaged 2.1 births, or pretty much the replacement rate. By having babies later in life, they caused a dip in reported fertility rates, just as younger mothers caused a boom in the 1950s. Fertility actually rose in the US from 1.77 to 2.08 births per woman between 1975 and 1990, as the daughters of the baby boomers stopped postponing having their own babies.

If we take stock of what's happening, it took many tens of thousands of years for the human population to reach about 15 million, about 12,000 years to reach 1 billion, a mere two centuries more to reach 6 billion and may take just one more century to reach 10.4 billion. On the face of it then, the very last problem humanity would seem to have is infertility. Remember all those billions of sperm produced by the world's men? All that untapped fathering potential? Surely there's no need to worry about a shortage of sperm or a bear market in Y chromosomes?

Yet that is precisely the paradoxical concern emerging from the insights we are gaining into men and sex, and from what seem to be disturbing new trends in male reproductive health. The more we look at this perplexing issue the more we see warning signs that all is not as it seems, or should be, in the human male reproductive tract. The unexplained increases in testicular cancer rates and genital malformations stand out, but there may be other, more subtle and as yet unrealised problems with the reproductive future for men.

We know, for example, that infertility is more common and more complex than previously thought. Infertility is defined as a failure to conceive after 12 months of regular unprotected intercourse (about 85 per cent of couples will conceive a child under these conditions). The problem is now recognised as being widespread throughout human communities – although infertility rates vary from place to place – and probably affects 10–15 per cent of all couples. A further 10–15 per cent of couples who are already parents would probably like to have more children, but cannot. There's also a growing awareness that men are more often the source of the problem than was once assumed, largely for sexist reasons. The woman in a childless marriage was often called 'barren' but that term was rarely applied to her husband. My dictionary, for example, gives the example of 'a barren woman' to indicate a common usage of the word.

As investigative tools and technological remedies for our reproductive problems grow more numerous and sophisticated, more subtle variants of infertility are being recognised. Where once a couple might be told bluntly, 'Sorry, you can't have children', doctors can now offer a wide range of tests to find out, in intricate detail, where the problem lies and perhaps to offer treatments to beat it. Those investigations have shown that 'multifactorial infertility' – where more than one problem exists – is more prevalent than was previously thought, largely because we have become aware of previously unrecognised male factors. Indeed, the largest single category (about a third) of known infertility worldwide is still classified as idiopathic – in other words, we simply don't know the cause. Idiopathic cases most commonly feature a male partner who produces very little or no sperm, or sperm that are malformed or have poor motility (they do not swim normally, or perhaps not at all). Increasingly, genetic disorders are being found that explain a large proportion of these cases.

If men's ability to father children by natural means is threatened, we surely need to know as much as is reasonably possible about what goes wrong and how to avoid it or treat it. But we need to know much, much more about men generally. Rising suicide rates spell big trouble for them in many nations; their needless risk-taking leads to much tragedy and heartache; their hunger for power, status and personal autonomy tends to make societies less egalitarian and dulls the voices of many women and other men in society; their tendency to aggression and violence – in life generally as well as in sex – causes untold damage and pain.

We know from the wealth of scientific evidence already available that men are subject to their own special biological imperatives. Some of those can help to explain the behaviour patterns that make men the way they are. They may explain why men tend to die younger than women, for example. Just three centuries ago human life expectancy at birth was less than 37 years. By 1900, everyone was living longer on average, but women were living 2.5 years longer than men, and the gap has since widened greatly and is expected to grow even more. Girls born in industrialised countries today can expect to live almost 9 years longer than their male counterparts. Most will live to become great-grandmothers, but they are unlikely to share their joy at doing so with their spouses. Public health programs aimed specifically at men will help to keep them alive and fruitful for longer, yet even in wealthy and otherwise enlightened nations such programs often have not gone much beyond being discussed, or have only just got under way.

There are also concerns that boys in many Western nations are being 'emotionally miseducated'. They have long been told to act tough and be independent, for example, and now they are being chastised for being insensitive and uncooperative. Confusingly, they are being urged to be less macho and yet are growing up with role models that have become increasingly hypermasculine – body images, behaviour and ethics based on weightlifters, professional wrestlers and barely verbal actors portraying unblinking killing machines. Just as Barbie has been remodelled for girls, GI Joe – and even Luke Skywalker – has become more muscular, claims a recent article in the *Journal of Eating Disorders*. The article suggests that the emergence of this 'super-male' concept may cause an increase in body image disorders in young men. 'The public is exposed daily, in magazines, motion pictures, and other media, to increasingly – and often unnaturally – muscular male images,' say researchers led by Harrison Pope Jr, of Harvard Medical School in Boston. Pope's team speculates that the growing incidence of muscle dysmorphia (desiring large muscles despite having a good body physique) may be linked to these images, in much the same way as anorexia and bulimia became more evident as 'desirable' female body images grew scrawnier. You can't help wondering if they will encourage more male violence as well. Pope's team measured the waist, chest, and biceps of GI Joe and Star Wars male action figures marketed over the past 30 years. Star Wars figurines have certainly bulked up since their introduction in the late 1970s, 'with particularly impressive gains in the shoulder and chest areas'. But in the case of GI Joe 'not only have the figures grown more muscular, but they have developed increasingly sharp muscular definition through the years.' The 1998 version of the GI Joe Extreme action figure 'dwarfs his earlier counterparts with dramatically greater musculature and . . . an expression of rage which contrasts sharply with the bland faces of his predecessors,' the team says. If the toy was life-size, he 'would sport larger biceps than any bodybuilder in history', probably exceeding what is humanly possible.

Ah, but new technologies may make it humanly possible to grow such muscles before too long. New ways to regenerate or build muscle are being actively researched for legitimate medical reasons. The elderly are potential beneficiaries, since everyone loses muscle mass as they age. Regular exercise can slow the rate of loss, but most people will lose at least a fifth of the muscle mass they enjoyed as young adults. Loss of muscle power can have serious implications, not least in making it more likely that a person will fall and suffer broken bones or head injury. Glenn Zorpette, a staff writer with *Scientific American* who has reported in depth on the subject, believes that science is now close to creating a muscle-building injection. Separate British and American teams have in recent years tested two kinds of 'vaccine' for this purpose, based on engineered genes. Injected into mice, they reportedly boosted the muscle mass in the animals' legs by between 15 and 27 per cent. Some scientists are predicting the first human trials within a few years.

While such a treatment might be a boon for the elderly and frail – helping to increase their mobility and independence – it also seems inevitable that it will find its way into bodybuilding and sports, especially those with professional codes. 'Compared with anabolic steroids, the modern-day illegal but ubiquitous muscle-building drug of choice, a vaccine based on an engineered gene would offer some major advantages,' says Zorpette.[3] 'It would need to be administered only one time, rather than periodically, and it would be essentially undetectable in the body.' That prospect, of course, is enough to give sweet dreams to muscle-junkies and nightmares to those trying to stamp out performance-enhancing drugs and revise the desirable male body image to something less extreme than that of Mr Universe, Hulk Hogan or GI Joe.

Other emerging technologies pose new questions for men and maleness as well. Predicting is a dubious business at best, but here's a starter for your thinking cap: sometime early next century, the intelligence of machines will exceed that of humans. 'Within several decades, machines will exhibit the full range of human intellect, emotions and skills, ranging from musical and other creative aptitudes to physical movement. They will claim to have feelings and, unlike today's virtual personalities, will be very convincing when they tell us so.' The pundit is Ray Kurzweil, the CEO of Kurzweil Technologies, a high-tech development company.[4] Kurzweil's forecast highlights how the gap between technology and human biology is narrowing. He predicts that by 2019 a $1000 computer will have matched the processing power of the human brain; that by 2029 an average personal computer will be the equivalent of 1000 human brains, and the software for intelligence will have been largely mastered; and that by 2055, $1000 worth of computer will match the processing power of all human brains on Earth. 'In the 2020s neural implants will improve our sensory experiences, memory and thinking. By 2030, instead of just phoning a friend, you will be able to meet in, say, a Mozambican game preserve that will seem compellingly real. You will be able to have any type of experience – business, social, sexual – with anyone, real or simulated, regardless of physical proximity.' The early forays into 'cybersex' on the internet today will be puny by comparison. What new pressures will cybersex place on men? Will the sophistication of such technology make them even easier prey for exploitative entrepreneurs? Will some men be more likely to stay home and have virtual sex with an ever-eager computer-generated persona who enticingly fits an 'ideal' woman concept, rather than risking failure seeking the real thing?

And does the advent of cloning technology threaten men? Within the next five years, a team of scientists somewhere in the world will probably announce the birth of the first cloned human baby, asserts ethicist Ronald M. Green. 'Like Louise Brown, the first child born as the result of in-vitro fertilisation 21 years ago, the cloned infant will be showered with media attention. But within a few years it will be just one of hundreds or thousands of such children around the world.' How the world proceeds on cloning of humans is yet to be seen, but it is of course a fact that the basis of the technology already exists. The cloning of Dolly the sheep in 1997 was an extraordinary development that stunned scientists, ethicists and legislators alike. It wasn't supposed to be technically possible, yet Ian Wilmut, Keith Campbell and their colleagues at the Roslin Institute near Edinburgh, Scotland, managed to engineer a virgin birth – a lamb with no father. Dolly developed from a sheep's egg in which the original DNA in the nucleus had been replaced by DNA taken from a cell in an adult ewe's udder.

If it is possible for us to clone such a large and complex mammal (goats and cattle have since been cloned as well), it is surely only a short technical leap to clone ourselves. In a roundabout sort of way, then, sex has come full circle – from the invention of males in the first place to the invention of a technology that could make them redundant.

Despite the disapproval expressed by ethicists, legislators and scientists alike, it seems inevitable that cloning will make its way into human reproduction before too long. Pressure groups representing those unable or unwilling to conceive a child genetically related to themselves by any other means will surely see to that.

Meanwhile, doctors are already growing or synthesising skin, cartilage, bone, ligament and tendon – novel applications of biotechnology that make the prospect of off-the-shelf organ replacements seem not just possible but likely in coming years. 'Indeed, evidence abounds that it is at least theoretically possible to engineer large, complex organs such as livers, kidneys, breasts, bladders and intestines, all of which include many different kinds of cells,' say David J. Mooney and Antonios G. Mikos of Rice University, in Houston. If so, it should be possible for our sons (and daughters) to swap dud pieces of their bodies – worn out by age, damaged by smoking or cursed by a lousy gene – and stay healthy longer. If a man is crippled, bio-sensors may help him walk. If he goes blind, retinal implants may help him see. If he goes deaf, vital parts of his inner ears may be regrown. If his reproductive organs fail, why not order a new penis, or prostate or testes? At the time of writing, testes transplants are on the verge of being conducted (the first crude transplant operations were tried early in the twentieth century, with doubtful results). But this operation requires a donor, and raises all manner of ethical and practical problems. Will it be possible one day for infertile men to receive healthy new testes, engineered to grow from their own cells and thus containing their own genes?

And as for our grandsons, how will sex and reproduction be for them? For one thing, the artificial womb is under development by Nobuya Unno, at the University of Tokyo. Anthony Atala of Harvard Medical School foresees a uterus being grown from an infertile woman's stem cells – undifferentiated cells – and implanted back into her; it might take just six weeks from placing an order to taking delivery of her custom-made womb. But why leave out men? Couldn't they have a womb grown for them as well and be implanted with a fertilised donor egg? Your son or grandson might decide to become a 'mother', having his baby delivered by caesarean section. And surely it would not stretch the imagination – nor the biochemistry – too far to picture him breast-feeding the child? If he should happen to be infertile, why, the baby might even be a clone of himself.

Now that would be weird. And, of course, it's wild speculation. But it's easy to see that men do face special problems right now, and that new ones will keep on emerging. They have reached a watershed, not only in their biological evolution but their social evolution as well, and it's well past time to get their house in order. The existence of the feminist movement means that the clock cannot just be turned back to the 'good old days' when men ruled the roost. Even the very concept of maleness and the neat divide between the genders has become blurred, and rightly so. We need to formulate a new view of men – one that accords with what science is telling us, not outmoded social conventions and tired slogans. We need new and more positive ways to educate and socialise boys. We also need a new view of successful aging in men – one that cherishes the experience they have to offer, not one that discards them when they no longer have the vigour of youth. Whichever way you look at it, the world will never again be the same for men. We are witnessing the reinvention of a remarkable and colourful character, the common man. Let's hope it makes this wonderful planet a better, safer, happier place. Here's to the new man!

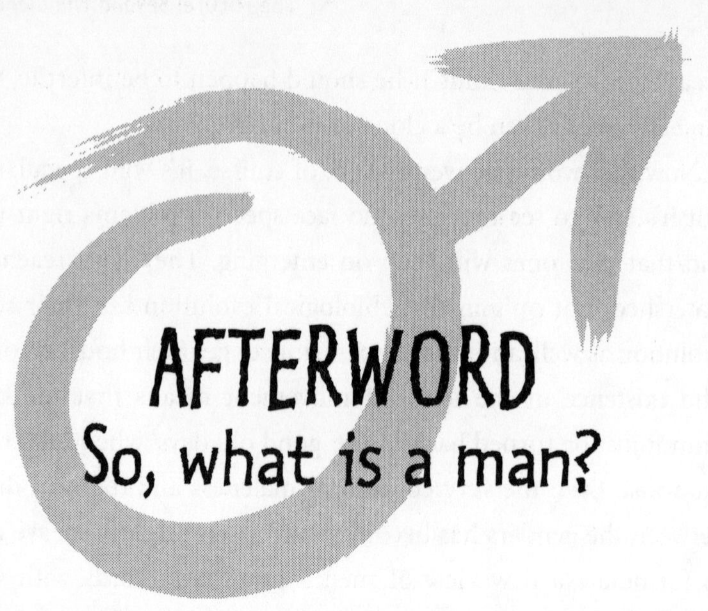

AFTERWORD
So, what is a man?

TWO LESBIANS, Roxxy Bent and Margie Fischer, proudly display their six-month-old daughter Ruth in a photograph on the front page of my local newspaper. They are newsworthy because my country's Prime Minister, John Howard, has stirred up an ethical hornet's nest. He opposes single women and lesbians having access to fertility treatment – and Roxxy, Margie and Ruth are just the sort of family he wants to prevent. 'I'm appalled that he thinks he can play God,' says Bent, who conceived Ruth with the help of donor sperm and in-vitro fertilisation.

As you'd guess, Howard is a devout and practising conservative struggling to deal with a world that is shifting fast beneath his feet. He is a product of his times and is clinging to the values of a post-war era when 'Father Knows Best' wasn't just the title of a trite black-and-white TV program but code for a whole male-dominated social system. Even his Christian God was personified as a 'male' who created women from Adam's rib. It was an age when men were supposed to be the main breadwinners and authority figures and sons were to inherit their wealth and power.

Well, it didn't work out that way and events since then have given me hope that his will be one of the last generations of its kind. I think my small childhood world – in Australia at least – was the poorer for its rigid adherence to 'traditional' male values and the brutalising of boys to 'toughen' them up. The larger world of my young adulthood was overshadowed by the appalling fear that the hairy-chested, male-dominated conflict of the Cold War might degenerate into a nuclear nightmare. The world of my middle age, however, seems to me to be becoming an altogether better place, as women have begun to gain something more like equal rights and influence.

Many societies, of course, remain locked into old ways. But I think the young men I meet are, in the main, gentler and more considerate souls, more emotionally mature, more empathic and better socialised than many of their fathers were at the same age. My daughters have more options open to them in career and lifestyle than many of their mother's generation did at the same age. As well, many oppressed minorities have been able to successfully ride the wake of the feminist wave and Western society is now more inclined to tolerate and even celebrate diversity than to fear it. Personally, I feel happier and more able to march to the beat of my own drum – a person first, a man second.

My wife reckons – correctly, I'm sure – that Howard's concept of a family is so narrow that lesbian parenthood is totally alien to him and that his sense of masculinity is somehow affronted by women who pursue a life without men. I don't know how Howard defines his manhood, but it seems to involve a belief that men are indispensable to women and to their children. Roxxy and Margie are living proof that he's only partly right, and good luck to them. Cloning may yet prove him totally wrong, at least as far as conception is concerned. If Howard is right about children needing the guiding influence of adult males, then most children of lesbian couples and those raised by single mothers can find plenty of other 'father' figures in their lives, through uncles, friends, teachers and so on.

Some men seem equally discomforted by gay males – their mere existence seems to unnerve them so much they feel the need to insult, abuse and even bash gay men. I'm not sure how these gay bashers define their manhood but they seem to believe that it entails not simply being heterosexual but being aggressive, predatory, coercive and violent if the mood takes them. Then again, as some theorists suggest, such men may harbour secret doubts about their own sexual orientation and are trying to resolve that inner conflict by emphatically distancing themselves in 'manly' ways from what they see as socially or personally unacceptable.

The malaise afflicting the thinking of so many Western men is surely linked to the loss of some key elements of the old masculine identity that Howard apparently wants to salvage and revive. Men had it good and are losing it, but nothing better has come along instead. In some cases, worse things have emerged. The new hypermale – his body obsessively sculpted by over-exercise and hormones into a bloated, muscular parody of vigour and health – seems no more desirable than the depressed, dispirited and self-destructive new hypo-male.

So what is a man? What the radical social changes of this past generation have made very clear, to me at least, is that he is much more a cultural invention than a biological entity. Indeed, like the experts whose opinions I sought, I find it impossible to define a man. He's a moveable feast, depending on the individual, his culture and his times. As a friend put it: 'Where do you start? With Robert Helpmann, all face powder, frills and dancing? With a beefy football player? The Pope? Prince Charles? An empathic social worker? A mercenary soldier? You'd have to interview half the world's population to get a decent answer. I can't tell you what a man is, but if you asked me how being one has influenced my life I could go on for hours.'

So flexible is the concept of a man that even a woman can become one. In Albania, for example, a little-known tradition exists whereby girls choose to give up their female identities and vow to live as 'sworn virgins'. They live and dress as men, assume men's rights and are accepted and even revered as such by their peers. The British anthropologist who has studied the custom, Antonia Young, has found it had its origins in a shortage of adult males as a result of blood feuds. Ironically, political change has meant the erosion of the equal rights formerly conferred on Albanian women under communist law, and the sworn-virgin custom has undergone a revival in remote rural communities. Not only have blood feuds returned, but some women have embraced the custom as a chance to enjoy the same privileges as men. Clearly then, a man is a social role, a malleable human construct.

There's no point in denying that there are biological differences between men and women, as some people seem to want to do – guys are not gals with penises. But there's every reason to rejoice in the distinctions between them. They may be small in most cases, but they are significant and they do make the world a far more interesting and dynamic place. Equally, however, it's utter nonsense to suggest that the differences are so great as to justify a whole social system based on some supposed innate superiority of men. I repeat, for emphasis, that all the scientific evidence points to the conclusion that men and women are simply different melodies played on the same instrument – the amazing human body.

Science has peeked beneath our underwear and into the microscopic reaches of our cells to confirm that there is a continuum of human sex, with maleness and femaleness at opposite ends. The people we call men at the maleness end are – on average – larger, stronger, hairier, more aggressive and probably more impulsive than the people we call women at the femaleness end. Men are better able to perform some mental tasks, and less able than women at others. Yet there is more physical and psychological variation between individual men than there is – on average – between men and women. A male jockey is more like a female jockey than either is like a brawny male wrestler. In the films *Tootsie* and *Mrs Doubtfire*, Dustin Hoffman and Robin Williams were able to tweak their characters convincingly from male to female, yet no amount of acting talent and make-up could have succeeded in making us believe they were male basketballers. Likewise, only men make sperm and only women make eggs, yet being unable to do either (by accident of birth, as a result of trauma, surgery or age) doesn't prevent you from being seen by others as a man or a woman, or prevent you from seeing yourself that way. Perhaps the clearest distinction is that only women are equipped for pregnancy and giving birth; yet some men can and do adopt a woman's identity and social role.

Some of the differences we attribute to men and women clearly have a biological basis and almost certainly reflect ancient evolutionary forces. Yet just as many are cultural. There's no convenient dividing line down the middle of the sexual spectrum, with men on one side and women on the other. And who can say whether men would be less aggressive, less risk-taking, less impulsive or less interested in sex if they were not given 'permission' by each other and by society to be that way? It will be a long time yet before we can be sure that genes dictate this and culture dictates that in a man.

One defining facet of men in most human societies – and throughout history – is that they are more likely than women to die at any age. Baby boys are more prone to childhood disease; teenage boys and young men take more fatal risks; men often work in more dangerous places or in more dangerous ways; men are more likely to be involved in violence and armed conflict; men are more likely to smoke or drink to excess; old men die some years sooner than old women. While behaviour accounts for most of these premature deaths, it is possible that men have been 'programmed' by evolution to live shorter lives than women. With a few exceptions, notably wolves, most male mammals perish sooner than females. To that extent, males are the disposable sex – one ram can inseminate many ewes. Yet among humans, men have been far more crucial than most other male mammals to the success of their species. Our big-brained helpless infants need years of care and teaching, and two people are much better able than one to meet those needs. A man and a woman are a custom-made fit for that role; they complement each other in conception. For that reason alone, I think it's a fair bet that no matter how sophisticated our reproductive technologies become, no matter how tolerant we grow of other types of families, men will continue to be seen by most women – and by most men – as essential to marriage and parenthood. And, in turn, most men will surely continue to willingly play that role. Yet there are many other kinds of men – infertile men, gay men, celibate men, sex-reversed men, transsexual men and more – who may never do so but nonetheless will continue to be accepted as men, and rightly so.

When my wife was pregnant, people would ask me: 'What do you want – a boy or a girl?' I'd say, 'I don't mind, so long as it's healthy.' I was not simply being diplomatic; I genuinely meant it. Given the great subtleties of sex and gender and the many mysteries that remain about them, we really should stop making so much fuss about being male and female, about the differences between men and women. We know enough now to stop being so dogmatic about all this – science has shown us that we've been so dazzled by the window display that we've overlooked the shop. As a first step to reinventing men, then, we could do worse than declare peace in the phony war of the sexes.

ENDNOTES

CHAPTER 1

[1] Personal communication.

[2] Ridley, M., *The Red Queen*, Penguin, London, 1994, p. 17.

[3] Personal communication.

[4] Personal communication.

CHAPTER 2

[1] Diamond, Jared M., *Why is Sex Fun? The Evolution of Human Sexuality*, Weidenfeld & Nicolson, London, 1997.

[2] Ibid.

[3] Lampl, M., in *The First Humans*, Burenhult, G. (ed.), University of Queensland Press, 1993, pp. 30–1.

[4] Ibid.

[5] Taylor, T., *The Prehistory of Sex*, Fourth Estate, London, 1996, pp. 116–41.

[6] Ibid.

[7] Burenhult, G. (ed.), *The First Humans*, University of Queensland Press, 1993, pp. 115–16.

[8] Personal communication.

[9] Taylor, T., op. cit.

CHAPTER 3

[1] Reiter, J., 'Life History and Reproductive Success of Female Northern Elephant Seals', in *The Evolving Female*, eds Morbeck, M., Galloway, A., & Zihlman, A., Princeton University Press, 1997, pp. 46–52.

[2] Personal communication.

[3] Personal communication.

[4] Pavelka, M., 'The Social Life of Female Japanese Monkeys', in *The Evolving Female*, eds Morbeck, M., Galloway, A., & Zihlman, A., Princeton University Press, 1997, p. 76.

[5] Draper, J., 'Institutionalised Gender Roles in !Kung', in *The Evolving Female*, eds Morbeck, M., Galloway, A., & Zihlman, A., Princeton University Press, 1997, pp. 225–6.

[6] Wallen, K., in *Sexual Nature, Sexual Culture*, eds Abramson, P. & Pinkerton, S., University of Chicago Press, 1995, pp. 177–94.

[7] Smuts, B., *The Evolving Female*, eds Morbeck, M., Galloway, A., & Zihlman, A., Princeton University Press, 1997, p. 65.

CHAPTER 4

[1] Sinclair, A. et al., 'A gene from the human sex-determining region encoding a protein with homology to a conserved DNA-binding motif', *Nature*, vol. 346, 1990, pp. 249–54.

[2] Lahn, B.T. & Jegalian, K., 'The Key to Masculinity', in 'Men: The Scientific Truth', *Scientific American* supplement, vol. 10, no. 2, 1999, p. 21.

[3] *The Differences Between the Sexes*, eds Short, R.V. & Balaban, E., Cambridge University Press, 1994, p. 403.

[4] *New Scientist*, 24 July 1999.

[5] Hansen, D., Moller, H. & Olsen, J., 'Severe periconceptional life events and sex ratio in offspring: follow up study based on five national registers', *British Medical Journal*, vol. 319, 28 August 1999, pp. 548–9.

[6] Media release, Cedars-Sinai Medical Center, Los Angeles, 14 June 1999.

[7] Jager, T. de & Bornman, M.S., 'Reproductive toxins affecting the male', *Proceedings of the 11th World Congress on In Vitro Fertilisation and Human Reproductive Genetics*, May 1999, pp. 265–76.

CHAPTER 5

[1] Money, J. & Ehrhardt, A., *Man & woman, boy & girl,* Jason Aronson, New Jersey, 1996, pp. 118–23

[2] Ibid.

[3] Diamond, M., & Sigmundson, K., *Archives of Pediatric Adolescent Medicine*, vol. 275, no. 5307, 21 March 1997, p. 1745.

[4] Colapinto, J., *As Nature Made Him: The boy who was raised as a girl*, HarperCollins, New York, 2000.

[5] Mead, M., *Male and Female*, William Morrow, New York, 1975, pp. 128–36.

[6] Morelli, G., *The Evolving Female*, p. 212.

[7] Blum, D., *Sex on the Brain: The biological differences between men and women*, Penguin USA, New York, 1998, pp. 18–19.

CHAPTER 6

[1] Johnson, M. & Everitt, B., *Essential Reproduction*, Blackwell Scientific Publications, Oxford, 1980.

[2] Max, B., 'This and That: hair pigments, the hypoxic basis of life and the Virgilian journey of the spermatozoon', *Trends in Pharmacological Science*, vol. 13, July 1992, pp. 272–6.

[3] Ralt, D., *Proceedings of the National Academy of Sciences*, vol. 88, pp. 28–40.

[4] Vacquier, V.D., *Science*, vol. 281, 25 September 1998, pp. 1995–8.

CHAPTER 7

[1] Silber, S., 'The Disappearing Male', *Proceedings of the 11th World Congress on In Vitro Fertilisation and Human Reproductive Genetics*, May 1999.
[2] França, L.R., Russell, L.D. & Cummins, J.M., 'Comparative and evolutionary aspects of human spermatogenesis and male fecundity', *Human Reproduction*, vol. 14, 1999.
[3] *Human Reproduction*, vol. 14, 1999, pp. 106–9.
[4] Potts, M. and Short, R., *Ever since Adam and Eve*, Cambridge University Press, 1999, p. 116.
[5] Baker, R., *Sperm Wars*, Fourth Estate, London, 1996.
[6] Fisher, R.A., 1958, *The Genetical Theory of Natural Selection*, 2nd ed., Dover Press, New York, p. 291.
[7] Cohen, J., 'Sperms Galore', *Science Spectra*, issue 16, 1999, pp. 14–20.
[8] Bonde, J.P. et al., 'Relation between semen quality and fertility: a population-based study of 430 first-pregnancy planners', *The Lancet*, vol. 352, 10 October 1998, pp. 1172–7.
[9] Carlsen, E. et al., 'Evidence for decreasing quality of semen during past 50 years', *British Medical Journal*, vol. 305, 1992, pp. 609–13.
[10] *Science News*, 6 August 1996, p. 365.
[11] *Seattle Times*, 25 November 1997.

CHAPTER 8

[1] Meggitt, M., *Desert People*, Angus & Robertson, Sydney, 1975, p. 262.
[2] *Journal of Sex Research*, vol. 29, no. 4, pp. 579–80.
[3] *Bluff Your Way in Sex*, Ravette Books, London, 1994, p. 7.
[4] Parsons, A., *Facts and Phalluses*, Watermark Press, Sydney, 1988.
[5] Roach, M., 'Intimate Engineering', *Discover*, February 1999, pp. 76–81.
[6] Diamond, Jared M., *Why is Sex Fun? The Evolution of Human Sexuality*, Weidenfeld & Nicolson, London, 1997, pp.150–5.
[7] Gallup, G.G., Jr, & Suarez, S.D., 'Optimal reproductive strategies for bipedalism', *Journal of Human Evolution*, vol. 12, 1983, pp. 193–6.
[8] Brownell, R.L. & Ralls, K., 'Potential for sperm competition in baleen whales', *Report of the International Whaling Commission*, special issue no. 8, 1986, pp. 97–112.
[9] *Encyclopaedia of Aboriginal Australia*, Aboriginal Studies Press, Canberra, 1994, p. 195.
[10] Laumann, E.O., 'The Circumcision Dilemma', in 'Men: The Scientific Truth', *Scientific American* supplement, vol. 10, no. 2, 1999, p. 68.
[11] *Ever since Adam and Eve*, Cambridge University Press, 1999, p. 228.

CHAPTER 9

[1] Melman, A., 'Impotence in the Age of Viagra', in 'Men: The Scientific Truth', *Scientific American* supplement, vol. 10, no. 2, 1999, pp. 62–7.

CHAPTER 10

[1] Janssen, E. & Everaerd, W., *Annual Review of Sex Research*, vol. 4, pp. 211–45.
[2] Sachs, B., 'Erection invoked in male rats by airborne scent from estrous females', *Physiology and Behaviour*, vol. 62, no. 4, 1997, pp. 921–4.
[3] Buss, D., *The Evolution of Desire*, Basic Books, New York, 1994, p. 77.
[4] 'Surgery, drugs, and the male orgasm', *British Medical Journal*, 1 February 1997.
[5] Ibid.
[6] 'Wine and women', *New Scientist*, 27 November 1999, p. 63.
[7] 'Real men don't drink', *New Scientist*, 27 November 1999, p. 58–62.
[8] Crenshaw, T., *Why We Love and Lust*, HarperCollins, London, 1997, p. 140.
[9] Abramson, P. & Pinkerton, S. (eds), *Sexual Nature, Sexual Culture*, University of Chicago Press, 1995, pp. 80–118.
[10] *Proceedings of the Royal Society B*, vol. 266, p. 2351.

CHAPTER 11

[1] 'Deadly Myths of Aggression', *Aggressive Behaviour*, 1998.
[2] *Scientific American*, vol. 272, no. 2, February 1995, pp. 76–81.
[3] *New Scientist*, 7 February 1998.
[4] Crenshaw, T., *Why We Love and Lust*, HarperCollins, London, 1996, p. 145.
[5] Interview with David Celemajer in the *Sydney Morning Herald*, 9 December 1999, p. 2.
[6] 'Health Matters', ABC Radio.

CHAPTER 12

[1] Allman, W., *The Stone Age Present*, Touchstone, New York, 1995, p. 133.
[2] *Science*, vol. 284, no. 5418, 21 May 1999, p. 1263.
[3] Nisbett, R.E. & Cohen, D., 'Men, Honor and Murder', in 'Men: The Scientific Truth', *Scientific American* supplement, vol. 10, no. 2, 1999, pp. 17–19.
[4] Allman, W., op. cit.
[5] Russell, D. & Judd, F., 'Why are men killing themselves?', *Australian Family Physician*, vol. 28, no. 8, August 1999, pp. 791–5.
[6] 'Sex Differences in the Brain', *Scientific American*, September 1992, pp. 119–25.

[7] *Cerebral Cortex*, vol. 9, no. 8, December 1999.

[8] Maccoby, E., *The Two Sexes: Growing up apart, coming together,* Harvard University Press, 1999.

CHAPTER 13

[1] Jones, S., Martin, R. & Pilbeam, D. (eds), *The Cambridge Encyclopedia of Human Evolution,* Cambridge University Press, 1992, p. 402.

[2] Bongaarts, J., 'Demographic Consequences of Declining Fertility', *Science*, vol. 282, 16 October 1998, pp. 419–20.

[3] Zorpette, G., 'Muscular Again', in 'Your Bionic Future', *Scientific American* supplement, vol. 10, no. 3, 1999, p. 27.

[4] Kurzweil, R., 'The coming Merging of Mind and Machine', in 'Your Bionic Future', *Scientific American* supplement, vol. 10, no. 3, 1999.

ACKNOWLEDGEMENTS

This book could not have been written without the help, encouragement, advice, answers, time, thought, information and inspiration generously provided by many people – I take full responsibility, however, for any errors of fact or interpretation and omissions. I am pleased to be able to acknowledge that help and sincerely thank them.

Jim Cummins stands out for his continuing interest, kindness and wise counsel. He and David Mortimer, Colin Groves, Marijo Kent-First, Jennifer Graves and Andrew Sinclair read and commented on various sections of the draft manuscript and gave invaluable advice. I would also like to thank John Alexander, John Archer, Michael Archer, Goran Arnqvist, Michael Babyak, Paul Bailey, John Bancroft, Mark Beale, Walter Boles, C. Loring Brace, Warwick Brady, James Brody, Stephen Burnell, Niccolo Caldararo, Kathryn Chouaf, Jack Cohen, Bryony Coles, Clare Coney, Alison Cowan, Julian Cribb, Tim Curnow, Mark Davoren, Leigh Dayton, Milton Diamond, Thorsten Diemer, Thomas Eisner, Howard Fienberg, Brian J. Ford, Clare Forster, Matt Fraser, Phillip Galbraith, Gavin Gilchrist, Peter Gill, Peter Gort, James Gruber, David Handelsman, Sheryl Hilton, Wayne Hutchins, Erick Janssen, Jessica Kernigan, Greg Laden, Marci Lobel, Oscar McMahon, Anne Musser, Harriet Bjerrum Nielsen, Paul Patterson, Anne Pusey, Robert W. Reasoner, Benjamin Sachs, Wijnand van der Sanden, Robert Sapolsky, Steven Schrader, William Scott, Roger Short, Deborah Smith, Laurajane Smith, Su Solomon, Jim Stevenson, Alex Stitt, Melissa Sweet, Martie Thompson, Alan Thorne, Terry Turner, Glenn Wagner, Lenore Walker, Max Walsh, Tim White, Michael Wilson and Antonia Young.

Some parts of this book have been previously published in other forms in the *Sydney Morning Herald*, *The Bulletin* and *Reader's Digest*. 'Jack's Story' (pp. 266–8) is an abridged version of an interview with Jessica Kernigan, reproduced here courtesy of the author and borders.com.

The author gratefully acknowledges permission from authors and publishers to reproduce extracts from the following works:

Why is Sex Fun?, by Jared Diamond, Weidenfeld & Nicolson. Copyright © 1997 Jared Diamond.

The Two Sexes: Growing up apart, coming together, by Eleanor Maccoby, Harvard University Press. Copyright © 1998 by the President and Fellows of Harvard College.

The Trouble with Testosterone, by Robert Sapolsky, Touchstone. Copyright © 1997 by Robert M. Sapolsky.

'Mammalian sex-determining genes', by Jennifer Graves, in *The Differences Between the Sexes*, eds Short & Balaban, Cambridge University Press 1994.

The Cambridge Encyclopedia of Human Evolution, eds Jones et al. Copyright © 1992 Cambridge University Press. Reproduced with the permission of Cambridge University Press.

The Evolving Female, eds Morbeck, Galloway & Zihlman. Copyright © 1997 by Princeton University Press. Reprinted by permission of Princeton University Press.

Sexual Nature, Sexual Culture, eds Abramson & Pinkerton, The University of Chicago Press. Copyright © 1995 by The University of Chicago.

INDEX

T